AF608255

UNTIMELY DEATHS IN RENAISSANCE DRAMA

Biography, History, Catastrophe

UNTIMELY DEATHS IN *Renaissance Drama*

Biography, History, Catastrophe

ANDREW GRIFFIN

UNIVERSITY OF TORONTO PRESS
Toronto Buffalo London

Toronto Buffalo London
utorontopress.com

ISBN 978-1-4875-0348-2

Library and Archives Canada Cataloguing in Publication

Title: Untimely deaths in Renaissance drama: biography, history, catastrophe / Andrew Griffin.

Names: Griffin, Andrew, 1978– author.

Description: Includes bibliographical references and index.

Identifiers: Canadiana 20190114347 | ISBN 978-1-4875-03482 (hardcover)

Subjects: LCSH: English drama – Early modern and Elizabethan, 1500–1600 – History and criticism. | LCSH: English drama – 17th century – History and criticism. | LCSH: History in literature. | LCSH: Death in literature.

Classification: LCC PR658.H5 G75 2019 | DDC 822/.309358—dc23

This book has been published with the help of a grant from the Federation for the Humanities and Social Sciences, through the Awards to Scholarly Publications Program, using funds provided by the Social Sciences and Humanities Research Council of Canada.

University of Toronto Press acknowledges the financial assistance to its publishing program of the Canada Council for the Arts and the Ontario Arts Council, an agency of the Government of Ontario.

Canada Council for the Arts Conseil des Arts du Canada

Funded by the Government of Canada Financé par le gouvernement du Canada | Canada

Contents

Acknowledgments

Like the figures I discuss here, this book would have died too soon if not for the notes, mentorship, kindness, criticism, and generosity of Helen Ostovich, Elizabeth Hanson, and Paddy Fumerton. They've been excellent guides and friends.

This project was born over a decade ago at McMaster University, where it was helped along by a number of friends and faculty, most notably Melinda Gough, whose careful, critical, encouraging voice lives in the back of my head whenever I write, and Gary Kuchar, who showed me that early modern literature and psychoanalysis were the only truly interesting topics. As is often the case, the work here grew largely from informal conversations with interested friends and colleagues, at bars and around seminar tables. Most immediately helpful for their notes and friendship were Stephanie Morley (on print history), Suzanne Rintoul (on trauma), Tim Kaposy (on Adorno's *Lectures on Metaphysics*), Emily Johansen (on urbanity), Shawna Ferris (on the history of sanctified prostitution), Kaley Joyes (on trauma), and Justin Sully (on intergenerational history). While Sylvia Bowerbank didn't live to see the work here, she introduced me to early modern literary studies and changed my life.

For the past eight years at the University of California, Santa Barbara, I've been lucky to enough to work with supportive, critical, careful, and – perhaps most important – interesting colleagues. Jim Kearney read several chapters of this book and gave invaluable notes. Heather Blurton and Brian Donnelly have each supported my work in more ways than I can enumerate here. Mark Rose has been unfailingly supportive and helpful. Tess Shewry has been a bulwark of humane sanity in a profession that seems to thrive on a variety of pathologies. Rachael King has talked me through a number of intellectual impasses with her great sense of print history. Josh and Murphy Epstein have vetted – in some form – most of the ideas that appear in this book. Scott Selisker helped to shape the book's introduction with his careful reading and his notes on most topics. I've also been lucky enough to learn from the bracingly bright graduate students I've worked with here, including Pav Aulakh, Megan Palmer, Chris Foley, Danielle Davey, Kristy McCants, and Katie Adkison; each of their projects has made an impact on my own work, and I'm sure each can find his or her influence in it.

Though frequently aflame and utterly incomprehensible to me, Southern California has been an excellent place to work as an early modernist, thanks in part to the Early Modern Studies Institute at the Huntington Library, run with intelligence and warmth by Heidi Brayman and Heather James. They have built an astonishingly amiable intellectual hub. The Renaissance Conference of Southern California is also an incredibly valuable institution that has welcomed me warmly; Martine van Elk and Andy Fleck introduced me to the RCSC and I thank them for that. The transient "w/Shakespeare" colloquia, sponsored by a grant from the University of California's MRPI program were also helpful to me as I thought through the book in its final stages; for those meetings I thank Jim (again), Julia Reinhard Lupton, and Lowell Gallagher.

Most of the chapters here have appeared in some form or another at one of the Shakespeare Association of America's annual meetings. In a number of SAA seminars, I've been lucky to be paired with bright and generous respondents, including Lara Bovilsky, Aaron Kunin, Alice Dailey, Lauren Shohet, and Genevieve Love. Conferencing has also introduced me to Stephanie Shirilan, whose influence – both intellectually and more broadly – rings through these pages. Also through the SAA, Gil Harris and Janelle Jenstad have offered quickening notes on Stow and London; these notes shape chapter 2.

This book wouldn't have been written without the financial support of the Social Sciences Humanities Research Council of Canada, the Hellman Family Faculty Fellowship, the UCSB Senate Faculty Research Grants, and the Canadian Federation for the Humanities and Social Sciences' Awards to Scholarly Publications Programme.

Of course, this book was written only after decades of care from my parents, Bob and Elaine Griffin, who have been consistently supportive even when confused by my choice of topics and methods. They gave me the tools I needed to write this and to live, and I owe them too much to repay. Recently, Ming Li and Zhisheng Cheng have welcomed me into their family, and I'm grateful for the generosity they've shown with their time and energy. Their work has helped me to finish this book.

Finally, this book is dedicated to June, Sam, and Noa. While Sam and Noa have been – to be frank – useless though delightful interlocutors, June has always helped me to think through the problems presented in this book as if they were her own. Most importantly, June, Sam, and Noa help me live each day in the shadow of Parolles's great promise, only available to him at the moment he's overlived his pretensions: "simply the thing I am / shall make me live." I love them dearly.

Toronto, 2019

UNTIMELY DEATHS IN RENAISSANCE DRAMA

Biography, History, Catastrophe

Biography, History, Catastrophe

Untimely Deaths focuses on the problem of narrative abruption in a selection of historically minded early modern plays, and it does so to explore the various strategies through which early modern historical culture made narrative sense of biography and fatality. When examining this historical culture – the "perceptual and cognitive web of relations between past, present, and future" (Woolf, *Social* 9) – the book both develops from and explains a set of related assumptions about biography, narrative, drama, and history writing in the late sixteenth and early seventeenth centuries. First, I claim here that an untimely death is best understood in terms of narrative abruption or disruption, meaning that an untimely death is a narrative problem in that it arrives before it should have according to available forms of narrative explanation. Such forms may be familiar biographical plots (e.g., "the seven ages of man") or they may be tied to conventional forms of temporal emplotment (e.g., a person dies a timely death if he or she dies after a readily comprehensible and thus established causal chain of events). In either case, a death might be understood as "timely" rather than "untimely" when it abides or provides a narratively coherent biography – when it "caps" a life, or when it seems to follow naturally from the pattern of life that came before it. Second, I argue here that, paradoxically, we can clearly see the narrative formulae through which early modern writers made sense of lives and deaths when we explore narrative failure. When narrative forms fail in the face of an untimely death, the disruption appears as matter of trauma or incomprehensibility, making the untimely death an epistemological problem as well as a formal problem. Such traumatic incomprehensibility is the hallmark of the untimely death as it appears in the plays I study here. Third, and finally, I argue in *Untimely Deaths* that the narrative formulae through which early modern dramatists make sense of lives and deaths draw heavily from and participate in the period's wider culture of history writing. This final assumption draws on revisionist accounts of early modern historical culture that have emerged over the past fifteen years. According to these new approaches, we cannot understand the historiographical *mentalité* or *mentalités* of the period without recognizing forms of historical writing such as those associated with drama and other disciplines that have previously been excluded from the canon of historical thought. Such previously marginalized forms of history writing exploit the innovations and habits of nominally more "serious" forms of historical writing and in turn influence these other forms which had yet to distinguish and institutionalize themselves in what we might consider the modern discipline of history. Consequently, by exploring the various forms of narrative historical explanation as they fail in early modern drama, we ultimately glimpse the unwieldy, fraught, and often conflicted set of ideas that might be characterized as the early modern "historical imagination."

Comparing the deaths of Richard II and Henry V in Shakespeare's plays illustrates the relationship between these various *topoi*. In *Richard II*, a play decidedly interested in narrative closure and untimely death, John of Gaunt notes from his deathbed that narrative ends wield outsized explanatory significance: "More are men's ends marked," he claims, "than their lives before" (2.1.11). This is an observation that many critics take to be true for both King Richard II and Shakespeare's play as a whole. As *Richard II* closes, we are often told, the king finally becomes himself in a cell at Pomfret Castle, embracing his status as a so-called poet-king rather than a divinely sanctioned sovereign. At this point, Richard's long, introspective, and knotty soliloquies recursively inform our understanding of all that came before: the vacillating poet-king should never have judged the conflict between Bolingbroke and Mowbray, he should never have sailed for Ireland, he should never have usurped Bolingbroke's birthright. He has somehow always been a gnomic poet rather than an effective king, and the play's closing scenes remind us that his life was forever headed in this direction. Like the stories of apocalyptic conclusion that interested Frank Kermode, Richard's death as dramatized by Shakespeare has led critics to suggest that his life concludes in apotheosis. The end, that is, crowns all, by capturing the essence of the life that led up to it. This end is the promised end because it retrospectively makes sense of the story that leads inevitably, tautologically, to it. Richard's self-reflecting, indecisive late style provides the truth of the life he lived.

But what about Henry V? Henry's death resists the biographical urge that Richard's death seems to satisfy. Such resistance and what it tells us about early modern historical culture are ultimately the focus of this study. Specifically, *Untimely Deaths* is interested in moments in which historical, biographical, and dramatic narrative forms fail when faced with catastrophes that make their structures appear inadequate. Both historically and in Shakespeare's plays, Henry's death is not "marked" more than his life before, and this failure poses problems for contemporaneous forms of narrative historical explanation. In the historical records from the late sixteenth and early seventeenth centuries, the scene of his death is largely ignored or is treated as a moot piece of trivia rather than a meaningful historical datum. In Holinshed, for instance, the circumstances of Henry's death are, if anything, a matter of curiosity rather than serious historical concern, and Holinshed blithely offers a number of hypotheses on his demise without comment. Perhaps it was pleurisy that killed him, as Peter Basset suggested in a now lost account referred to by Holinshed; or perhaps it was venereal disease, as the "Scots and French" claimed, or an acute skin infection, as Enguerrand de Monstrelet proposed in his manuscript *Chroniques* (c. 1450), or a "sharpe fever" made worse by the "dog daies" of summer, as Christopher Ocland stated in *Anglorum Praelia* (1580) (6.583). Holinshed, borrowing from Hall, ultimately identifies this biographically unsatisfying death, in fact likely from amoebic dysentery, as "untimely": "Thus ended this puissant prince his most noble and fortunate reigne, whose life (saith Hall) though cruell Atropos abbreuiated; yet neither fi[...]e, malice, nor [...] fretting time shall appall his honour, or blot out the glorie of him that in so small time had doone so manie and roiall acts" (6.584). Recently married, recently named Regent of France, and father to a young son unready to wear the crown, Henry seems to have lived an "abbreviated" life and his death comes "before his tyme," even if death by dysentery was frighteningly common among medieval warriors such as the king.

On stage, too, the death of Henry was a moot point, though Shakespeare (or Nashe)[1] was more sensitive to the disturbing affective and historiographical effects that his biographically unsatisfying death produced. Unlike all other kings in the history plays, Henry dies outside the diegetic frame of the drama, in part because unfulfilling biographies make for narratively difficult drama. This narrative and theatrical failure is clear in *1 Henry VI*, when Henry's coffin appears on stage in a play whose plot seems always on the verge of collapse. As the play opens, mourners repeatedly attempt and fail to make sense of Henry's death in biographical or narrative historical terms. The play opens with John of Lancaster, the Duke of Bedford, expecting some grand cosmological crisis that never arrives:

> Hung be the heavens with black, yield day to night!
> Comets, importing change of times and states,
> Brandish your crystal tresses in the sky,
> And with them scourge the bad revolting stars
> That have consented unto Henry's death!
> King Henry the Fifth, too famous to live long!
> England ne'er lost a king of so much worth (1.1.1–7)

Bedford situates Henry's death in a broad providential frame, attempting to summon the portents that would make sense of the king's catastrophe as part of a meaningful historical situation. Like Hamlet, who worries that time is out of joint, Bedford is bothered that Henry's death is out of joint with a providentially ordained historical time. Because comets refuse to appear and ratify the divine ordination of Henry's demise or to make it somehow meaningful, the rest of the scene features similar attempts to explain his death in historical terms. For Exeter, we might "curse the planets of mishap," though it seems better to blame the "subtle-witted French" who "By magic verses have contrived his end" (1.1.23, 25). Or perhaps, as Gloucester suggests, it was the fault of churchmen who hoped for the king's death in order to shore up their status: "Had not churchmen pray'd, / His thread of life had not so soon decay'd" (1.1.33–4). The scene subsequently invokes sublunary forms of historical explanation in ways that trouble the portentous language that suffuses its opening: the French are succeeding against the English not because of magic power or subterfuge but for England's "want of men and money" (1.1.69). History unfolds the way it unfolds, that is, either because willed by God, because one's enemies are too savvy, or because armies need adequate supply chains. No one seems to know exactly why they face the tragedy they do.

Staging a history without *telos* or readily comprehensible motive forces, the remainder of *1 Henry VI* tarries with the historical confusion offered in its opening scene, refusing to offer a coherent plot in either dramatic or historiographical terms. The play offers no central character – its eponymous king only appears at the start of the third act – and the play's sense of historical causality is confused: it engages seriously with secular *realpolitik* and the politics of faction but also with a providentially plotted morality play featuring Joan of Arc and her demonic familiars. In Clifford Leech's reading, this narrative confusion mars the play, rendering it a "fairly shapeless piece of writing" and "an anecdotal kind of drama in which incidents are presented in turn for the sake of immediate dramatic effect rather than for their contribution to a total pattern" (14). But the narrative "shapelessness" of this play – which Brian Vickers suggests is "the most disorganized play in the canon" – seems a self-conscious, apt response to the catastrophic and surprising death with which it opens ("Incomplete Shakespeare" 324). Certainly the play is like the other *Henry VI* plays, in that they are all marked by what Barbara Hodgdon identifies as "closural deficiences" that refuse to provide a sense of narrative wholeness. But *1 Henry VI* is more specifically characterized by a poetics of abruption rather than by the "stubbornly refractory" anecdotalism of the picaresque that Hodgdon identifies with the entire series (44). As Bedford attempts to put Henry to rest in an elegy, for instance, his mourning rite fails: "A far more glorious star thy soul will make / Than Julius Caesar or bright – / *Enter a Messenger*" (1.1.56). The failure of apotheosis offers the truth of the play's abrupted narrative form as it stutters forwards. Like Bedford's abbreviated apotheosis, Henry V's funeral, proceedings in Parliament, and, pointedly, the coronation of Henry VI in Paris are all interrupted before they might unfold.[2] This preoccupation with interruption and narrative failure becomes clearest not as *1 Henry VI* begins but as it ends: instead of concluding with a betrothal, as in a comedy or as in *Henry V*, this play ends with a betrothal *and* the breech of a betrothal, a promise of futurity *as well as* its foreclosure.[3] In light of these interruptions, diversions, and disruptions throughout the play, the conclusion of the first scene feels ominously prophetic because there is no stage direction for the removal of Henry V's coffin. Though typical of the folio's sparse stage directions, the play printed in that edition features a coffin that sits on the stage for the duration of the performance, providing a resonant stage image for the play's hobbled plot.[4] Time seems confused here, and unable to move easily forwards into the next king's reign.

Critics have often made similar arguments by suggesting that Henry V's coffin looms large over *1 Henry VI*, and they have convincingly deployed the language of trauma to negotiate the sense of catastrophic disruption that Henry's untimely death inspires. For Phyllis Rackin, for instance, the play stages "a struggle on the part of the English to preserve [Henry V's] rapidly disappearing legacy of national unity and French conquests" (29). But the quick delineation of "before" and "after" in Rackin's observation, which would mark Henry's death as a watershed moment, obscures the traumatic temporality that subsequent scholars have noted when negotiating the *Henry VI* plays. This weird sense of historical unfolding is characterized by belatedness, haunting, anachronism, and a sense of failed historical supersession. In this sense, the temporality of trauma is at odds with those attempts to plot historical and biographical spans into narratively satisfying wholes. Recognizing trauma's temporal disruptions at work in *1 Henry VI* and in the opening scene, specifically, Thomas Anderson is struck by Gloucester's "inability to speak" and by Bedford's worry that news of English military losses in Rouen and Paris will make the deceased, coffined king "burst" his lead-lined casket and "rise from the dead" (2–3). In the shadow of Gloucester's inarticulacy, Anderson suggests, Bedford is anxious "over the restless nature of Henry's corpse" and evinces "reluctance to confront" the past that lingers there in Henry's coffin, always ready to repeat itself and to deform the present with its unwillingness to remain part of the past (3). Laurie Ellinghausen similarly finds a struggle with trauma that "troubles the heroic narrative [the play] purports to offer," constantly reiterating a pattern of violence inspired by misrecognition and shame (279). Again, that is, the language of trauma intersects with the language of narrative, and catastrophe inspires a sort of temporal drag or confusion.

While recognizing the significance of trauma theory, as invoked by the characterization of staged time in the Henry VI plays discussed above, *Untimely Deaths* teases out Ellinghausen's passing reference to "narrative." In doing so, this study emphasizes specific features of trauma, catastrophe, and time as they are rendered in early modern plays and historical writing. Rather than reading trauma as a "breach experience," characterized by the apparent extremity of an event, I read trauma as a breach of narrative, or as a failure to find a compelling explanation for a given disruptive event. When Bedford and Gloucester point to a certain form of traumatic temporality at the start of *1 Henry VI*, they suggest that Henry's death is troubling not only because a paragon of virtue and chivalry is lost, but also because they have no way to explain the loss, no narrative through which to both feel and understand how their world has arrived at the present moment in which the coffin of a king lies before them. The traumatic event is traumatic because it overwhelms, shocks, and disturbs one's sense of the world, but also, as Freud saw, because it troubles familiar understandings of time's regular unfolding.

Freud's most influential discussion of trauma emerged from his treatment of soldiers who, after the First World War, were unable to overcome their wartime experience, returning to the scene of disaster in their dreams at night and, in the process, contradicting Freud's earlier theory of dreams (*Beyond* 55–6). The crucial feature of the traumatic event in this aetiology is its unpredictability rather than its sheer violence.

Traumatic neuroses and repetitive behaviour may appear after "severe mechanical accidents," but, he noted, "the same symptoms arose from time to time in the absence of any gross mechanical violence" (55). The problem is not "violence" but "accidents." As Cathy Caruth notes, the "breach experience" is measured not in terms of an event's extremity, but in relation to "an ordered experience of time" that it disrupts ("Violence" 25), breaching "the mind's experience of time, self, and the world" relative to what should be the case (*Unclaimed* 4). Returning to Freud, she emphasizes that the traumatic circumstance is "not just any event" that happens to be unsettling or disturbing, but is instead, "significantly, the shocking and unexpected occurrence of an accident" (4). To be traumatically untimely, then, a death must run contrary to a schedule so regular that it has come to be presumed inviolable.

When exploring the various strategies available to early modern writers as they attempt to make narrative sense of lives, we begin to recognize the myriad narrative tools they had at their disposal. This repertoire was incredibly diverse, featuring forms of historical explanation that seem both familiar and decidedly foreign to modern ears. In *1 Henry VI*, for instance, Exeter explains Henry's death by appeal to French magic, pointing to the "the subtle-witted French / Conjurers and sorcerers that, afraid of him [the King], / By magic verses have contrived his end" (1.1.25–7). Such an explanation seems absurd to modern readers because we assume that the French never successfully used magic as a tool of combat or foreign policy. Yet the play's ultimate treatment of Joan of Arc and her fiends gives us pause, reminding us of our considerable distance from the forms of historical explanation that Shakespeare deploys in his play. In the opening scene of *1 Henry VI*, we see more causative instruments in the heterogeneous early modern historical tool kit, as the play's characters offer a variety of explanations for the historical events they experience, from providence to the sublunary "facts" of a failed military supply chain, to the failure of political machinations. According to one practical interpretation, made by a messenger who seems to have read the secular and more broadly social histories of Machiavelli, Guicciardini, and Bacon, "No treachery" caused Henry's death and the English losses in France, "but want of men and money" (1.1.69).

Further complicating the question of causality in historical sources are the generic conventions of drama. A play operates within traditions of narrative explanation that are native to the form – comedy, romance, tragedy, and so on. When Joan suffers death at the stake for invoking evil spirits, we might recognize that her life and death make sense according to the logic of a morality play, where the burning stake replaces the mouth of hell as the site of subjective catastrophe brought about by one's guilt. Following different conventions, New Comedy tacitly explains its outcomes by appeal to a natural social order: the aspiring young lovers are successfully joined in marriage and the obstructive *senex* learns his descendent role in the world. And early modern tragedy (including a hybrid "the moral-tragedy of Joan")[5] might tacitly explain the events it stages by appeal to character or type, rather than by appeal to social and political forces. To recognize the historicity of narrative historical resources available to playwrights ultimately means recognizing that these resources derive not only from contemporary prose historiographies but from formal habits of dramatic narrative construction that bear within them complex understandings of temporal unfolding.

In focusing on forms of narrative historical explanation as filtered through the drama of the early modern period, I am here indebted to Michael Neill's work on tragedy and the "teleological violence of narrative form" (*Issues* 205). Yet I treat a wider variety of narrative forms available to early modern playwrights, as suggested above. While Neill focuses on generically self-conscious tragedies that foreground their inherited narrative conventions, I argue below that early modern dramatists often relied on and participated in the strikingly diverse field of history writing at the end of the sixteenth and the beginning of the seventeenth centuries, from the providential, to the mythographic, to the humanistic, to the antiquarian and its sensitivity to the forces associated with "social history." When playwrights wrote plays, that is, they also relied on forms of narrative explanation that were not, in any obvious way, native to the theatre. Further, I argue that the theatre was seriously engaged with the intellectual and methodological conflicts that characterized early modern historical thought more generally. Contrary to Steven Mullaney's claim that the early modern theatre was a site in which "cultural fault lines" could be addressed and "brought to a partial and imaginary resolution" (82), I propose, through the plays that I read here, that the theatre was simply one more venue in which the intellectual messiness around questions of historical processes was represented, in often unsatisfying or critical ways. By combining narrative forms native to drama with the diverse narrative forms from the extra-dramatic field of historical thought, the early modern stage operated as a kind of historiographical laboratory in which playwrights with considerable historiographical sophistication could experiment; sometimes, these experiments would go awry, as critical accounts of *1 Henry VI* suggest. When exploring the results of these experiments, we ultimately find evidence of complex narrative formulae through which history was understood and represented in England in the late sixteenth and early seventeenth centuries.

In outlining this knotty conceptual territory, the remainder of this introduction falls into two distinct parts. In the first section, I offer a schematic vision of the lifespan of an individual as a conceptual object and explain some of its uniquely early modern features. This section considers the distinctly theatrical or dramatic logics that are brought to bear on the untimely death of a person as depicted in early modern plays. The second section situates my project within the now familiar argument about the place of drama in the world of early modern historiography, which has established the legitimacy of a capacious "historical culture" as an object of study. In order to understand this revisionist project, my divergence from it, and the importance of drama, I first describe the forerunner of the revisionist project, which distinguished between the sorts of history writing that would become central to the discipline of history in the later seventeenth century – humanist historiography and antiquarianism, for instance – and the forms of history writing that would come to be treated as marginal or "parasitical," to use D.R. Woolf's evocative phrase. Revisionist historians have tended to play down rather than emphasize the methodological conflict in the field of early modern historical writing. But in revisiting this field, I find methodological diversity and contention alongside weird moments of synchrony. Humanist historians such as Sir John Hayward might think in providential terms, for instance, even while dismissing mythic stories of Brute. Closing this section with a focus on the special status of the period encompassed by *Untimely Deaths*, between 1574 and 1623, I argue that at this moment in time we find the gradual institutionalization of historiography in England, after which it in fact becomes reasonable to imagine the distinction between serious and non-serious forms of history writing, primarily because history gradually establishes itself in the university as a discipline rather than a topic.

Plotting Lives and Deaths

To imagine the lifespan as a meaningful whole has often meant imagining the intersection of material necessity and cultural habit before conceiving that they operate naturally in tandem. In the familiar "ages of man" *topos*, for instance, the process of aging becomes a narrative of incremental maturation and "life phases"; these phases are then tautologically invested with an air of biological inevitability. This model of the lifespan – one that appeals to the materiality of human life as its ultimate foundation and cause – is most famously drawn in the riddle of the Sphinx in which the transition from morning to noon to night offers a model for individual human growth in terms of ability: "What is that which in the morning goeth upon four feet; upon two feet in the afternoon; and in the Evening upon three?" By superimposing generic human identity – "Man" – upon apparently age-appropriate forms of movement and the diurnal arc of a day, contingent facts of age-related mobility are identified as essential aspects of human life as it unfolds predictably through time.

This naturalized and standardized plot of the human life is commonplace in classical and early modern literature, appearing in almost every medium and form.[6] Peter Fancy's popular seventeenth-century ballad "The Age and Life of Man" is typical of the figure. It describes the (male)[7] human lifespan through familiar tropes such as the running of the "glasse" and, in its custom-made woodcut, by reference to the human ascent and descent on life's podium (Figure 1). According to the ballad's arbitrary scheme of periodization in seven year intervals,

> When man is born he in a Cradle lyes,
> At one time seven a Hoby-horse devise,
> At two times seven a Book to Read with all,
> At three times seven a Bandy and a Ball,
> At foure times seven a wife he seeks to know,
> At five times seven the Horn of Strength he blow,
> At six times seven Time standeth by him still,
> At seven times seven his Bag begins to fill,
> At eight times seven his Bags are filld each nuke [sic: "night"?],
> At nine times seven, he to the Earth doe stoop,
> At ten times seven his Glasse and time is run,
> Into the Earth Man falls, and so hes gone. (1–12)

Traversing the arc of a biography and a career, the ballad explains its generic biographical plot by appeal to a material ground: "Man he is clay, that came from Earth"; "it is man, that is but clay"; "he to the Earth doe stoop"; "Into the Earth man falls." Mixing comments on both social and biological transformations in human life, Fancy's ballad offers a model of the orderly lifespan against which, I argue, the untimely death becomes both a conceptual possibility and disruption, as well as an occasion for rethinking the complex relations between individual lives and the broader unfolding of history.

Despite its familiarity and superficial intuitive sense, the ages-of-man *topos* is troubled by empirical experience and by its conspicuous conceitedness, as Jaques recognizes in *As You Like It*. In a speech that insists on the

1 Peter Fancy's *Age and Life of Man* (Euing Ballad 11, EBBA: 31654).

theatricality of daily life and on the performativity of identity, the predictable entrance, exit, and biographical plotline of human life is imaginable only ironically. "All the world's a stage," Jaques declares to Duke Senior,

> And all the men and women merely players:
> They have their exits and their entrances;
> And one man in his time plays many parts,
> His acts being seven ages. (2.7.138–42)

The equally familiar *theatrum mundi* figure[8] that Jaques invokes when he offers the seven-ages-of-man narrative reminds us that both *topoi* seemed hackneyed by the early modern period to a savvy critic of poetry and life, especially when questions of biographical emplotment are concerned. The "strange, eventful history" that Jaques provides is neither strange nor eventful, and it can be rattled off in a set piece that draws attention to its artifice. The scene of the speech's first articulation at the Globe, probably in 1599, compounds the speech's ironies, reinforcing the sense of artifice associated with visions of the smoothly unfolding biography. As theatre historians often point out, Jaques's speech was first performed in the recently built theatre with its self-consciously metatheatrical *genius loci* and motto: on the Globe's sign, Hercules hoists the planet aloft and is accompanied by a motto that speaks to the interrelation of life and performance, *"Totus mundus agit historionem"* ["all the world plays the actor"]. Reading Jaques's metatheatrical speech in *As You Like It*, critics tend to focus on the relationship between performance, artifice, and identity, and to ignore the fantasy of predictable biographical narrative that shapes his observations on the performativity of identity. If the role of the actor and the role of the audience member might blur together in terms of their social identities because both actors and audience members play roles, then the stories that people tell about their lives *as* lives seem contrived in the same way. Stories of biographically whole lives are as aesthetic as social roles when they attempt to render haphazard biographical plots into naturalized and essential truths.

Just as Jaques's speech imagines identity in performative rather than essential terms, its vision of narrative biographical wholeness becomes similarly performative, producing the life span only by transforming the life into an aesthetic object. As Paul Kottman argues when reading this speech, Jaques offers a vision of life which corresponds with the creative spectacle of art rather than with the mundane biology of the organism (*Politics* 193–200). "My life" is an object of aesthetic enquiry and labour, the speech declares, rather than a fact of brute biology. In this mixture of life and art, Jaques's ironic sensibility complicates the language of natural biological plotting that courses through the play, and yet the fantasy of such plotting remains persistently generative in the forest of Arden. In the world Shakespeare stages, human time moves predictably through seasons, from life to death by way of marriage and (re)incorporation in the social world. Repeatedly thematizing the seasonal – winter and spring appear frequently as metaphors in the play – Shakespeare continually invokes the natural plotting of human life. Contra Jaques, the play concludes with a song about spring and natural seasonality before the masque of Hymen unites lovers and puts everyone in their right role for a given time of life. Jaques may tell us that the biographical span is natural only in contrived ways, and yet the play's plot follows familiar narrative arcs, thematizes the naturalness of these arcs, and finally authorizes this sense of natural order with the imprimatur of Hymen's divinity. The play makes us leery of naturalized biographical narratives while it also traffics in them joyfully. In its canny double vision, *As You Like It* suggests both that imagined biographical wholeness is a tired trope, rather than an existentially meaningful truth, and that fictions of a biographical order conceived according to nature remain central to the understanding and representation of human life. The hyperbolically pastoral style of the closing scene, rubbing against the play's broad realism, suggests a certain irony with which Shakespeare deploys idealizing narrative fictions.

When visions of essentialized, prescriptive temporal order remain compelling despite their artificiality, they do so because the organic lifespan is a valuable or useful resource for thinking, even if the normative conventionality of the ages-of-man formula is ultimately too coarsening. To imagine life as plotted is both an aesthetic contrivance and a necessity. This salutary and ironic fact about embracing the integrity of biography is clear in the variety of narrative forms that produce the feel of a "complete" and coherent life while being subtler and more dialectically responsive than the ages-of-man model. A more sensitive model is familiar from the arguments of narrative theory which claim, in Marshall Grossman's concise phrase, that narrative "gives form to exigent experience" (18). When the exigent experience under consideration is the matter of a human life, the act of narration is ultimately the only means through which individuals persist meaningfully over time. In Hayden White's influential argument, narrative "might well be considered a solution of general human concern, namely ... the problem of fashioning human experience into a form assimilable to structures of meaning that are generally human" (5). Such life-sustaining narratives, however, emerge not from a predetermined or preordained order, as we see in Fancy's ballad – where matter determines the inevitable arc of a life and its events – but from the desire to imagine narrative order and to imagine that the principle of that narrative order emerges from the idiosyncratic events of the life under consideration (17). "My life" unfolds in the way that it unfolds because it reflects the temporal instantiation of "my self," or "my self" becomes the retrospectively posited object that one can recognize only once time has unfolded.

Hannah Arendt and many of her recent followers tarry provocatively and extensively with the relationship that White raises between human forms of being and the act of narration. Human self-narration is not simply a method whereby lives are given human meaning, they note, but is foundational to the creation of human life *as* human life, at least in the terms drawn from Aristotle, according to whom human *bios* is distinguished from *zōē*, or from not-yet-human animal life. In her extended engagement with Arendt, for instance, Julia Lupton focuses on Arendt's "concern with the conditions of human action and its intimate relationship with both storytelling and drama." In a provocative and dense reading of Arendt and Aristotle, Lupton ultimately points out that "Arendt distinguishes the activity of labor from human action in the political sense" associated with human *bios*: life is "itself always full of events which ultimately can be told as story, establish a biography" (*Thinking* 4). The result of this *bios*-making activity, Lupton concludes, is the idea of a self that coheres over time and might also take responsibility for itself.

Adriana Cavarero expands on the same aspect of Arendt's thought when claiming that the subject is a subject only through narration. Illustrating this claim with a thought experiment that asks about an amnesiac's self-understanding, Cavarero notes that in so far as the amnesiac "is a *victim* of amnesia, she finds herself being someone who has suddenly become no one, because she is now merely a sort of empirical life without a story" (35).[9] Additionally offering a vision of biographical narration that responds to the idiosyncrasies of individual lives, Cavarero begins *Relating Narratives* with another evocative illustration. Paraphrasing Karen Blixen's fictional account of a man, a dike, some fish, and a stork, Cavarero tells a story:[10] an unnamed man lives by a pond and wakes in the middle of the night because he hears an unusual noise. He wanders and stumbles through the dark, searching for the sound's source; he finds that his dike was leaking, allowing his fish to escape, and he fixes the problem. In the morning, when he awakes, he looks out "his little window" to find that his apparently aimless footsteps have traced the shape of a stork on the ground (1). Reading this story as an allegory for human lives generally – lives that appear aimless only to reveal at their ends a meaningful coherence – Cavarero asks a question to which she responds in the affirmative: "does the course of every life allow itself to be looked upon in the end like a design that has a meaning?" (1).[11] In this vision of human lives, deaths are meaningful as the inevitable end of material processes and also as conclusions around which individual biographies are built.

Though compelling and evocative, as the example of the biographical urge in *Richard II* suggests, such a vision of human life is troubled by its unidirectionality, as if lives intersect with narrative only retrospectively. In both Cavarero's vision and the biographical urge, narration transforms lives into temporally coherent wholes and enables a sense of subjective consistency across time. But there is an important difference. Biographies are lived and narrated, as Grossman argues, both proleptically and retrospectively, or according to a habit of "anticipatory retrospection" (58). Through this sense of forward-looking biographical narration, the untimely death becomes a meaningful concept not only beyond the rudimentary form offered in the ages-of-man formula. The recognition of biographical pre-emplotment also suggests that the untimely death may be a meaningful category despite Cavarero's claim that the biography – though artificial – becomes whole only at the moment of death. But the untimely death is a traumatic irruption which interrupts the imagined futurity built into a proleptically constituted biography, even if one might imagine a variety of potential futures.

This biographical urge is strong and extends even to critical representations of life and death. In *Issues of Death,* Michael Neill in fact suggests that a proleptic form of biographical self-understanding is a key theme in early modern revenge tragedies. From this observation, he then reads *The Spanish Tragedy* as a play about the teleological drive of Hieronimo's life once he writes for himself a revenge plot that runs parallel to the revenge plot of his wild play-within-the-play. According to Neill, "it is the revenger's task," in Kyd's self-consciously metadramatic vision, "to steer this narrative to its necessary resolution; but that does not grant him any autonomous power – to the contrary, as the man 'born to set it right,' [the revenger] is in every sense the agent of plot, his life is *a function of its prescribed end*" (211; emphasis original). Neill's reading of Kyd's play and his thematically similar reading of the more ambivalent *Hamlet* point to the experience of proleptic autonarration – the revenger is a revenger even prior to his act of revenge – and yet it overlooks the play's richest engagement with the question of biographical narration and its disruption. By staging a ghost who experiences the disruption of an anticipated biographical plot, and is suddenly forced to reimagine his life in different narrative terms, *The Spanish Tragedy* makes visible the complex forms of autonarration that make the untimely death a conceptual possibility while also enabling the project of backward-looking self-creation that Cavarero imagines. In his opening speech, the ghost of Hieronimo's son, Andrea, borrows the language of natural biographical unfolding familiar from the riddle of the Sphinx, as in Fancy's ballad and Jaques's ironic speech on the ages of man; he does so in order to describe the injustice of his death at the hands of Balthazar, a Portuguese prince. Invoking the rhetoric of organic seasonality, Andrea imagines that the impending marriage to Bel-imperia was that time when he would have achieved "the harvest of my summer joys," a harvest never reaped because "Death's winter nipped the blossoms of my bliss" (1.1.12–13). Here, the untimely death emerges as a disruption of biography wherein biography and nature are imagined to coincide with the social imperatives of matrimony and the socio-biological imperatives of reproduction.

The disruption of Andrea's apparently organic biography becomes something else, however, when he is unable to descend to hell because "rites of burial" have yet to be performed (1.1.21):

he comes to recognize that his biography might be re-emplotted according to the narrative demands of revenge rather than biology. He might only conclude his now-spectral life and find a way to cross the river Styx once Proserpina introduces him to a personified Revenge. He then becomes a subject emancipated by the fantasized revenge plot of a tragedy that will, Revenge promises, unfold in a predictable form:

> Then know, Andrea, that thou art arrived
> Where thou shalt see the author of thy death,
> Don Balthazar, the prince of Portingale,
> Deprived of life by Bel-imperia.
> Here sit we down to see the mystery,
> And serve for Chorus in this tragedy. (1.1.86–91)

When Don Andrea finds fault in his biographical narrative before re-emplotting his life according to a different set of narrative possibilities drawn from revenge tragedy (or from the logic of revenge in general), Kyd's play points out the double vision involved in the imagination of biographical wholeness. Andrea's destiny was interrupted, and yet, as Revenge insists, Andrea relearns "What 'tis to be subject to destiny" (3.15.28). It is only once revenge has been exacted that Andrea can finally recognize himself at the end of his life: "Ay, now my hopes have end in their effects, / When blood and sorrow finish my desires" (4.5.1–2). Dwelling on the language of conclusion – "end," "finish" – Andrea's life is able to conclude after its interruption only when he and the play adopt a different fantasy of what might make a fitting end. On the one hand, a whole of a life is lived proleptically *in media res* when Andrea imagines biographical fruition, first in reproductive futurity and then in revenge; on the other hand, individual lives can only be narrated retrospectively, once they have been fully lived. As Neill argues, then, *The Spanish Tragedy* is characterized by a "ferocious concentration upon ending" (214), and yet, I argue, the play is willing to renegotiate the ending that provides the conclusion of a life around which biography might be built. In this move, *The Spanish Tragedy* stages the untimely death as a psychological if not ontological truth, and it also draws attention to the self-consciously performative attempts to mitigate the traumatic fact of biographical disruption by appealing to other forms of self-understanding. Andrea may be able to live and die after his new biography has been imagined and played out, but he does so only in an alienated, aestheticized mode as the "Chorus in this tragedy" (1.1.92).

Thinking History on Stage

Kyd's play, as Neill points out, suggests the various forms of biographical emplotment available to early modern dramatists. Specifically, it suggests various ways that a scripted death might be made meaningful according to the logic of teleological organic development or according to the narrative plan associated with retributive justice. And yet to focus exclusively on the dramatic narrative forms available to early modern dramatists – tragedy, revenge tragedy, and so on – means ignoring their intellectual promiscuity and engagement with forms of broader historical explanation. In the first scene of *1 Henry VI*, for instance, the play not only turns to tragedy or revenge tragedy to explain Henry V's death or the in-fighting and political turmoil that caused the Wars of the Roses, it also emplots action according to broader historical logics, staging kinds of narrative explanation that would have been more familiar in the period from the chronicles or from humanist historiography than from the morality play or the Senecan tragedy. The Wars of the Roses unfold onstage as plotted not simply because certain character arcs play out in ways familiar from the period's drama, but because politics and history are also related to supply chains ("want of men and money") and technological or strategic innovation (the French ability to use magic). Henry V's life is not a tidy arc with beginning, middle, and end, yet his death remains meaningful and comprehensible within broader forms of explanation, which contemporaries would have understood as "historical."

Thanks to a series of revisionist critical arguments that have emerged in the past two decades, it has become plausible to take seriously plays like *1 Henry VI* as works of history rather than simply as plays. If we can see the play as a work of serious history writing rather than as a weak imitation of the real thing, we can do so in part because our understanding of early modern historiography has changed since the 1960s and in part because scholars have changed their critical focus as they explore the early modern culture of history writing. This new revisionist program has taken on a set of ideas associated with a previous generation of scholars such as F.J. Levy, Arthur Ferguson, Peter Burke, and F.S. Fussner, each of whom contributed to a set of arguments that identify the emergence of modern historiography in England in the sixteenth and seventeenth centuries. This earlier modernization thesis was itself a radical and much-needed revision of previous accounts of early modern English historiography that treated it as a superficial, uncritical, and unsophisticated account of the past, and yet these claims for the modern sophistication of early modern historiography tended to occlude as much as they revealed, concealing the real heterogeneity of early modern historiography at a moment when it had yet to become institutionalized. Scholars reacting to the work of Levy, Ferguson, Burke, Fussner, and others tend to respond critically to three distinct facets of the arguments offered by this loosely assembled school. More recent revisionists first claim that the methods of early modern historiography were far less homogeneous than the earlier revisionists allowed, and that the innovations of modern humanist historiography or antiquarian research were frequently combined with earlier, non-modern forms of history writing. Second, recent revisionists note that many writers could write both serious modern historiography and forms of history that were putatively less rigorous or serious; such promiscuity suggests that early modern writers did not recognize the strict distinction that subsequent scholars claim to recognize in their works. Third, recent revisionists point out that we make an anachronistic distinction when assuming that "serious" (i.e., methodologically modern) historiography could exist *as* serious historiography without the institutions such as the university or the scholarly press through which seriousness and marginality would subsequently be determined; instead of looking at the seriousness of a discipline that did not yet exist, we might be better served by looking at the wider array of ideas about the past that circulated in the period. Below, I briefly sketch out these debates and explain their relationship to *Untimely Deaths* before ultimately making a claim for the particular distinction and richness of the period that is the focus of this study.

When an earlier generation of revisionists argued for the comprehensive modernity of early modern historiography, they considered this modernity in methodological terms, though they frequently disagreed in their explanations for its emergence. This methodologically modern practice was marked by (1) an increasingly secular explanation of historical processes; (2) a philologically informed scepticism of sources; (3) a broadly "social" sense of history that thinks of the past in terms of populations, governments, technologies, and resources; (4) a sense of historical difference and a worry about the intellectual problem of anachronism; and (5) a sense that history writing was different in the early modern period from other forms of writing, such as poetry, myth, and drama. While broadly agreeing on this idea of modern historiography, however, the sources for the rise of the innovative historiographical practice were often debated. Fussner, for instance, identifies a "historiographical revolution" in the late 1500s that "helped to create those historical attitudes and questionings that we recognize as our own" (xxii), but disagrees with Ferguson over their source.[12] For Fussner, who was followed by scholars such as Donald R. Kelley, Anthony Grafton, and Peter Burke, this modern sense of history emerged from the work of French jurists such as François Baudouin, Jean Bodin, and Pierre Grégoire, from whom it was imported by their English counterparts, many of whom were members of the Elizabethan Society of Antiquaries. Following Ferguson, other scholars such as Joseph Levine, Timothy Hampton, Angus Vine, Robin Headlam Wells, and Philip Schwyzer suggest that historiography became modern earlier in the fifteenth century under the influence of Italian humanists who taught the English to relish curiosities of the past while maintaining philological rigour. As Levine puts it, humanists such as More, Grocyn, and Colet "deliberately turned their backs upon romance and hagiography" – the prevailing "premodern" forms of history writing in England – and "denied both their values and premises" (*Humanism and History* 48). Levine posits that this turn was inspired by exposure to the historicist philology of earlier continental peers or to the "politic histories" of Machiavelli and Guicciardini. Whether borrowing from French jurists or Italian humanists, early modern historiography in these accounts is marked most clearly by the nascent modernity of its method.

Considering the sophisticated historiographical writing produced in sixteenth- and seventeenth-century England, it seems unsurprising that historians would identify it as a watershed moment. No matter which features the scholar privileges as essential to "modern historiography," one can certainly find them in English histories written as early as the 1520s. If focusing, for instance, on typically modern histories that account for historical change by appealing to social and cultural forces, then one can see modern historiography emerging around More, whose history of Richard III demonstrates a meaningful awareness of social forces.[13] If focusing instead on the antiquarian sensibility characteristic of modern historiography – an "unswerving belief in the importance of antiquity and antiquities, a recognition of the value of ancient remains and traces," and a sense of the past's radical difference from the present (Vine 17) – then one might turn instead to members of the Elizabethan Society of Antiquaries, such as William Camden, John Selden, John Stow, and William Lambarde. This latter approach would find that historiography had become modern in England around 1570 with the publication of Lambarde's *Perambulation of Kent* or in 1577 with the publication of Camden's magisterial *Britannia*. Whatever the hallmarks of modern historical method, we can find them at the end of the sixteenth century: a scepticism about sources, a sense of historical difference, a resistance to providential explanation, and a sensitivity to broadly cultural forces.

To follow this critical trajectory and to insist on modernization of early modern historiography, however, means that one draws striking, exceptional works from their immediate historical contexts and then treats them as if they were typical, coherent, and part of a larger, organized program. Focusing on distinctly modern works of historiography or on distinctly modern sections in works of historiography ultimately misrepresents the field of historical writing in the period. For in fact at this moment in time, modern historiography ultimately applied, and would usually operate in tandem with other, non-modern methodologies. In terms of method, personnel, and disciplinary coherence, early modern historical culture is best characterized by appeal to heterogeneity and variety in a way that the modernization thesis contradicts. Certainly, Selden's *History of Tithes*, for instance, contains an astonishingly modern account of a tithing, signalling its modernity by describing in historically responsible terms the institution's transformation over time and in different social contexts. Yet Selden's historicism is far from typical among serious early modern writers of history. In fact, as I discuss below and in chapter 3, this serious, secular, modern method is not even typical within Selden's own corpus.

Perhaps more perversely, as David Womersley notes, when we read early modern historical culture through a sense of its incipient methodological modernity, we ultimately treat some of the period's most typical and important histories as if they were outliers, antiquated, or uninteresting. Foxe's *Actes and Monuments*, for instance, was among the most influential and widely read works of historical scholarship in the period, receiving regular updates and appearing in new editions over the course of a century, and yet the work is relegated by the revisionists to the "ghetto of 'ecclesiastical history'" (Womersley 102).[14] Because writers like Foxe owed debts both to religious sources and to uneven innovations in early modern historiographical method, the modernization thesis and the ghetto of ecclesiastical history seem to rely on "a falsely schematic teasing apart of elements that existed in close entanglement" (96). In this sense, modern methods come to seem less modern because they operate alongside other forms of writing – "romance and hagiography" – from which they might seem mutually exclusive in the world of modern historical thought.

The falsity of these schemata is perhaps clearest when considering even the most sophisticated, most modern works in the *artes historicae*. Taking, for instance, the first theoretical reflection on the practice of history writing to appear in English, Thomas Blundeville's *True Order and Method for the Reading and Writing of History* (1574), we recognize that history writers in the period – both in England and on the continent – rarely bracketed theological concerns and would mix different kinds of historical explanation quite comfortably, refusing to recognize category errors between religious and secular forms of explanation. Blundeville, translating the work of continental historians Francesco Patrizi and Jacopo Aconcio, situates himself in the traditions of Renaissance humanism, and yet neither he nor his sources seem bothered by their simultaneous providentialism, even when insisting on the practical value of historical knowledge for men at court. According to Blundeville, a sovereign's advisers need to read about how governors have ruled in the past in order to predict the future: "bycause we finde manye tymes, that like meanes haue bene used to the obtayning of like endes, (as we suppose) & yet not with like succcesse, we ought therfore diligently to consider the diuers natures of thinges, and the differences of tymes, and occasions, and such like accidents, to see if we can possibly finde out the cause why mens purposes have taken effect at one time, and not at an other" (H1). In this claim – politically sensitive, historically astute, aiming towards historiographical utility – Blundeville (via Patrizi) situates himself, as noted above, in the centre of the characteristically modern historiographical practice associated with humanist historians such as Guicciardini and Machiavelli in Italy and Bacon in England. As Lisa Jardine points out, Bacon's history of Henry VI was at the cutting edge of English historiography when, like Blundeville, he concentrated on "social and geographical details, as well as the details of policy" (156). By emphasizing questions of causality and recognizing the specific claims of historicity – "social and geographical details" – Blundeville thus contributes to that distinctly modern humanist historiographical practice, one that moves beyond the early humanistic focus on "great men."[15]

But this account of Blundeville's *True Order* is decidedly partial. Though Blundeville describes and idealizes the secular and deeply historicist intellectual project associated with historiographical modernity, its fundamental ground of historical explanation remains providential, and its fundamental end of historical enquiry remains a mix of moral and political edification. On the page immediately after that where Blundeville identifies the methodological imperative to document social history, for instance, he claims that historians show modern readers "prosperous success, which God hath gyuen as iuste rewardes to those, that woorke according to vertue: the great good will and love that allmen haue towardes them" (H1v). The historian, furthermore, should record the effect of "unlawfull meanes" and should "note what revenge God is woont to take of such doinges, and howe short a tyme & with what trouble, hee suffereth vs to enjoy them" (G1v).[16] From the perspective of the discipline that history would become later in the century, Blundeville seems to be making a serious category error when imagining that the historian functions in such didactic terms. But the document shows no sense of self-contradiction, as if it were not even thinkable that the two forms of writing might be at odds. Indeed, Woolf seems to miss the easiness of Blundeville's conclusions when claiming that Blundeville reconciles humanist practice with a clumsy providentialism in order to produce a surprising model of historical change (*Idea* 5). In fact, Blundeville's argument is striking because it fails to acknowledge any underlying conflict that *requires* arduous reconciliation. Such comfort deploying apparently contradictory forms of historical explanation, one "modern" and one "premodern," was, I posit, typical in the period, which is why it inspires little obvious hand-wringing. The same observation might be made Ralegh's *History of the World*,[17] for instance, or in the multivocal chronicles that I treat in the first chapter of this book.

Contrary to the modernization thesis, then, early modern historiography is, in general, characterized by an methodological heterogeneity inconsistent to modern eyes. Also troubling to the modernization thesis, the field of early modern history writing is far less stable and coherent from a disciplinary perspective. According to the modernization thesis, historiography became modern in the sixteenth century in England when it became a form of writing concerned with social and political facts, diverging from other forms of poetic or literary writing. Following from this thesis, poets and playwrights in the sixteenth century were suddenly free to be autonomous, proto-Romantic creators, unburdened by the world of historical fact, which was a preserve for historians alone. In the fifteenth century, as Levine argues, Caxton believed that Aeneas and Arthur were historically real figures and that Galfridian history was true, but "it was William Camden, finally, who set out all the evidence and politely disposed of it [Caxton's belief] once and for all in the *Britannia*" (*Humanism and History* 49); intimating a curious chronology, he also claims that "by Bacon's time ... the poets were exulting openly in their new-found freedom and autonomy" from the demands of historical factuality, turning away from history and enthusiastically towards romance (51). As with most stories of radical, sudden intellectual-historical transformation, Levine's story obscures more than it clarifies. The popularity of history plays in print continued well into the seventeenth century, for instance, even if few history plays were being written for the stage,[18] and the world of history writing overlapped considerably with the world of fiction, verse, and drama.

The complementarity between works of history and literature is perhaps most obvious in the multidisciplinarity of early modern writers at a moment when historiography had yet to become a discipline in the modern sense. Considering the serious historiographical work of poets and playwrights, the overlap in personnel is hardly surprising: Jonson wrote a prose history of Henry V that was lost in his library fire; Middleton was appointed the Chronologer of the City of London; upon Middleton's death, Jonson assumed this position, followed by Thomas May, who would be the third playwright in the role and would subsequently write a history of Parliament; Thomas Heywood took up mythic history in *Troia Britannica*, wrote several history plays, and demonstrates serious antiquarian sensitivity and numismatic knowledge in his *Apology for Actors*, just as he demonstrates philological acumen in his translation of the historian Sallust; Barnabe Barnes wrote a history of Elizabeth and Essex for James; John Bale participated in the compilation of the *Magdeburg Centuries*; Cyril Tourneur (discussed in chapter 4) also wrote military history; Thomas Legge was also a professor of civil law (an essentially historical topic in the sixteenth century); Thomas Lodge translated Josephus, the first century Jewish-Roman historian; and Arthur Wilson wrote a history of Britain.

But to point to playwrights who also wrote prose history assumes an erroneous distinction between literary history and "serious" historiography. Recently, following upon Woolf's capacious vision of historical culture, critics such as Blair Worden, Richard Helgerson, Benjamin Griffin, Teresa Grant, Barbara Ravelhofer, Alex Davis, and Paulina Kewes, among others, have insisted on the historiographical sophistication of early modern plays. As Reid Barbour points out, historiography, "like drama, was conceived as an exercise of the imagination, in which historians, like dramatists, asked themselves what a given character would have said or done in a given situation" (59, see also Worden, "Historians and Poets," *passim*). For Grant and Ravelhofer, history writing is best understood in the period as a "fluid and unfixed entity which encompasses as many different meanings as there are commentators" (14). These assertions of a homology between historians and poets – and their insistence that both types of writers aim towards some sort of realism with respect to the past and its processes – remind us that, in the early modern period, drama was a medium for significant historical thought rather than a parasitical genre rehashing information from other sources (Woolf, *Reading* 26).[19] Indeed, those features of critical enquiry characteristic of serious historiographical practice are features that we find in plays as well, leading F.J. Levy to suggest that "organized" history (as compared with chronicle history) "became much more common with the 'politic' historians" but "appeared first in the theater, and Sir John Hayward and Lord Bacon ... were well aware of the fact" (233). While Levy perhaps overstates the case when suggesting that humanist historiography owes a considerable debt to drama, he is correct to recognize that the demands of the theatre for plot, setting, and action require a sophisticated sensibility that might be best called "historical." When we witness bishops cynically debating Salic law at the opening of Shakespeare's *Henry V*, for instance, the play stages the same sort of philological concern that was characteristic of Lorenzo Valla's engagement with the Donation of Constantine. When Jonson published comprehensive annotations to his 1604 *Sejanus*, he produced a document of considerable philological rigour that, he declares, "shew[s] my integrity in the story" and "save[s] myself in those common torturers that bring all wit to the rack" ("To the Readers"). It seems unsurprising that, when released from prison after the *Eastward Ho!* scandal, Jonson, a serious historian as well as a playwright, would celebrate at a banquet with Camden and Selden, the two writers of history most closely associated with the modernization of early modern English historiography.[20] It makes similar sense that Selden would subsequently contribute Latin verses to Jonson's 1616 folio.

If it is difficult to identify the centre and periphery of early modern historical culture, this is likely because the world of history writing existed without a disciplinary infrastructure that could police its boundaries. Instead of operating within a strict – modern? – disciplinary form, the practice of history writing was instead decidedly undisciplined, disarticulated from various agencies and institutions through which it could become standardized, through which methodologies could be authorized and discarded, or through which historical thinking could be vetted *as* historical thinking by individuals who wielded symbolic and material authority. Ad hoc organizations such as the Elizabethan Society for Antiquaries flourished, and historical thought circulated in the universities, and yet it was only in 1623 that the first professional historian was installed in England, when Degory Wheare was seated as the Camden Chair of Ancient History at Oxford. Certainly, a discipline is more than a position in the university – it is an established set of methods, a writing practice, a network of commentary, a vocabulary, and so on – but a position in the university provides at least one site of authority through which such an institutionalized field can produce and reproduce itself, underwritten as it is by "courses and professorships, scholarly correspondence, monographs, textbooks, and scholarly journals" that render certain forms of thought authentic (Kelley, *Foundations* 19). This is not to say that Wheare's instalment offers a clear start date for the emergence of history as a recognized academic field. Wheare was neither original nor originary. He drew on earlier historians from the Basel Anthology in his *Method and Order of Reading both Civil and Ecclesiastical Histories*. And certainly serious historiography continued to be written outside the university after Wheare won his appointment. But his tenure at the university and the publication of his *ars historica* provide a useful, heuristic waypoint in the development of historiographical culture in the early seventeenth century, after which it makes more sense to imagine dominant or authoritative forms of historical writing.

Wheare's appointment suggests an increasing disciplinary centralization in the history of historical thought, moving the practice of history writing and reading away from the practical interests of the court and towards disinterested academic enquiry. Consequently, a comparison of his *Method and Order* to Blundeville's *True Order and Method* is illustrative, not least because Blundeville wrote the first English contribution to the tradition of Renaissance *artes historicae* and Wheare wrote the last. Blundeville's contribution to the *artes historicae* was at the cutting edge of humanist historical practice when it was published in 1574, and yet it was, as Blundeville claimed, authorized and made significant for practical rather than scholarly reasons. Dedicated to the Earl of Leicester, the work's value is, he insists, political and instrumental. Following rhetoric familiar from *artes historicae*, Blundeville claims to outline a practice of reading and writing that would enable a statesman to "gather" from histories "such judgement and knowledge as you may ther[e]by be the more able ... to direct your private actions, as to give Counsell lyke a most prudent Counseller" (A2). A gentleman scholar, Blundeville often thinks in such practical terms about the political ends of study and scholarship, treating history as a skill or, as we saw in the passage cited above, a set of useful facts about the past, rather than a discipline. In his *Brief and Profitable Treatise* on counsel to princes (1570), for instance, Blundeville insists that the "qualities of the minde requisite in anye counseler in generall, are in number ... xv":

1. To be wise.
2. To be eloquent.
3. To speake dyuers languages.
4. To be a good Hystoriographer.
5. To be a good Morall Philosopher ... (D2v–D3)

In such a list, which continues to include such courtly features as the "right judgement in all thinges" (D3), to be a historiographer or moral philosopher is a skill that one has or a feature of general competence rather than a vocation.

While Wheare's *Method and Order*, first published in 1625, shares with Blundeville's *True Order* an intellectual debt to continental humanists, the scene of his work's production and its investment in university pedagogy suggest that it aims to perform very different work. Outlining his book in its first English translation of 1685, Wheare explains his project succinctly:

> the first [part] ... shall containe the principal Authors which are to be read, and shall also shew the Order in which they are to be read, the second shall teach who is to be Esteem'd a Competent, well qualified reader of History; the third shall shew an Excellent way of gathering the fruits of History, and Explain the orders and Method of disposing them into Cells or Storehouse. (C2v)

Because Wheare's *Method and Order* is an edited version of a lecture that he gave to the university prior to assuming the Camden Chair, the pedagogical goals and the institutional language are unsurprising. Wheare considers history in terms of the university's disciplinary ends when describing the "well qualified reader of history." For instance, he offers the student mnemonic tips and promises the development of a curriculum or an orderly system for reading classical history. As the title page insists, the project Wheare outlines is properly reflexive and programmatic: it looks upon itself in order to reproduce itself and to build on a tradition. In the *True Method and Order*, "The most Excellent Historians are Reduced into the Order in which they are Successively to be Read; and the Judgments of Learned Men, concerning each of them, Subjoined." The ends and system of scholarly evaluation are determined for Wheare, in sum, by appeal to intellectual expertise and judgment rather than by appeal to a civic or courtly value. Certainly towards the end of his book, Wheare echoes the humanist claims of civic instrumentality that appear throughout the tradition of Renaissance *artes historicae*, but he seems less interested and engaged in the book's closing passages: rather than critically examining claims to extra-disciplinary utility, he turns over these discussions largely to Bartholomäus Keckerman, Gerardus Vossius, and Simon Grynaeus, from whom he cuts and pastes extensive notes on the "fruits" of historiography.[21] Broadly disinterested in the instrumental application of knowledge, Wheare aims primarily to program a discipline that measures itself on its own terms and then reproduces itself through "well qualified" disciples.

Though Wheare might not provide a hard start point for a phenomenon as amorphous as the modernization of historical thought in England, the distinction between Blundeville's and Wheare's works – between

1572 and 1625 – offers a heuristic period through which we can usefully consider the character of historical culture in early modern England and its relationship to the early modern stage. Between the publication of the first and the last English contributions to the tradition of Renaissance *artes historicae* we must recognize a wide and diverse field of learned historical enquiry, one that had yet to be bound up with the language of authority associated with disciplinarity and the modern university. This is not to say, of course, that all history writing was treated equally or that early modern writers of history were unable to distinguish between fiction and fact until a discipline emerged. Rather, to recognize the undisciplined character of history writing in the period means recognizing that historical thought proliferated outside of the university and that meticulous historiography was often combined with providentialist fantasy and fiction, among other approaches. Camden, for instance, provided intellectual foundations for the English legal system and modern historical thought, and yet he also remained agnostic on the question of Brute's role in England's past and the role of divine intervention at the battle of Agincourt. In such a field of enquiry, we need to take seriously the historical work that early modern dramatists performed, to recognize that they were often writers of savvy, non-dramatic history, and that the distinction between literary, dramatic, and serious historiography was only just emerging.

Because early modern playwrights had access to (and often produced) serious historical writing, drama is an ideal medium for any attempt to understand the workings of early modern historical culture. To read drama in terms of history is not to assert that early modern dramatists reflected prevailing notions of historical change or operated with respect to history writing at a remove that allowed them critical distance. Instead it is to recognize that early modern dramatists were seriously engaged with discussions of history. In acknowledging this facet of early modern drama, the recent calls by scholars such as Kewes for not only interdisciplinary approaches to the literature but a broader understanding of what counts as a historical genre in the first place. As Kewes notes, despite the influences of new historicism and cultural materialism, our knowledge of early modern historical culture "is still constrained by disciplinary divisions between history and literary studies. Although scholarly accounts of individual forms of historical writing – the chronicle, antiquarian tracts, the history play, politic historiography, urban histories, and so on – have proliferated in recent years, there has been a corresponding narrowing of the corpus of genres discussed in general studies of early modern historiography" ("History" 3). This disciplinary retrenchment is ultimately problematic if we hope to approach the archive without anachronistically applying post-Enlightenment ideas of disciplinarity to a pre-Enlightenment culture: we must engage with a "variety of genres" if we hope to understand "early modern historical culture since, even if many of those genres are no longer recognized as history, early modern writers and readers treated them as such" (5).

Ultimately, Kewes and other recent historians have established a new area of enquiry when they reimagine the world of history writing in the sixteenth and seventeenth centuries. When we look at "early modern historical culture" through this reimagining, we no longer see the same field as that which a previous generation of revisionists saw. As the phrase "historical culture" signals, this new vision, in which *Untimely Deaths* participates, treats a wide and amorphous array of phenomena rather than a constricted discipline. In such a vision of the historical past, as Matthew Neufeld points out, the "focus is less on the problem of determining the truth about the past ... and more on what the past meant for early modern people, and on the way it impinged on a range of social and cultural practices" (485). Crucial here is an expansive sense of how history is put to work beyond the confines of a university or, as the humanist historian might have it, beyond the confines of a court. It is this complex field that I explore in *Untimely Deaths*, highlighting the various forms of historical explanation accessible in early modern England by studying their failure, or those moments when it seems impossible to explain the unfolding of history, even when using the wide array of a contemporary's available narrative tools. These tools, I argue, are ultimately the foundation of the culture of history.

Outlining *Untimely Deaths*

The first chapter of *Untimely Deaths* turns to *Richard II* in order to further develop the discussions of historiography outlined above by challenging the familiar reading of the play's historical vision and its explanation of Richard's death, a death that Bolingbroke declares untimely in the play's final line. Following work from the 1990s by scholars as diverse as Phyllis Rackin and Richard Halpern, recent scholars such as Zenón Luis-Martínez continue to turn to E.M.W. Tillyard as a strawman, and find in Shakespeare's play the renunciation of providential historiography and the insistence on a secular, humanist, "Machiavellian" historicism. According to this reading, when Richard dies at the end of Shakespeare's play, his death arrives at the right time not because providence ordains it, as Tillyard suggests, but because secular forces of history necessarily topple inept sovereigns. Such a reading of Shakespeare's play is problematic, I argue, because it elides the play's radical and self-conscious narrative-historical confusion and because it imagines humanism and providentialism as the only two options available to early modern writers of history. I show instead that *Richard II* offers a variety of historical accounts for the action it stages, and that it carefully withholds information that would confirm any of the given narrative possibilities to which it points. In doing so, the play emphasizes the overabundance of potential historical causes of Richard's death that were circulating in the chronicles, pamphlets, and ballads that served as Shakespeare's sources. For a play that features so many characters who obsessively meditate on the historical causes of the world in which they live – from *de casibus* providence to social history to a great-man model of humanism to a stoic insistence on chance – *Richard II* is astonishingly short on the sort of evidence that an audience would need to explain Richard's death in historical terms.

Having explored the fragmentation of historiographical thought in the chapter on *Richard II*, my focus turns, in the second chapter, on Thomas Middleton's *Chaste Maid in Cheapside*, to explore the ways that myriad historiographical methods might work syncretically to explain the unfolding of history and the position of the individual within history. Struggling to account for the surprising deaths and resurrections at the end of Middleton's play, critics disagree over the nature of the historical world in which the play is set. On the one hand, the play is situated in London at the end of Lent and is saturated with allusions to the Christian story of redemption, which suggests that London somehow participates in the story of salvation typical of romance; on the other hand, the play's deep cynicism, its preoccupation with London's vices, and its focus on commerce potentially ironize these allusions, transforming the story of urban redemption into a story of charming and urbane, but amoral, savvy. In the latter reading, the world of London is somehow beyond the Christianized, romantic processes of death and redemption, while in the former reading, even a debased urban space participates in the salvation typical of a Christianized romance narrative. Such debates seem wrongheaded, I argue, because they ignore the ambivalent vision of London that we find in various histories of the city, such as those written by Middleton himself in his mayoral pageants, as well in the cycle plays that *Chaste Maid* cites. To choose between a debased "citizen time" and a sacramental "romance time" in reading the play is to ignore contemporaneous descriptions of urban life, which imbricate civic institutions and commercial trade *within* historical narratives of sacred redemption. To find romantic redemption in the institutions of civic life was a familiar gesture in early modern histories of London, which regularly used the aggrandizing of romantic plots to celebrate civic development. As Middleton's play suggests, urban history was also often sacred history in early modern history writing, and the redeemed untimely deaths of his protagonists participate in the sacred as well as secular histories of the city.

In the third chapter, I argue that Marlowe responds differently to historiographical overdetermination than either Middleton or Shakespeare. Compared with Shakespeare's historical agnosticism and Middleton's historical syncretism, Marlowe's approach seems utterly sceptical of grand historical narratives and explanations. Specifically, *Dido Queen of Carthage* speaks to a growing sixteenth-century scepticism about the mythic and epic roots of "Britannia," the archipelagic proto-nation imaginatively constituted from the ashes of Troy through the *translatio imperii* and through further exploration by Aeneas's grandson, Brute. Dramatically, however, the play also articulates the human cost of this historical scepticism, or the price paid by individual human beings once mythic history fails to seem plausible. Here, *Untimely Deaths* argues that the critical tradition has widely misread the relationship between tragedy and epic history in Virgil's poem and in Marlowe's play. When critics maintain that Marlowe transforms Aeneas's epic history into Dido's tragedy by desublimating the historical machinery of Virgil's epic and by focusing on Dido's death, they ignore that Virgil's story of Dido borrows heavily from the tradition of classical tragedy – emphasizing a tragic *telos* in the Dido plot – and that Marlowe's account of Dido's story refuses to explain her death in satisfying, tragic terms. When Marlowe renounces epic history in *Dido* – when he reduces epic history by offering a story of debased gods and equally debased human beings – he ultimately eliminates any sense that Dido's death is "tragic," or that its end might be understood in terms of tragic narrative with a beginning and middle that somehow cause its end. Dido's death is irredeemably untimely in Marlowe's play because history for Marlowe, following a narrow stream of historiographical trends, is fundamentally shapeless.

Whereas the preceding chapters explore the engagement of early modern dramatists with extra-dramatic historiographical forms, the final chapter, on Tourneur's *Atheist's Tragedy*, works in the opposite direction, discussing how drama *as* drama participated in the field of early modern historiography. Tourneur's play is, in some respects, a typical revenge tragedy, even though it was first produced after the fad for revenge tragedies had waned. Suffused by melodrama *avant la lettre*, it is typical of the genre, featuring a hyperbolically villainous antagonist, a pathologically virtuous hero avenging his father's murder, and an angry ghost faithful to revenge tragedy's Senecan roots. And yet

The Atheist's Tragedy also features an elaborate set piece describing the notoriously bloody Siege of Ostend, in which English forces defended Ostend for three years between 1600 and 1603, before surrendering to the Spanish and returning home after 20,000 English soldiers had died. The set piece is astonishing for its accurate historical detail, describing idiosyncratic military manoeuvres determined by Ostend's unique geography. By situating the Siege of Ostend and other historical military catastrophes within the narrative logic of revenge tragedy – a narrative logic that satisfies demands for inevitable punitive justice – Tourneur's play struggles to make sense of a historical catastrophe that made little sense in early modern England. At the moment when Tourneur wrote his play, the Siege of Ostend had yet to be "historicized," or subjected to the logic of historical explanation; no English writer had attempted to represent or account for the combat in the Low Countries in historical terms, even though various news pamphlets were circulating that described the violence of the battle and the massive number of English casualties. In light of Tourneur's famous elegy for Prince Henry and his clear allegiance to an idea of bellicose Protestant irredentism, the play becomes an explanation of recent English history through the logic of revenge tragedy, finding a narrative historical reason for national catastrophe in the subject-centric plotting of the dramatic tradition when no other explanation was forthcoming from other quarters.

The concluding chapter of *Untimely Deaths* reads Jonson's late plays against the considerations I deal with in the rest of the book, exploring specifically how Jonson understands his own lifespan. A sophisticated historian, a masterful plotter, and a self-conscious shaper of his persona, Jonson attempts in the paratexts of his late plays to establish the wholeness of his life against contemporaries who imagine the apex of his career a decade earlier with the publication of his 1616 folio *Workes*. While critics both modern and early modern imagine that Jonson somehow lived "too long" – he "enfolioed himself [...] as a dead classical author" in Lynn Meskill's phrase (*Envy* 187) – Jonson asks his readers to imagine the cursus of his career differently. Rather than producing dotages, that is, or rather than writing after-works that lamely followed upon his accomplishing his greatest *Workes*, Jonson insists on framing his late works as the culmination of a life, as a return to and perfection of earlier projects. In this sense, Jonson's ultimate act of authorial self-figuration appears not in the folio, as is often argued, but in the late plays that meditate on the fullness of a life – his own life – as a whole.

Chapter One

Richard II, Problem Tragedy

In the final lines of *Richard II*, Bolingbroke attempts to cement the legitimacy of his reign by initiating the funeral of his predecessor. Ironically, however, as he walks Richard's corpse towards its grave, he draws attention to the potential illegitimacy of his succession. Inaugurating the process of mourning that will mark the absolute end of his predecessor's claim to the throne, Bolingbroke closes the play by insisting that his court "March sadly after, grace my mournings here / In weeping after this untimely bier" (5.6.51–2). If Bolingbroke means to mark the end of Richard's reign, then his recognition that Richard's bier is "untimely" raises difficult questions. Richard is dead too soon, it seems, and history has been disrupted, no matter what a funeral procession might signify. As we have learned from de Certeau, Derrida, Caruth, Dominick LaCapra, and many others, rites of mourning attempt to entomb the past *in* the past under the guise of commemoration so that the living can live unhaunted lives. But Bolingbroke's recognition of untimeliness draws attention to the problematically instrumental utility of mourning: he seems aware that putting the dead in their place by mourning them requires us to overlook or conceal the traumatic character of some deaths that arrive before their time. "Richard should be alive and I shouldn't be king," he says, "but let's ignore that." Considering the ironies of this funereal gesture, it seems fitting that Richard continues to live as a spectral agent in Shakespeare's later history plays, even after his interment. Three plays later in the second tetralogy, Bolingbroke's son reminds audiences that he has had to rebury the king whose untimely death has disrupted the logic of natural succession: "O! not today," Henry V implores God on the eve of the battle of Agincourt, "think not upon the fault / My father made in encompassing the crown. / I Richard's body have interred anew" (4.1.275–7).[1] The ghost of Richard lingers in the second tetralogy, requiring more than one burial, as his corpse is moved from Langley Abbey to the Abbey of St Peter, Westminster. Because his death comes somehow too early, he continues to linger and refuses to be part of the past, no matter how often he finds himself entombed.

But what does Bolingbroke mean when he identifies Richard's death as "untimely"? As the modern critical tradition suggests, Richard's death seems "timely" because it arrives at the correct point of a coherent and familiar narrative arc. Indeed, a substantial portion of this critical tradition over the whole span of the past fifty years spends time explaining Richard's death in terms of its narrative satisfactions. Surprisingly, however, this tradition offers a number of mutually exclusive explanations of Richard's biographical plot. Richard Halpern, for instance, argues that the play is a *Trauerspiel* because it stages a "tyrant figure of *Trauerspiel* as, precisely, indecisive: buffeted by his own creaturely passions, the tyrant finds himself unable to wield his own sovereign power ... [and] is upended by the courtly intriguer" (72). In such a reading, Richard's death seems timely, emerging organically from a weakness in his character. James Phillips similarly sees in Richard "a king whose half-hearted tyranny proves fatal to him" (161). Hugh Grady sees "a deficient Machiavellian who needs to study the details of his *Prince* much more closely" (134), and Peter Ure sees a monarch who overreached when he seized Bolingbroke's inheritance and fell as a result (lxvi). Moving from secular to providential explanations of Richard's death, Phyllis Rackin finds a king who lives in a "providential world" but who has "dispersed" his own sacred legitimacy and dies as a result (76). Robert Rentoul Reed identifies "God as the avenger of the deposed Richard II" (21), and Paul Budra finds a monarch punished by God, even if the play is less pious than a standard *de casibus* tragedy. Contrasting these readings that find political or moralized history in the play, Bernard McElroy claims that the meditative and often plodding *Richard II* is "not really about issues at all but about characters who must face those issues in a specific context" (14); if the play is more interested in character than politics or providence, then Richard Wheeler is compelling when he psychologizes Richard, arguing that the king is driven by a sense of guilt or shame, and that he "collaborates in his own destruction" (159). In the shadow of these debates about the historical cause of Richard's fall, Anthony Dawson and Paul Yachnin, the play's most recent Oxford editors, have chosen agnosticism. Following Steven Mullaney's vision of the early modern theatre as an interrogative space that allowed early modern audiences to "sound out the gaps" of their contemporary world, Dawson and Yachnin claim that the play is "a complex, unfolding action intended to entertain, arouse strong feelings, and make possible disciplined political thinking," without insisting on one interpretation of the plot's motive forces (Introduction 21).

If we agree with Dawson and Yachnin that the play stages an ambiguous "complex, unfolding action," then we also seem unable to agree with them that the play is also Shakespeare's "most austere achievement in the genre of tragedy" ("Introduction" 42). No matter which vision of tragedy we might invoke – from Aristotle's idea of tragedy in c. 335 BCE to Paul Kottman's in 2012 – tragic narrative imagines a relationship between character and catastrophe, meaning that its "complex, unfolding action" is, in some sense, anathema to the form, according to both classical and early modern theories of the genre. To be tragic rather than pathetic or absurd, Aristotle claims, a tragedy's final catastrophe must be "necessary or probable" relative to character, meaning that it must fit a specific character at a specific historical moment (Aristotle 50b30). In other words, it must be "timely," or narratively satisfying, however necessity or probability are mediated by historical assumptions. Kottman similarly points out that a "tragic *mythos*" by definition is a "series of consequential actions, reversals, and recognitions" that speak to a sense of necessity rather than offering a "summation of disjointed facts" ("Defying" 4). As he says elsewhere, "tragedy stages the different forms and meanings that a given subject's fate may take," and it explains why rather than how "this destiny comes about" ("Slipping" 7). In a specifically early modern context, Sidney makes this connection between tragedy and character clear: if "evil men come to the stage," he insists, "they ever go out – as the tragedy writer answered to one that misliked the show of such persons – so manacled as they little animate folks to follow them" (*Defence of Poetry* 24). As I discuss below in a reading of Marlowe's *Dido*, Sidney's vision of tragedy relies on a ubiquitous early modern idea that ties tragedy's didactic function to the relationship between character (rather than action) and catastrophe.

Instead of attempting to finally identify the "real" tragic *mythos* of Shakespeare's play, I argue here that *Richard II* locates the cause of Richard's death in too many distinct, often contradictory, potential causes; it is self-consciously and ironically *too* successful a tragedy. Is Richard's death "necessary" because he is a medieval king, invested in the idea of sacred authority, who lives in a modern, Machiavellian world? Is his death "probable" because God punishes monarchs who abuse their divinely sanctioned authority? Does he die because of a division in his character or because of an impulse towards self-destruction? Critics responding to Shakespeare's play answer these questions in different ways, and so too do characters within the play.

More than in any other play in Shakespeare's oeuvre, characters in *Richard II* seem intent on describing the processes of history that shape their world, and they do so in compelling, if contradictory, ways. By drawing attention to these questions of historical interpretation without ever answering them conclusively, *Richard II* seems like a "problem tragedy." It refuses to provide the answers that tragic narrative *as* tragic narrative is expected to provide: how did we get here? Why did this catastrophe befall this figure at this moment? Such explanatory work is the work of tragic narrative, and Shakespeare's plot in *Richard II* refuses to perform this work by performing it too readily.

The problem of plot in Shakespeare's play ultimately reflects what I describe here as a historiographical problem in his sources. The narrative problem in Shakespeare's play replicates the confused state of early modern historiography around Richard's death, and it does so self-consciously. If, as I claim in the introduction to *Untimely Deaths*, the main stream of historiographical theory around the turn of the seventeenth century was broadly incoherent when it came to questions of historical causality, then the stories that Shakespeare inherited about Richard's death concretize these theoretical confusions. Richard's death, depending on a given historian's methodological practice, was rationalized in myriad ways. Rather than identifying the narrative problem of Shakespeare's play as a symptom of his promiscuous reading, as if he consulted too many sources, I would suggest that this confusion is internal to the individual sources to which he turned. By recognizing the historiographical confusion of Shakespeare's sources, we can better recognize Shakespeare's intervention as a historian in contemporaneous historical debates around Richard's fall. When he concludes his play by drawing attention to the untimeliness of Richard's death, Shakespeare reminds his audience that questions of timeliness and historical causality are fraught, and that they fail to abide in any straightforward way the characterological focus of tragedy, no matter how insistently Richard and other characters in the play attempt to think of his downfall as a tragedy with an identifiable, characterological cause. In a play that seems conspicuously confused about such questions of history, in the same way that early modern historiographers were confused about history, *Richard II*'s narrative ambiguity appears to be symptomatic of a methodologically overdetermined historiographical culture.

As I discuss below, a substantial strain of criticism treating *Richard II* and historiography has treated early modern historiography as a space in which writers exclusively debated the question of providence. The discussion of providence in human affairs is central to contemporaneous historiographical theory and practice (Thomas Blundeville, Edmund Bolton, Degory Wheare, and Sir John Hayward all explicitly ask questions about providence), and yet debates among early modern historiographers moved well beyond the discussion of God's hand in sublunary affairs. Writers of history also tarried with questions about the role of "social" forces, chance, character, the economy, and popularity in the broad transformations of political history. These complicated considerations of history suffuse early modern discussions of Richard's reign just as they suffuse Shakespeare's play. If Richard fails to die a death proper to some characterological cause, then he fails not because providential order has been replaced by chaos but because the play has too many stories to tell about his death, none of which fits perfectly.

From a reading of *Richard II* that situates the play within the context of early modern discussions of Richard's reign, we can also rethink the broad narratives surrounding Shakespeare's development as a dramatist and historian. As I discuss at length in the conclusion to this chapter, familiar stories of professional development suggest that Shakespeare is overwhelmed by the contingencies of history in his early, unwieldy *Henry VI* plays before he subjects history to the workings of tragedy in *Richard II* and *Richard III*. He then matures so that he can treat history in a character-driven, humanistic, potentially triumphalist mode in the *Henry IV* plays and *Henry V*. This teleological fantasy of Shakespeare's growth falls apart when we recognize in *Richard II* a more complicated story of the relationship between theatre and historiographical methods: here, generic habits vie with common historical methods and a variety of historiographical assumptions as Shakespeare attempts to explain the unfolding of a specific reign and the downfall of a specific king. Rather than following the story of Shakespeare's development as a dramatist, we can just as easily recognize that Shakespeare's historical vision in the tetralogies corresponds with contemporaneous historical discussions of the individual reigns that he stages. A good historian recognizes that different political forces operate more or less powerfully at different historical moments, meaning that early modern history writers could more easily write a *de casibus* plot about the fall of Richard III than they could write a *de casibus* plot about the fall of Henry VI. Sometimes God punishes evil kings for their sinfulness; sometimes barons punish weak sovereigns for their weakness. This, famously, is Sidney's great criticism of historiography when one looks to it for moralistic lessons that can teach virtue. As Shakespeare recognized, this didactic failure is the result of history's variety: different times call for different measures of history.

Shakespeare's Sources and Their "Sundrye Vices"

The story of Richard's fall was a popular topic for historians and poets during the latter half of the sixteenth century, in part because it spoke so evocatively to the contemporaneous political climate. Even if Elizabeth had never actually identified with Richard – "I am Richard 2d. know ye not that?" she reportedly asked William Lambarde – the monarchs had much in common. They dealt with similar conflicts when they faced antagonistic Parliaments, factious courts, and potential threats from popular members of the nobility.[2] When the republican Sir John Hayward dedicated his history of Richard's fall to the Earl of Essex, for instance, he was imprisoned because the resonance between the two reigns seemed dangerously clear, where Bolingbroke might serve as a heroic antitype to Essex. Pointing to this historical echo, jurist and prosecutor Edward Coke insisted that Hayward had worked against the interests of the crown when he "fetche[ed] a storie 200 yere olde, and publish[ed] it this last yere, intendinge the application of it to this tyme" (NA SP 12/275, no. 25.i, fol. 42v).[3] The histories seemed so easily comparable that historical analysis of one "tyme" felt like historical analysis of the other. Beyond the immediately topical resonance of Richard's life, the story was redolent in the period because it spoke to fraught questions about divine right, royal prerogative, and Parliament's role in governance. While these questions of political philosophy and theology would come to a head catastrophically in the 1640s, they were percolating intellectually and practically for a century prior to start of the civil war.[4]

Despite this obvious topicality, contemporary historical accounts disagreed over the lessons that readers should glean from the history of Richard because they disagreed over the nature of the plot and its motive forces. Even if these historians never intended to be topical, the methodological distinctions between their practices correspond loosely with various positions in contemporary philosophical debates about England's constitution. To draw a quick, illustrative distinction, familiar from critical discussions of the play's politics: Hall's providentialist account of Richard's reign implies an argument for divine sovereignty, while Hayward's socially minded history imagines a secular, modern political world in which popularity is a powerful political weapon. When the engine of history is imagined differently – shifting from the hand of God to the force of "the people," who have a voice in Hayward's history – political order and the lessons of history are also imagined differently.

Such a claim is, doubtless, unsurprising: different historians with different methodologies and assumptions produce different sorts of stories about history. Crucial to our understanding of Shakespeare's play, however, is that none of the sources to which he might have turned was methodologically "pure." Though the critical tradition since Tillyard has treated Hall as the font of a naïve providentialism, for instance, his *Union* regularly tempers its providentialism by focusing on secondary historical causes and on the authority of Parliament in the process of succession. "[N]oble menne murmured" during Richard's reign, he notes, "and the comon people grudged, and all menne wondered at his unprincely doynges" (A2v). More significant, however, is that the long speech he attributes to the Archbishop of Canterbury implies that such grudges are politically and historically meaningful: "wee miserable subjectes have so long borne the yoke of wa[n]ton unwitty kyng Richard, and have paciently tollerat the parnicious persecucion of his gredy and avaricious councellers ... And therfore necessitie, and not will, reason, and not affeccion" inspire the political efforts to end Richard's reign (fol. v). Rather than finding simple providentialism in Hall, we find instead an account of Richard's fall that takes seriously a complicated set of political affairs and stakeholders, including the Commons, the nobility, and (in the body of the Archbishop) the church.[5] When Tillyard turned to Hall to argue that early modern writers thought of history in providential terms, he ignored these sorts of complications that characterize all of Shakespeare's sources.[6] To use Christy Desmet's phrase, Shakespeare's potential sources for his Richard were "*already* dialogized" because they incorporated material facts and interpretative gambits from a variety of previous histories (11, emphasis added). As Desmet, Annabel Patterson, Peter Herman, and Paulina Kewes have shown when discussing the developments of early modern historiography, these historians tended as a rule to mix sources; consequently, the also mixed methods. Feeling relatively little institutional compulsion to theorize and standardize their practices, they regularly cobbled together sources that disagreed with one another on questions of historical causality.

Because early modern writers of history operated in this methodologically overdetermined and underpoliced field of historical enquiry, Shakespeare never dealt with a single document that was uniformly humanistic, providentialist, or "antiquarian" when he tarried with his source material.[7] Rather than simply wrestling with the distinction between "Machiavellian" and providential modes of historical thought as they were applied to Richard's story – the historiographical tension that Phyllis Rackin teases out in *Stages of History* – Shakespeare inherited a more complexly variegated tradition than the distinction between these poles would suggest. Drawing from the sophisticated humanist tradition, these historiographers also thought in terms of legal history, and they worked with the "social" or "material" history that was made popular in England by Camden and other members of the Elizabethan Society of Antiquaries.[8] This antiquarian history, as well as the legal sophistication of many humanists, falls outside the quick distinction between Machiavelli and God; it turns to legal, economic, and technological history as it explains historical events, rather than to great men or Providence as the engines of history.

To frame this confusion in terms of histories treating Richard's reign, I want here to turn briefly to Baldwin's *Mirror for Magistrates* and then to Holinshed's *Chronicles*. The choice of these two sources is, in part, rhetorical. Baldwin's *Mirror* is usually treated as a stridently monological history that works according to a straightforward vision of vengeful providential punishment;[9] by recognizing methodological heterogeneity in this most putatively monovocal source, we can see the very real confusions in early modern historiography as they apply to the story of Richard. When I subsequently turn to Holinshed and emphasize the inconsistency of his history on questions of causality, I turn to Shakespeare's most important source to demonstrate the same fact. In doing so, however, I work against the now seminal revisionist reading of Holinshed that Patterson offers in *Reading Holinshed's Chronicles*. Here, I return to an unreconstructed Holinshed, or a Holinshed who is unwieldy in a way that recent critics, following Patterson, have tended to ignore. Only by returning to this knottier, pre-revisionist account of Holinshed can we actually see what Shakespeare does with his sources in *Richard II*.

To claim that the *Mirror* is methodologically heterovocal is to disagree with its own explicit claims about historical causality. Stridently moralistic, the *Mirror* claims in its induction to show "[h]ow [God] hath delt with sum of our countreymen your auncestors for sundrye vices" in order to "move you to the soner amendment" (65–6). As the title page insists, history here is the story of catastrophes whereby "greevous plagues [and] vices [are] punished in great Princes and Magistrates." And yet, as Donald Jellerson and Paul Budra each point out, the *Mirror* regularly fails to make good on this promise of edification, occasionally looking to the past only to find a curious mixture of "divine Providence and irrational Fortune" (Budra 330). Where Budra ultimately reasserts the relative homogeneity of the *Mirror* by insisting on the exceptionality of non-providential falls, Jellerson makes a more compelling claim, pointing to the *Mirror*'s form as a source of its "dialogic sensibility": the prosopopoeic form of the *Mirror*, he argues, poses intractable interpretive problems, as voices from within the history often disagree with the poem's didactic paratexts.

These instabilities are more or less meaningful at different moments in the *Mirror*, but they are particularly significant in Richard's monologue as Baldwin interprets his fall in various conflicted ways. When introducing his case, he treats it as an exemplary instance of punishment:

> Happy is the prince that hath in welth the grace
> To folowe vertue, keping vices vnder,
> But wo to him whose will hath wisedomes place:
> For who so renteth ryght and law a sunder
> On him at length loe, al the world shall wunder. (1.107)

He subsequently blames Richard's fall, however, on his unwillingness to take "good counsayle," as his tone changes from regret to lament: Baldwin's original sense of Richard's culpability becomes a declaration of his status as a victim, murdered "causeles [sic] ... agaynst all lawes" (116). From a story that demonstrates the moral causes of his death, Baldwin suddenly turns to a vision of his death's unlawful "causelessness." If we attempt to lay this confusion at the foot of form – prosopopoeia makes such irony possible – then we still recognize that questions of causality are confused in the *Mirror*, treating Richard's fall as a story of crime punished as well as a story in which Richard is the victim of a different crime. Suddenly, justice begins to work through injustice, and claims of historical causality in Richard's death become more difficult to parse. Where Richard claims that "rulers" might look to his biography and learn that they should "beware / Good counsayle, lawe, or vertue to despise" (97), the majority of his account offers few details of providence, focusing instead on the problems that occurred in England when he was at war in Ireland: "while I fought in Ireland with my foes / Mine uncle Edmund rebelliously arose" (148); ultimately, it was "Henry puft with pride" – not God's providence – that "Causde see resigne my kingly state and thorne" (188). As various agencies operate in tandem, the question of agency ultimately becomes insolubly muddled.

This muddle of historical causality and internal inconsistency is also characteristic of Holinshed's *Chronicles*, the source to which Shakespeare is most obviously indebted. Such a reading of Holinshed corresponds with a long tradition of criticism on Holinshed's history that began with Edmund Bolton's 1621 *Hypercritica*, in which Bolton complains about the *Chronicles*'s incoherence. In his short treatise on the "Rule of Judgement, for writing or reading of our History's [sic]" Bolton argues for a humanist historiographical practice, focusing on the character of monarchs and other great men while also demonstrating a sensitivity to the insights of antiquarians, especially those like Camden who work diligently with artefacts and etymologies (229).[10] In this humanistic/antiquarian mode, Bolton's work is stridently secular in orientation, resisting facile providential historiography that "shuffle[s] up the reasons of events, in briefly referring all causes immediately to the Will of God" (224). Against this simple providentialism, he chastises historians who "neglect ... to inform their readers" of secondary historical causes, or "the ordinary means of [God's] Carriage in human Affairs" (224–5). Chroniclers such as Holinshed and Grafton are similarly inadequate in Bolton's reading because they "relate ... Events, without their Premisses [sic] and Circumstances" and consequently ignore the real "Causes of things" (224). For Bolton, that is, chronicles such as Holinshed's are "vast vulgar tomes" (237), not only because they seem unwieldy and indecorous in their content, but also because they fail to make historical causes clear. Whether or not Bolton's dismissal of the chronicle is inspired by snobbishness towards the predominantly "middle-class citizens" who wrote them (Patterson, *Reading* 7), he seems correct to point to the sheer incomprehensibility of history – "the ordinary means of Carriage in human Affairs" – as it appears in chronicle history. Peter Heylyn argues along the same lines in his 1639 *Mikrokosmos* when criticizing the "voluminous *Holingshead*" for being "full of commixture of unworthy relations" (23), and this sense of Holinshed's voluminousness and incoherence persisted over centuries until recent revisionist accounts have attempted to smooth over, rationalize, and justify what seemed a historiographical inadequacy to previous generations of scholars.

I return to this older tradition of criticism on Holinshed because recent scholars have tended to ignore the shapelessness of Holinshed's history in order to identify a deeper truth in the *Chronicles*. Rackin, for instance, finds in Holinshed a sense of coherence that few modern readers of the *Chronicles* might actually feel when sitting with his volumes: "Monologic, they obscured the differences between the disparate authorial voices, opposed discursive positions, divergent accounts, and contradictory interpretations" (25). Even Holinshed's most careful, generous, and engaging modern readers such as Patterson and Cyndia Clegg tend to ignore Holinshed's incoherence on the question of historical causality. As a fundamental premise of *Reading Holinshed's Chronicles*, for instance, Patterson points out that the volumes contain contradictory opinions regarding parliamentary authority and England's "ancient constitution." Assiduously revisionist in her reading of Holinshed, she ultimately claims that the volumes are proto-liberal in their form, where they abide a "principle of diversity and multivocality," a "principle ... of evenhandedness," an "egalitarian principle," and a "democratic principle" (*Reading* 33, 35, 179); these principles of composition and exposition reflect – in a nascent form – the workings of a Habermasian public sphere. From such a critical viewpoint, Holinshed – contrary to Bolton and Heylyn – thinks of history in consistently "social" terms, treating it as a matter of institutions or broad cultural forces. Patterson's chapter headings suggest as much – "Economics," "Government," "Religion," "Law" – and she explicitly says as much when she identifies in Holinshed a form of "economic self-consciousness" (*Reading* 73). Such a reading of Holinshed – attentive to the myriad ways that the volume can be decidedly sophisticated and nuanced – ultimately reclaims a partial vision of the work and occludes huge swaths of the work's historical analysis. As often as Holinshed's history is secular and social in its vision of historical agency and change, it is also humanistic when preoccupied with "great men" and historical personality history, and it remains exhaustingly providentialist in its regular polemical moments.

To pay attention to the rhetoric and form of the *Chronicles* means acknowledging this incoherence, whether one identifies it as a strength or a weakness. The *Chronicles*'s debt to humanism, for instance, is clear in its sensitivity to character and to its repeated use of marginal tags. These tags are a hallmark of the humanist practice as it attempted to distil for readers the lessons of comportment and practice that they might apply to their lives. In the case of Richard, for instance, readers are reminded in the margin that certain passages illustrating the dangers of pride are "worthy to bee well wayed, and diligently marked" (1107). On the next page, Holinshed offers a truism illustrated by Richard's fate: "Where fortune fauoreth, thyther the peoples fauor fleeth" (1108). The marginal gestures here are significant where they imply how a reader might use Holinshed, and where they suggest that history is a storehouse of exempla from which a reader might draw. Readers of the chronicles may find a "history of institutions," but they also may find a history that ignores institutional forces, or combines these institutional forces with a focus on the agency of individuals.

In its humanist mode, the *Chronicles* suggests that history is a process shaped by the activity of individual decisions, and that Richard died as a result of flattery and poor council rather than because history was moving towards a form of republican democracy characterized by impersonal institutions and a wide distribution of authority. Susceptible to wantonness, Richard dies due to a failure of character, even if Holinshed sounds less moralistic than Baldwin:

> that this Henrie duke of Lancaster should be thus called to the kingdome, and haue the helpe and assistance (almost) of all the whole realme, which perchance neuer thereof thought or yet dreamed; and that king Richard should thus be left desolate, void, and in despaire of all hope and comfort, in whom if there were anie offense, it ought rather to be imputed to the frailtie of wanton youth, than to the malice of his hart: but such is the

> deceiuable iudgement of man, which not regarding things present with due consideration, thinketh euer that things to come shall haue good successe, with a pleasant & delitefull end. (1107–8)

Holinshed here thinks like a humanist who treats human frailty and personality as crucial engines of history: because he was "prodigall, ambitious, and much giuen to the pleasure of the bodie," Richard's fall was inevitable as a matter of his character rather than a matter of cultural transformation. Missing here is any story, say, of taxation, parliamentary authority, or a faith in juridical autonomy that Patterson detects.

But if in the *Chronicles* Holinshed seems certain about how to draw lessons from the past, he also demonstrates considerable sensitivity to the force of contingency, which ultimately works against his sense that Richard's death was necessary or inevitable based on his character. Although Richard's character is seen as contributing to his fall, bad luck, too, seems to play a significant role in the historical events leading to his death. On Richard's rush back to England from Ireland in order to defend against Bolingbroke's forces, for instance, the *Chronicles* reminds readers that Richard

> made hast to returne into England, in hope with an armie to incounter the duke, before he should haue time to assemble his fréends togither. But here you shall note, that it fortuned at the same time, in which the duke of Hereford or Lancaster, whether ye list to call him, arriued thus in England, the seas were so troubled by tempests, and the winds blew so contrarie for anie passage, to come over foorth of England to the king, remaining still in Ireland, that for the space of six weeks, he received no advertisements from thence. (1106)

A victim of weather, Richard is undone by poor travel conditions and failed communications as much as by his moral weakness, God's hand, or the rise of Parliament in a long history of democracy's ascent. Had weather been better, Richard would have arrived at Conway earlier, and he would have found a supportive army of 40,000 Welsh soldiers, who only disbanded because they thought Richard dead and thus "tooke from the king all occasion to recover afterwards anie forces sufficient to resist him" (1106).

Besides chance, the character of great men, and a broad social energy, the *Chronicles* also recognizes a providential hand in the history of Richard's reign. The providentialism here is multifaceted, ranging from the oblique claims of God's overarching plan to the more explicitly moralistic claims of direct intervention, and thus it disagrees with itself on the question of divine action and historical change. At one moment, for instance, the *Chronicles* makes obscure and noncommittal statements about "Gods wrath and displeasure" (1039). Later, however, the will of God is more carefully delimited with respect to Richard:

> Moreouer there reigned abundantly the filthie sinne of lecherie and fornication, with abhominable adulterie, specially in the king, but moste chiefly in the prelacie, whereby the whole realme by such their euill ensample, was so infected, that the wrath of God was dayly prouoked to vengeance, for the sinnes of the Prince and hys people. (1117)

Curiously, just as God was "prouoked to vengeance" against Richard, the will of God also works in the opposing political direction. As the story of Richard's fall concludes, the *Chronicles* insists that Bolingbroke's "l[in]neal race were scourged afterwardes, as a due punishment with rebellious subiects, so as deserued vengeance seemed not to stay long for his ambitious crueltie, that could not be contented to driue king Richard to resigne his Crowne and regall dignitie ouer vnto him, except hee also shoulde take from him his guiltlesse life" (1117). This is the sort of passage from Holinshed that could lead Tillyard to make claims about the providential forces driving the Wars of the Roses.

Troubled that this ham-fisted providentialism in Holinshed is at odds with her sense of the *Chronicles* as a whole, Patterson suggests that such passages do not necessarily "contribut[e] to a providentialist grand narrative" as Tillyard and others suggest: "[t]he facts of the reign" somehow "continue to speak for themselves" in opposition to the narrative in which they exist (*Reading* 116). Complicating matters, however, is that Holinshed never lets us know which facts are historically meaningful and which facts are trivia. Is the institution of Parliament and its transformation during the late Middle Ages a fact that we need to consider when struggling to understand why Richard's history unfolds as it does? Is the question of character a fact we need to consider? And if we need to think about character when dealing with the broad movements of history between reigns, is the historical effect of character meaningful because God declares it so or because political actors are subject to forces that are purely social? Does Richard fall because he is weak or because he is sinful? Or does his usurpation become a fact in a longer story of strife among Bolingbroke's "lineal race"? We might assemble some of these facts to produce a coherent narrative, and yet Holinshed's account of history around the fall of Richard contains too much contradictory data and too many different interpretations of that data to say what really counts as a fact and what counts as historical noise. Moments of astute social and historical analysis fail to override a sense that Holinshed might be problematically "voluminous."

Shakespeare and the Secrets of History

Shakespeare was sensitive to the myriad, often conflicting, visions of historical causality in his sources when working on *Richard II,* and yet criticism on the play's historiographical vision consistently debates whether the play is "providentialist" or "Machiavellian" in its treatment of history, as if these must be the two, mutually exclusive, possibilities in the period's history writing. On the one hand is Tillyard's now notorious reading of the play that sees in *Richard II* a dramatic version of the "Homily against Disobedience and Wilful Rebellion" (1570), a document that Tillyard treats as quintessentially early modern in its political outlook. According to this reading, *Richard II* is a conservative play, and it treats Bolingbroke as a usurper who contradicts divine right. Growing from this vision of *Richard II,* the Henriad becomes for Tillyard a story of redemptive purgation: the Wars of the Roses mark a period of suffering that purges Bolingbroke's crime. On the other hand are readings of the play that still treat Tillyard as a strawman, and they tend to situate Shakespeare at a critical juncture in the history of political thought as it grows modern. As Martin Coyle makes the familiar argument, "The world of medieval refinement is indeed the main object of presentation, but it is threatened and in the end superseded by the more familiar world of the present" (115). This reading of the play treats Richard as the deluded medieval monarch in a modern world, and it claims that a thoroughly modern Shakespeare staged a usurper who was successful because he mastered the putatively modern art of political theatre.

More recent criticism moves away from the coarse distinction between Machiavellian and providential accounts by becoming wider ranging in its historicism, though it continues to smother the play's historiographical variety. Jeff Doty, for instance, turns to the emergence of "popularity" as an operative political category in the 1590s to explain the play's vision of political history:

> If *Richard II* dramatizes a transition in the understanding of the English monarchy – and most critics suggest that some change occurs – the foundation of that change is how members of the ruling elite relate to the people. At the time of the composition of *Richard II* in 1594–95, popularity was controversial because its users inducted people into political matters and deployed their affections in factional rivalries. (205)[11]

Doty's reading ultimately finds in *Richard II* an "onstage commons" that operates as a meaningful political force. Halpern also becomes more historically specific by turning to the sovereign's right of taxation as it was debated in the Middle Ages (73), while Phillips thinks about a longer philosophical and constitutional tradition that treats the sovereign's subjection to the law. For Doty, Halpern, and Phillips, then, the play continues to be historiographically modern, and it seems so because it accounts for the power of a nascent public sphere or because it clearly considers the position of the sovereign as a subject of the law that he or she embodies.

The problem with these readings of the play – despite their rich insights – is that they fail to acknowledge that the play strategically obfuscates the causes of the history it stages. The play is filled with characters who interpret their own history in various ways, and all of these historical interpretations offer compelling visions of the plot they describe. If modern critics debate the historical vision that Shakespeare's play offers, then it seems useful to recognize that these debates are internal to Shakespeare's play. Beyond this thematic engagement with questions of historical causality, however, *Richard II*'s dramaturgy and plotting seem designed to foreclose the possibility of comprehensive historical interpretation. Repeatedly, the play draws our attention to material facts that it withholds, refusing to provide its audience with the sort of information about character, for example, that an audience needs before it is able to interpret the play's action with confidence. If those attending the performance could see the off-stage action that it hears reported, then the ambiguities that have inspired critical debates would vanish. In this sense, the play taunts us, reminding us of the secrets that it keeps from us while maintaining the plausibility of the varied historical interpretations that its characters offer. This theatre of secrecy ultimately troubles Rackin's reading of the play, in which she claims that Shakespeare puts "conflicting propositions about historical truth and historical causation to the tests of dramatic action" (46). What is distinctly aggravating about this play, instead, is that it points to crucial historical propositions – "Bolingbroke is an unwilling usurper" – that it refuses to subject to the "tests of dramatic action." Only by recognizing these historiographical confusions that frustrate interpretive energies can we recognize the character of Richard's tragedy as a search for historical explanation within a superfluity of possibilities. Both Richard's and Shakespeare's audience live in a world that refuses to offer the information that one needs if one wants to explain the historical cause of his death, even if such narrative explanations also seem ready to hand.

When Mowbray and Bolingbroke feud about the past in the opening scene, they remind the audience how little it knows about the staged world. As the play opens, they argue about events in Calais the previous autumn when Bolingbroke's uncle Thomas of Woodstock, the Duke of Gloucester, was murdered while under Mowbray's protection. The record – historically and in Shakespeare's play – is unclear about the circumstances surrounding Gloucester's death, though it seems likely that he was murdered at the behest of Richard for his role in the Merciless Parliament a decade earlier. The record also suggests that Mowbray was somehow complicit in the murder. In the debate between Bolingbroke and Mowbray about the precise events in Calais, even the few established facts remain obscure. Bolingbroke imagines a scene in which Mowbray "did plot the Duke of Gloucester's death ... / And consequently, like a traitor coward, / Sluiced out his innocent soul through streams of blood" (1.1.100, 103–4). In response, Mowbray offers a claim striking for its ambiguity: "For Gloucester's death, / I slew him not; but to my own disgrace / Neglected my sworn duty in that case" (1.1.132–5). Whether he admits here that he "allowed" the murder by making Gloucester available to murderers, much as Richard's keeper will make Richard available to Exton, or whether he suggests pure neglect, the debate about history remains unresolved. In *Richard II*'s opening scene, then, we are compelled to acknowledge that we have no real idea what happened in Calais, though the murder there inaugurates the play's tragic action. Beneath the slanders and the innuendos, apart from the claims of justice, is an attempt to "prove" a story about history, which is perhaps another way of imagining justice in the historiographical mode.

While pointing towards the historical unknown, the first scene's promised trial-by-combat also implies fantasies that historical ambiguity can be readily resolved. The proposed combat between Mowbray and Bolingbroke assumes not only a certain model of providential justice, but also a model of historical analysis in which combat can provide the truth of history: a prepared combat between Bolingbroke and Mowbray will make plain the contested truth about Calais because God will stand behind the victor. When Bolingbroke insists that he will "in battle prove" his claims about Mowbray (1.1.92), he assumes that history – barring the occasional disruptions – follows God's will and can be used tautologically to evaluate propositional truths. In such a world, one can produce a truth machine by engineering a historical event – the trial-by-combat – whose outcome will speak to divine necessity. For Rackin, this moment is crucial to the play because, when Richard suspends the combat, he demonstrates his unwillingness to abide the providential claims that undergird his claim to legitimacy; consequently, he "dissipates" his authority and dies as a result. Whether or not Rackin is right here, the scene is perhaps more crucial thematically because it forecloses the possibility of establishing historical truth in a play whose characters seem obsessed with understanding the history they live. At this moment, we experience again the foreclosure of historical truth; more radically, however, we are also forced to recognize that the processes of history may or may not be regular in the way that the ritual trial imagines. When Mowbray enters the lists, he seems sceptical that the trial by combat can reveal truth, insisting on his virtue regardless of the combat's outcome: "However God or fortune cast my lot, / There lives or dies, true to King Richard's throne, / A loyal, just and upright gentleman" (1.3.85–7). In Dawson and Yachnin's words, "Mowbray introduces a note of doubt into the proceeding by suggesting that the outcome might be the result of either divine judgement or chance" (153 n. 85), which means that our historical judgment is doubly troubled in the scene: we never get to see how the trial resolves the factual question of Calais, and we never get to really believe what the trial by combat can tell us about Calais.

At the level of metatheatrical self-commentary, the play often follows Mowbray and treats providential fantasies with ambivalence, even if it seems unwilling to fully exclude providential interpretations of the history it stages. As many critics point out, for instance, when Richard implores his followers to "sit upon the ground / And tell sad stories of the death of kings," he summons a *de casibus* model of history that describes the fall of monarchs as a matter of divine retribution. In his reading of *de casibus* logic, however, he engages with these providentialist stories while also insisting on fatal contingency: some fallen monarchs in these familiar sad stories may be exemplars of the punitive *de casibus* fantasy, and yet others "have been deposed; some slain in war, / Some haunted by the ghosts they have deposed; / Some poison'd by their wives: some sleeping kill'd; / All murder'd" (3.2.153–6). While *de casibus* poetry so often insists that kings fall when God punishes them and that their stories are consequently didactic, Richard recognizes that other kings fall when their wives poison them, and that sometimes these deaths are acts of murder rather than sentences from heaven. In a similarly conflicted vision of divine providence, the next scene points to the force of divine necessity while staging it as potentially fantastical. As Richard is preparing for war against Bolingbroke, sympathetic Welsh forces have disbanded after reading the stars and sensing futility. The short scene again reminds us that the play is about historical self-interpretation, by offering the superstitious Welsh army as they read the firmament:

> The bay-trees in our country are all wither'd
> And meteors fright the fixed stars of heaven;
> The pale-faced moon looks bloody on the earth
> And lean-look'd prophets whisper fearful change
> ....
> These signs forerun the death or fall of kings.
> Farewell: our countrymen are gone and fled,
> As well assured Richard their king is dead. (2.4.8–11, 15–17)

As the Welsh captain suggests, one might see in the events of history a grand cosmological force, and yet the play is keen to put such ominous fantasies into the mouths of the stereotypically superstitious Welsh; in doing so, it introduces the fantasy of overarching providence, points to ominous tokens that might be historically meaningful, and then restricts the value of the interpretation by making it Welsh. A decade later, Hayward will insist that the withering bay trees are historically meaningless, and that they only seem ominous in retrospect: "prodegies [*sic*], either forged in that fabulous age, or happening commonly and of course, are then only noted, when any notable accident doth ensue" (51). And yet for Shakespeare (as for Holinshed) such providential explanation remains open and plausible, even if not fully compelling.

If the providential interpretations of history fail to be fully compelling in *Richard II*, then they fail in part because the play offers so many competing explanations of Richard's fall. The juxtaposition between secular and providential modes of interpretation is clearest in the scenes where Aumerle and Carlisle advise Richard on his response to Bolingbroke. The debates between Aumerle and Carlisle are not only debates about strategy and virtue, or the sorts of debates one finds in cerebral sixteenth-century dramas such as *Gorboduc*. They also point to varied historical assumptions that one must make before advising a monarch. As they plan a response to Bolingbroke's gathering forces:

> CARLISLE:
> Fear not, my lord; that power that made you king.
> Hath power to keep you king in spite of all.
> The means that heavens yield must be embraced
> And not neglected. Else heaven would,

And we will not: heaven's offer we refuse,
The proffered means of succor and redress.

AUMERLE:
He means, my lord, that we are too remiss,
Whilst Bolingbroke through our security
Grows strong and great in substance and in power. (27–35)

"He means, my lord": here Aumerle attempts a work of translation between forms of historical interpretation. On the one hand is Carlisle's devout understanding of history's mechanics and the consequent necessity of action against Bolingbroke. Like the Carlisle in Holinshed's *Chronicles*, Hayward's *Henry IIII*, and Hall's *Union* – a prelate who speaks passionately about Richard's divine right before Parliament – Shakespeare's Carlisle is certain in Richard's divine authority and in the inevitable providential retribution that will befall a king who refuses to defend these providential rights. Transposed into a secular register, Aumerle tells the story of defence in a wholly pragmatic language that one might find in a humanist history: a king should stop rebellion at its inception before rebels can grow strong.

The point that Aumerle makes about strategy and secular combat is repeated later in the play in the strange set piece featuring the Gardener, invoking the familiar analogy between kingdom and garden and speaking a language that makes him sound more like an allegory-minded humanist historian than a horticulturalist:

O, what pity is it
That [Richard] had not so trimm'd and dress'd his land
As we this garden! We at time of year
Do wound the bark, the skin of our fruit-trees,
Lest, being over-proud in sap and blood,
With too much riches it confound itself:
Had he done so to great and growing men,
They might have lived to bear and he to taste
Their fruits of duty. (3.4.56–64)

In *Richard II*, however, both explanations ably explain the action that will subsequently occur: Richard will fall to a more powerful Bolingbroke, and no one seems able to agree why this fall occurs. He may fall as a *de casibus* prince or as a victim of his own political weakness. He falls and we see him fall, and yet we never know whether Aumerle or Carlisle has read the world correctly.

In this second register of secular historical interpretation, the play offers other historical evidence that points to extra-personal social forces that Aumerle and the Gardener elide. Against the Gardener's insistence that history is determined by the strategy of great men, Doty's argument about popularity is valuable here. When the play speaks of restless populations, taxation, famine, and Bolingbroke's courtship of "the people," and when it features York's moving speech about a city that celebrates Richard's downfall (5.2.23–40), we find a very different vision of secular, historical causes. The play reminds us that Bolingbroke doffs "his bonnet to an oysterwench" (1.4.30), and that he taps into historic resentments inspired by overtaxation during a time of dearth, and it consequently suggests that politics – even in an age of monarchy – is largely a matter of population management. Even Richard recognizes as much, as when he claims to usurp Bolingbroke's inheritance to "deck our soldiers for these Irish wars" against rebellious populations in the realm (1.4.61). After Richard returns from Ireland and recognizes Bolingbroke's strength, he begins to speak a language that is introspective and melancholic or maudlin. This second Richard is the "poet king" we find so often in the criticism on the play, but, earlier, Richard seems to recognize the need for thinking in terms of populations. In the first two acts of the play, seizing an inheritance is a matter of governance in the modern sense, whereas protecting a realm is an act of taming peoples rather than taming individual persons, and history moves according to the force of such extra-personal energies.

If these varied historical interpretations all seem plausible, then they seem plausible because the play withholds information that would move an audience to find certain interpretations more credible than others. *Richard II* is scrupulous in these key obfuscations. Among the crucial facts that the play never reveals: why does Bolingbroke return from his exile on the continent? On this point, *Richard II* is notoriously muddled, even though clarifying the point would help an audience to decide why the action of the play unfolds as it does. If Bolingbroke returns simply to reclaim his inheritance – as he claims explicitly – the play feels more like a story of inevitable processes of history rather than the story of an over-proud, politicking usurper. Bolingbroke would become king because he stands ready to claim a crown that falls from Richard's head. If he returns with plans to claim the crown, the play's history would feel more like the history offered by Aumerle and the Gardener, or a history where a savvy nobleman outmanoeuvres a monarch. On the question of Bolingbroke's return, however, the play is double-voiced. In 2.1 for instance, Bolingbroke's homecoming seems to be a matter of usurpation rather than reclamation. Immediately after Gaunt's death – in the same scene in which Richard lays claim to Bolingbroke's patrimony – Ross, Northumberland, and Willoughby explain that Bolingbroke has already sailed for England and that they vow to support him. If Bolingbroke has intended only to reclaim his patrimony when he returns, then he had no time to gather a fleet of ships because he lost his patrimony just a few moments before. But Northumberland subsequently insists in 2.3 that "The noble Duke hath sworn his coming is / But for his own / ... / And let him never see joy that breaks that oath" (147–8, 150). To see that Bolingbroke returns from England for the sake of the throne requires us to be more suspicious of Bolingbroke than Northumberland is, even though Northumberland clearly and obviously knows that the return involves more than the reclamation of a title, deeds, and rents. So why does Bolingbroke return? Does he cause Richard's catastrophe? Does Richard fall or was he pushed?

The ambiguity surrounding the cause of Richard's downfall is repeated in the confusing deposition scene, a scene that critics problematically treat as though it makes sense. As the scene opens, Bolingbroke vows his fealty to Richard, sending Northumberland to tell Richard that "Upon his knees [he] doth kiss King Richards hand, / And sends allegiance and true faith of heart" (3.3.35–6). Subsequently, Northumberland approaches Richard on Bolingbroke's behalf and tells Richard that Bolingbroke's "coming hither hath no further scope / Than for his lineal royalties and to beg / Enfranchisement immediate on his knee" (3.3.111–13). Bolingbroke then attends Richard, repeating his story that he aims only for the return of his inheritance. Richard then explains that he will do "what force will have us do" and asks whether Bolingbroke intends to imprison him in the Tower: "Set on towards London, cousin, is it so?" (3.3.205, 206). Here we find a textual crux that may be answered in the theatre, but it remains a textual crux that refuses to be soluble according to any critical method. Directors may need to decide what happens at this moment in 3.3 – conventionally, Richard descends from the upper area to hand over the crown – and yet the textual openness of this crucial moment points to the instances of undecidability and opacity that lurk at the heart of the play.

Bolingbroke's character – crucial to the understanding of the play's historical vision – is also obscured in the final movement of the play when Richard is murdered in prison. The play's audience hears from Exton that Bolingbroke, in the shadow of the Winchester plot to restore Richard, has asked publicly and rhetorically in regard to Richard, "Have I no friend will rid me of this living fear?" (5.4.2). Exton, claiming that Bolingbroke subsequently "looked on me, / As who should say, 'I would thou wert the man / That would divorce this terror from my heart'" (5.4.7–9), takes Bolingbroke's cue and ultimately kills the king. But an audience never sees this loaded look, never hears the tone in Bolingbroke's voice, never has the chance to determine whether or not Bolingbroke is actually winking and nudging in Exton's direction. Here we might detect an analogue in the awkwardly punctuated note in Marlowe's *Edward II*: one reading of the note sent by Mortimer to Edward's guards demands that they protect him while an equally plausible reading of the note insists that Edward be executed. But while Marlowe offers his audience a speech by Mortimer to indicate that the latter version is the version he intends and that he intends this deniability, we never hear the truth – or see the truth – of Bolingbroke's potentially murderous intimations.

The obscurity of Bolingbroke's character seems more like a strategic choice than a failure of art. The theatrical void at the centre of Bolingbroke's character is perhaps most palpable when we recognize that, apart from Henry VII, he is the only sovereign in the history plays who never speaks a soliloquy, and Henry VII is largely a cipher who only ever stands on the very edge of *Richard III*'s action. The absence of a soliloquy for Bolingbroke is particularly apparent in a play that exploits so effectively the device's expository and poetic value. Richard's soliloquies are famous because they remain somehow subtle despite their emotional ostentation, and because they make palpable a rich inner world of motives and ambivalence, desire, and shame. Bolingbroke is a similarly "deep" character, but Shakespeare produces Bolingbroke's depth by way of a contrary strategy: he provides an audience with compelling reasons to imagine something like an inner life, and yet that inner life remains meticulously locked away. Exposed to the audience, this inner life would clarify the play's action and would help us to see the truth of its historical world; it would inspire us to think one way or the other about the reason for Richard's fall. Like Holinshed, however, Shakespeare offers instead historical ambiguities and historical polyphony, producing a plot that moves forwards quickly without letting us know why it moves in the direction it does.

Against the background of the play's confused historical vision, Richard's sense of his own tragedy begins to look different, a matter of temporal dislocation rather than "hysteria." Critics often argue that Richard's tragedy is at least partly existential: when he loses his crown, "he is confronted with the void of his subjectivity outside the symbolic mandate-title 'king,' and is thus forced into a series of theatrical, hysterical outbursts, from self-pity to sarcastic and clownish madness" (Žižek 9). As he is formally deposed and responds to Bolingbroke's question, "Are you contented to resign the crown?" (4.1.190), Richard insists on this loss of himself: "ay no; no ay" – homonymic with "I no, no I" – "I must nothing be" (4.1.191–2). For Judith Brown, we find here a king (or former king) who imagines himself according to the imperatives of a queer aesthetics, or a poetic project of self-fashioning that refuses to fashion a self and that instead "hinges on undoing" (288), scuttling all sense of identity. In a play so concerned with questions of historical meaningfulness, however, Richard's self-loss seems a matter of historico-narrative loss as well as social or symbolic loss. He loses himself because he is unable to think of himself in historical terms, or to imagine the biographical line through which his fate relates to previous action. Sensing his end, he has trouble identifying the nature of his life's beginning and middle. Prior to his usurpation, he appeals to various narratives that describe his life and his fall. He invokes the story of Christ's betrayal by Judas, for instance, as well as the *de casibus* tradition and its familiar plotting. But after he loses his crown and is imprisoned in Pomfret Castle, plots seem to fail him when he hears a song from the world that now excludes him. He lives on, somehow, without a plot that lets him explain himself to himself:

> Ha, ha; keep time! How sour sweet music is
> When time is broke and no proportion kept.
> So is it in the music of men's lives.
> And here have I the daintiness of ear
> To check time broke in a disordered string;
> But for the concord of my state and time
> Had not an ear to hear my true time broke.
> I wasted time, and now doth time waste me,
> For now hath time made me his numb'ring clock.
> My thoughts are minutes; and with sighs they jar
> Their watches on unto mine eyes, the outward watch
> Whereto my finger, like a dial's point,
> Is pointing still in cleansing them from tears. (5.5.42–54)

Richard registers his experience of negation ("I must nothing be") in a language of historical trauma. He has lost himself because time has been broken. The "disordered string" that he hears – or that he overhears, because the song is performed for someone else – is disordered because he finds himself unable to "keep time" and because the regular time kept by the "music of men's lives" is a metaphor that no longer works. Out of step with time and continuing to live after his story has ended, he is "broke" because his "true time" is "broke." Even if not "broke," time is no more saturated by meaning than the meaning that one finds in the mere chronicity of a watch. The jarring metre of the first line here – "Ha, ha! keep time: how sour sweet music is" – only emphasizes how far out of time the poet king seems to have fallen; Richard is a watch that fails to tick and tock according to the regular measure of iambic verse.

Such an account of his historically unanchored life seems dissonant when measured against his earlier speech about lives and their trajectories, and it retrospectively casts that earlier speech – so certain in biographical predictability and order – in an ironic light. Beyond the broad historical contours of a monarch's life, Richard had already described how lives should play out. Speaking to York in an earlier scene, Richard invokes a familiar horticultural metaphor when describing Gaunt's impending death:

> The ripest fruit first falls, and so doth he.
> His time is spent; our pilgrimage must be.
> So much for that. (2.1.154–6)

"So much for that": the glib half-line speaks to a casual if absurd assumption that biographies unfold naturally, as if fruits never suffer blights and as if lives somehow exist apart from the tumultuous history in which they happen to be imbricated. Read against his earlier assumptions about biography, Richard's tragedy comes to seem like a tragedy of recognition, where the recognition is epistemological. Just as the play's audience is lost when attempting to explain why the play's action has unfolded, even though that action has already been explained a number of ways, Richard is lost as he attempts to explain his life according to the imperatives of the narrative forms that he has inherited. In this respect, Richard is lost in history as the play's audience is lost in history, and as readers of Holinshed, perhaps, would have been lost in history before him.

The sense of historical dislocation is ultimately the only effect the play might produce because of a profound ambiguity over what counts as historical evidence and because of a strategic withholding of any information that might point to a compelling form of historical explanation. This disturbed relationship between narrative and evidence becomes particularly clear when considered against Joel Fineman's account of the tautological structure of all historical narrative. In his reading of Thucydides' *History of the Peloponnesian War*, Fineman points to the mutually constitutive relationship between events and the historical explanations given of those events: "events derive historical significance because they fit into a representative narrative account, and ... the narrative account derives its historical significance because it comprehends significant historical events" (64). By withholding apparently crucial historical facts – facts that would be central to familiar forms of historical explanation – Shakespeare's play emphasizes the difficulty that one faces when struggling to understand historical causality, and it draws attention to the difficulties that early modern history writers faced when attempting to identify historical facts in a powerfully overdetermined historiographical field. The problem here is not a paucity of historical evidence, but a confusion over what might count as evidence at all.

The self-conscious narrative confusion in *Richard II* is ultimately a problem that makes Shakespeare's play a "problem history" or "problem tragedy," and it also troubles the sorts of stories that we might offer about Shakespeare's development as a playwright or about the *cursus* of his career. These stories tend to conceal more than they reveal. We might think that Shakespeare grew more introspective over the course of his career, as Edward Dowden claims, or we might follow Northrop Frye and imagine that he grew more interested in social rather than personal concerns, or follow Tillyard to suggest that Shakespeare grew more generously humane as he aged.[12] As the dates of these readings suggest – ranging from 1875 through 1965 – recent critics have generally abandoned projects that imagine a coherent logic of Shakespeare's development, with Patrick Cheney's 2008 work on the shape of Shakespeare's career offering a noteworthy exception. But if recent critics resist the idea that one can explain Shakespeare's development according to a single principle (e.g., increasing introspection, increased attention to the social, increasing "humaneness"), the story of Shakespeare's maturation or development remains current in discussions of the history plays. In the broadest version of the story, we find Shakespeare overmastered by his historical source material in the *Henry VI* plays, which offer incident without meaningful shape, before ambivalently providing a providential view of history in *Richard III*. He then works as a humanist historiographer and a sophisticated historical dramatist in the "mature" second tetralogy, where he successfully binds history to character, or where he binds the matter of his plays to the imperatives of his medium. Dawson and Yachnin make the claim explicitly on the first page of their introduction to the most recent Oxford edition: "the play marks a transition from the earlier history plays (the 'first tetralogy' comprising the three parts of *Henry VI* and *Richard III*) in which the terrible mechanisms of civil war and naked power dominate the scene ... Here a new note is audible, a more nuanced representation of the political conflicts of the English past in which character and politics are so deeply intertwined as to be inextricable." The changing "notes" of Shakespeare's career – from "terrible mechanisms" and "naked power" to something else – mark the steps in his *Künstlerroman*.

The still familiar sense that Shakespeare developed as a writer of history over the course of the tetralogies might be revised, and we might think differently about this apparent development, if we recognize that his histories of individual reigns relate to and comment upon contemporaneous discussions of those same reigns. Where *Richard II* responds to early modern discussions of Richard's reign – discussions around the question of divine right, providence, motivating forces of historical change, and so on – it seems responsible to think of Shakespeare's play by recourse to the sources that inspired it rather than by appeal to its position in his career. Such a vision of Shakespeare's development ultimately offers a better and more interesting sense of his historical work as a writer who reads historiography seriously before subjecting historical facts to the logic of the stage.

Following this vision of Shakespeare-the-history-writer rather than Shakespeare-the-evolving-author, the story of his "growth" falls apart and reorders itself anew. Specifically, thinking of Shakespeare as a writer of history who engages with other historians writing on similar matter makes better sense: his plotting changed not because he matured – he wrote plots well even early in his career – but because he responded to the historiographical accounts that he treated as sources. If the *Henry VI* plays feel shapeless and overfull of action, for instance, then we might recognize that this shapelessness speaks to the confusions in the chronicles to which Shakespeare turned when negotiating a reign that was characterized by decentralized conflict that aggravatingly refused to focus on a monarch. Alexander Leggatt points out that "the first half of *1 Henry VI*, like the Roman plays, is set in a kingless world" (*Shakespeare's Political Drama* 1); the observation reminds us that the play's messy plotting recalls similar difficulties faced by historians who attempted to describe political history at a moment when such political history refused to centre around a sovereign. We should note here that Holinshed's account of Henry VI's reign is similarly messy. Indeed, even though Holinshed's *Chronicles* is divided by appeal to the logic of the reign, the messiness in his history of Henry VI's reign is more obvious than in his accounts of other reigns. And Budra reminds us that even *de casibus* accounts of Henry VI's weak reign are about "the falls of *many* people" rather than the fall of a king (80). Perhaps Shakespeare's clumsy plotting marks a sensitivity to the historiographical and poetic visions of Henry VI's rule that he inherited from his sources? Perhaps, that is, his dramatic untidiness responds responsibly to historical material?

To follow this logic to its end: if we find a transformation in Shakespeare's writing of *Richard III* after the *Henry VI* plays, where he suddenly offers a mixture of humanist and providentialist historiography, then we might recognize that Shakespeare responds in the latter play to More, to the Tudor myth that villainized Richard III, and to the increased power of the sovereign that characterized Richard III's reign. If this logic holds, then Shakespeare's apparent maturity in the second tetralogy – where "character and politics are deeply intertwined"– makes sense not within a *Künstlerroman* as Yachnin and Dawson suggest, but within contemporaneous historiography. Sources to which Shakespeare turned when writing on Henry IV, as another example, assiduously focused on the agonistic struggle between Richard and Henry IV before focusing on the combative tensions between Henry IV and "the north." Historical sources, similarly to Shakespeare, treat Henry V in terms of political centrality: his heroism, his grandeur, and his glory. As a writer of history rather than a maturing writer of drama, Shakespeare followed suit, every step of the way. When we focus on Shakespeare as a writer of history who spoke to other writers of history who were writing on the same historical material, we are left with the conclusion that the *Henry VI* plays and *Richard III* would look much the same as they look now, even if they were written after, rather than before, the second tetralogy. Shakespeare's development as a playwright might have little to do with the curious fantasies of maturation and everything to do with his engagement with history, one that registers in each of the history plays as it registers so profoundly in *Richard II*.

Chapter Two

A Chaste Maid in Cheapside and the Histories of London

The fundamental claim of *Untimely Deaths* is that we can best recognize the underlying assumptions of early modern historical thought by looking to a specific selection of plays and exploring points at which, according to conventions of historical explanation, their narratives are problematically abrupted. Such a claim relies on the revisionist assumptions that drama is a crucial part of early modern historical culture and that it operates in conversations with other forms of historical writing in the period. Growing from this sense of the period's intellectual culture, the modernization thesis – or the claim that modern historiographical practice "emerges" in England at the end of the sixteenth century – obscures much more than it illuminates, succumbing to the allure of a Whiggish intellectual history that finds heroic innovators throwing off the shackles of providential explanation and unrigorous "literary" mythography. Instead, we find in the period that there were no purely modern historians and that poets or providentially minded writers were often sophisticated and "modern" in their methods.

Thomas Middleton's career speaks explicitly to the variety of historical thought in the period and to the absence of any institutional, authorizing infrastructure that might distinguish between serious and non-serious writers of history, or between writers of history with more or less legitimacy. With various individuals and institutions demanding historical writing for a variety of ends – from civic authorities who wanted to establish the historical borders of an *urb* to noblemen who wanted aggrandizing stories about their families – history writers were called upon to perform various sorts of work. Similarly, many men with different talents or interests were called upon to write history. Occasionally, one would need a sophisticated antiquarian. At another time, one would require a poet to write a history foregrounding the accomplishments of one's ancestors.[1] Middleton performed all varieties of historiographical work, and recognizing this variety helps us to approach his plays with a greater sensitivity to the ways in which they make meaning and make sense of the world they stage.

When considering Middleton's vision of urban life in *A Chaste Maid in Cheapside,* I argue that Middleton, as Shakespeare does in *Richard II,* offers a variety of competing historical accounts in his vision of historical unfolding, but does so in a more syncretic, less agonistic way, an approach that perhaps spoke more clearly to an early modern historical culture that treated mythopoetic and providential history far more seriously than is usually supposed. Further, I posit that unless we acknowledge the various kinds of urban history being written in the early seventeenth century – forms with which Middleton was well versed – the play inevitably seems confused or incoherent. Featuring the shocking but ultimately false deaths of Moll and Touchwood Junior, Middleton's play considers the possibility of urban rather than pastoral romance; this potential catachresis – "urban pastoral" – has inspired a critical debate around the play's sincerity, and such disputes can only be resolved when we address the various sorts of history being written about London, from the providentialist and the romantic to the chorographical antiquarianism associated most famously with John Stow and his *Survey of London.* To choose between a debased "citizen time" and sacramental "romance time" as we read the play, however, is to ignore contemporaneous descriptions of urban life, which imbricate citizen institutions and commercial trade *within* historical narratives of sacred redemption. As Middleton's play suggests, then, urban history was also often sacred or mythopoetic history in early modern history writing, and the redeemed untimely deaths of his protagonists participate in the sacred rather than secular histories of the city. While *Chaste Maid* isn't a "history play" as the genre is conventionally understood today, it speaks in surprising ways to the historical culture of early modern England: with its porous borders and internal variety, historical writing in the period provided a *lingua franca* or *linguae francae* through which to understand the world. Middleton wrote fluently in these languages, and he draws attention to their significance repeatedly in his play.

Middleton's career and his various skills as a writer of history demonstrate that modern thinking about the distinction between poetry and historiography – between, say, providential fantasy and antiquarian rigour – fails to match the practices of early modern historical culture. By exploring his role as a Chronologer of the City of London, and by exploring that institution more broadly, we might also get a better sense of how this dynamic historical culture affects the sense of history with which he works when he puts the city on stage in his city comedies. More specifically, the various Chronologers of the City of London and the work they perform demonstrate a characteristically early modern standpoint that various forms of history might be treated with equal value, that they may be mutually supportive, and that writing in these various forms might require a similar set of skills. We know that London's aldermen, who established the position, were serious about historical enquiry: by the middle of the sixteenth century, city authorities were invested in the protection and recovery of historical records, realizing that antiquarian scholarship was particularly valuable in a nation where custom and common law determined legal rights, obligations, and liberties.[2] Emerging from this antiquarian impulse and the fastidiousness of some civic record keepers such as William Fleetwood and William Smith, the close relationship between the City of London, its Remembrancer, its Recorder, and the Elizabethan Society of Antiquaries seems inevitable. And yet within this apparently modern historico-administrative bureaucracy, the first City Chronologer tasked with recording crucial civic events for historical record was Middleton, a playwright, who was replaced by Jonson after his death. When trying to fill a crucial role in its historically minded bureaucracy, that is, the Court of Aldermen turned to playwrights and poets. The choice of two poets as Chronologers seems at first to suggest that the role simply required a poetic touch, but Jonson was replaced after his death by Edmund Howes, an antiquarian who continued Stow's *Survey* after Stow's death.[3] After Howes died, the position was returned to the poets when emblematist Francis Quarles was appointed, and then it went back to the antiquarians with the appointment of Walter Frost, the city's Swordbearer, responsible for the preservation of ancient customs (Thomas 2.287). The City Chronologer, then, could emerge from any number of professional spheres, could write in any number of forms, and would be expected to perform the same work in the service of the city.

While the practical responsibilities of the City Chronologer remain unclear, they were likely more intellectually demanding and politically sensitive than the existing civic records suggest, and they were likely less *pro forma* or ceremonial than most modern accounts of the position suggest. Middleton's appointment and his contribution to the city illustrate the role's intellectual heft, and they testify to his capacity for rigorous and "modern" historical thought. As recorded in the *Remembrancia*, Middleton's appointment required him to "collect and set down all memorable acts of this City and occurrences thereof, and for such other employments as this Court shall have occasion to use him in" (Anon., 305 n.2); for the service, he was awarded a stipend of £6 13s 4d, which was subsequently raised to £10. The stipend and job description initially suggest that the appointment was a lucrative sinecure, rewarding Middleton for his close relationship with Lord Mayor Thomas Cokayne,[4] but the city clearly valued Middleton's research: London's Court of Aldermen encouraged him to produce more writing in 1626, threatening to withhold payment if he failed to submit his history (Cogswell 1909; Anon., *Remembrancia* 306 n.2). The results-oriented council, then, did not treat Middleton as a mere patronage appointee.

The material that Middleton covers in each of his two submitted volumes further belies the sense that the position was light and ceremonial. The volumes are lost but the eighteenth-century antiquarian William Oldys recorded their contents when he saw them prior to an auction. The first volume, titled the *Annales* (perhaps by the seller), contained "Passages and Occurrences" in London for the two years following Middleton's appointment through 1622; included were accounts of the death of London's bishop, the imprisonments of Sir Francis Bacon and Sir Edward Coke, and the burning of the Fortune Theatre. The second volume, the *Farrago*, moved beyond the focus on London and covered events that took place throughout England over the subsequent years until 1626. That volume, according to Oldys, featured a discussion of the contentions between the Earl of Essex and Viscount Wimbledon, notes on the marriage contract between Charles I and Henrietta Maria, and two sections entitled "Parliamentary Matters, 1625–26" and "Habeas Corpus 1627."

Critics writing on Middleton's role as the City Chronologer tend to do so in relation to his city comedies or his satirical pamphlets, following T.S. Eliot and suggesting that Middleton would have been a good Chronologer because his plays prove him to be ("merely") "a great recorder."[5] But the material covered in the historical volumes and their audience suggest that his work was sophisticated in ways that we might associate with modern historiography rather than encomiastic celebration or careful social observation. The contents of the *Annales* and *Farrago* suggest that Middleton's histories were more interested in politics than manners, in the processes of history than the vices of urbanites, and in the state of the nation's constitution than the wit of young gallants. In his excellent account of the *Annales* and the *Farrago* – the first commentary on the works to take them seriously – Thomas Cogswell emphasizes the political volatility of the material Middleton worked with, all of which (apart from the Fortune's destruction) touches on matters relating to the major political crises that troubled James' reign throughout the 1620s. When dealing, for instance, with the death of John King, London's bishop, Middleton was addressing gossip about alleged Catholic sympathies in James' court. King was a staunch defender of James' pacifism against Spain, constantly checking the bellicose anti-Catholicism that circulated among London's more zealous preachers and in Parliament; at his death, he was (falsely) rumoured to have converted to Catholicism, a rumour that would imply James' sympathy towards Spain and would also suggest that his hopes for a Spanish match were motivated by a similar crypto-Catholicism. The imprisonments of Francis Bacon and Edward Coke were likewise politically volatile topics because they emerged from the constitutional debates around parliamentary privilege that would inspire regular and heated conflict in the coming decade. Bacon, the Lord Chancellor, was imprisoned under orders of Parliament only after it appealed to medieval custom and reclaimed its right to imprison royal ministers. James, handcuffed by his need for parliamentary subsidy and by multiple witnesses attesting to Bacon's graft, acquiesced and allowed Bacon's trial. This dangerous friction between James and Parliament grew further with the imprisonment of Coke in 1621 after parliamentary debates about James' pacifism against Spain. Attempting to make a Spanish match for Charles, James curtailed Parliament's right to free speech relating to Spanish foreign policy and questions of the prince's future marriage; in the tumult that followed, James imprisoned Coke, a prominent jurist, onetime Lord Chief Justice, and regular supporter of parliamentary rights, as well as other political opponents for insisting too vociferously on Parliament's right to free speech. When Coke, Bacon, and King are central to Middleton's account of the years 1620–2, that account is inevitably something greater than the straightforward civic encomium that previous scholars have suggested.

The *Farrago* picks up the key themes of the *Annales*, recognizing the longer history of the debates that flared up in the early 1620s. Parliament was particularly worried about the potential for Catholic toleration in England that would ensue with Prince Charles' marriage to the Bourbon Henrietta Maria, and it insisted on seeing the marriage contract; instead, it received a promise from the prince that all English laws would be enforced after his marriage. To Parliament's dismay, the prince's promise was clearly disingenuous, as became clear when then-King Charles, married by proxy to Henrietta Maria in 1625, implemented a policy of *de facto* toleration for her retinue of twenty priests, allowing them to walk openly in London's streets. In this second volume, then, Middleton continued to recount constitutional tensions or frictions between Parliament and the crown. Further expanding on this theme, the feud between Viscount Wimbledon and the Earl of Essex was a proxy-conflict between Charles and Parliament. Parliament wanted withdrawn from leadership roles both Edward Cecil, Viscount Wimbledon, and the king's favourite,

George Villiers, Duke of Buckingham and Lord High Admiral, in the English war against Spain, a new conflict that Parliament supported. Charles rebuffed Parliament. When Wimbledon subsequently commanded a failed Anglo-Dutch expedition against Cádiz, Charles blamed his own officers, including Robert Devereux, 3rd Earl of Essex. The next meeting of Parliament – as Middleton surely recounted in "Parliamentary Matters, 1625–26" – picked up on these tensions between Charles and his favourites, and the Commons. Parliament in response voted to impeach Buckingham. Reacting to the call for impeachment, Charles quickly dissolved Parliament, a decision that proved problematic because he was fighting a war against Spain and needed Parliament to ensure that the war was funded. Without subsidy from Parliament, Charles implemented an unpopular "forced loan" to the crown, which raised the problem of "Habeas Corpus": men of rank who refused to pay the forced loan were imprisoned without trial.

When reading the *Annales* and *Farrago* in light of Middleton's politically explosive (and career-ending) *A Game at Chess* (1624), Cogswell emphasizes the incendiary content of Middleton's volumes. As he does in *A Game at Chess*, Middleton demonstrates a "fondness for tackling sensitive issues" and a willingness to enter the "innermost chamber of the *arcana imperii*" (1910). His audacity here is certainly striking, though it seems readily explicable when considering the nature of Middleton's audience. As the *Remembrancia* suggests, Middleton was writing his chronology exclusively for a group of sophisticated, politically connected men of the city, and they wanted to be sure the work would be written with their needs in mind. Tacitly acknowledging that a useful bit of poetical history would require a dangerous degree of candour, a clause in Middleton's appointment insists that "the said Thomas Middleton is not to put any of the same acts so by him to be collected into print without the allowance and approbation of this Court" (Anon., *Remembrancia* 306 n.2). The nature of the work undertaken for the council, then, was not in any obvious way ceremonial, nor was it written for the aggrandizement of the city. Instead, it was a critical analysis provided for political actors who often had to deal with both Parliament and the crown, thus necessitating clear-headed thinking on the state of the city in power politics.

While Cogswell is right, then, to claim that the *contents* of Middleton's volumes are fascinating, what interests me here is what the tables of contents imply about the form and methods of the volumes. The statement of contents not only implies an appreciation of political scandal and tumult, it also points to the contours of critical humanist or antiquarian historiography, genres quite different from the social satire or city comedy with which critics generally associate Middleton's work as a civic "recorder." The tables of contents imply an implicit (and plausibly explicit) analysis of the state; this politically engaged, thematically coherent history necessarily deals with key political questions about sovereign authority, customary rights, and the power of Parliament. This is not a mere chronicle or "notebook," as Trevor Howard-Hill suggests (52 n.36), simply listing a year's major events. What Middleton produces instead of a chronicle or a list of "all memorable acts of this City" is a compendium of politico-historical analysis of the sort that Bacon would produce in the same year in his *History of the Reign of King Henry VII*, or that had already caused political problems for Sir John Hayward when his history of Henry IV was published. Apart from humanist political analysis, the works' obvious interest in institutions and social practices, including a discussion of *habeas corpus*, seems closely related to the antiquarian analysis that characterizes John Selden's work, as in *Analecton Anglobritannicon* (1615), his history of civil administration in England, or in his famous *History of Tithes* (1618), which unpacks the legacy of another institution related to both church and state.

Considering the work that Middleton was performing for London in the early 1620s, his appointment offers insight into the city's historical culture. When the Court of Aldermen was looking for historical or political analysis, they turned to various sources and refused to discriminate based on the profession of the writer. That the Court renewed Middleton's tenure after he submitted the *Farrago* suggests that this critical work fit their requirements, and subsequent appointments imply that it was critical work that others, they thought, might perform with similar distinction, regardless of their professional background or previous writing. Playwrights, poets, or men of the city working in clerical roles were all considered, by a group of historically savvy men, to be "professional" historians, or at least to be the sort of writers who could record history for serious people and then be paid for it. Before the birth of an institution like the university, able to certify historians as such, this imprimatur, perhaps even more than the imprimatur of publishers, can stand as a mark of historiographical legitimacy.

But why would the aldermen choose Middleton? To answer the question, we need to recognize that Middleton's work as a writer of the past in civic pageants and on stage might well have demonstrated the sort of historiographical skills they were looking for. Appointing Middleton seems like a wise decision, that is, if one assumes that his creative output before 1620 demonstrated a thoughtful engagement with history, even though he had no record as a writer of critical prose histories. When Middleton was appointed City Chronologer by the Court of Aldermen his reputation as a writer of history would have originated not from previous political histories, but from his various historical accounts of the city and kingdom on stage and in civic pageantry. He had recently completed the popular *Hengist, King of Kent* (c. 1616–20) on the matter of Britain, and had possibly started his career writing plays about history: he was paid in 1602 for a lost chronicle history, *Chester's Tragedy,* and for a lost Caesar play, *Caesar's Fall.*[6] Middleton's civic pageants complement the historical focus of these history plays: they mythologize the city's past in broadly providential terms while turning regularly to the recorded chronicle history of the city and its civic worthies.[7] His civic pageantry may have impressed the Court of Aldermen when it idealized the city, and they may have offered Middleton the position of City Chronologer as a patronage appointment, but the members of the Court would also have recognized his commitment to historical thought. As Gail Kern Paster notes, Middleton's civic pageants combine allegorical mythologizing with "an explicit recognition of the past," and she points to Middleton's *Triumphs of Love and Antiquity,* produced the year before his appointment, as a key example of this historical interest: it features figures "personifying Example and Antiquity" who praise "worthy former mayors from the Skinners' Company" (*Idea* 143).

Reading these pageants in terms of Middleton's literary biography, we come to get a sense of the various forms of historical understanding with which he worked contemporaneously and simultaneously. In the world of the early 1620s where "History" was yet to be a carefully regulated discipline Middleton was untroubled by work as the city's in-house historian while also serving as its piecework mythologer: writing his *Annales* between 1620 and 1622, Middleton also wrote two mayoral pageants including *The Sunne in Aries* (1621), which imaginatively imbricates the new mayor, Edward Barkham, in a cosmological scheme corresponding, astrologically, to the rejuvenation of nature "for the comfort and refreshing of the creatures" (l.25).[8] The Court of Aldermen wanted both hard-headed critical analysis of political affairs and fantastical, providentialist fantasies of the city and its place in the world or cosmos. Middleton provided both, and we see in his pageants and *Chaste Maid* how the focus on urban institutions and historical facts was readily absorbed by schemes we might now recognize as antithetical to serious historical thought.

Instead of thinking of Middleton's "historical imagination" as contradictory, however, his practice is best understood in terms of discursive variety and professional imperatives. Middleton was a writer who responded to various demands that he represent the same set of objects in diverse registers. Indeed, this sense of variety has come to be seen as a hallmark of Middleton's writing since the publication in 2007 of Middleton's *Collected Works*. As Gary Taylor argues in his introduction to the *Works*, the variety of Middleton's creative output embodies the skills taught in the grammar schools that Middleton attended. In grammar school and in his time at Cambridge, Middleton cultivated a "myriad-kinded copiousness ... [A]n ability to write prose, verse, comedy, tragedy, tragicomedy, history, allegory, masque, pageant, satire, poetry commendatory or commemorative, biblical commentary, annals" (32). With respect to Middleton's drama, Suzanne Gossett concurs, insisting that even individual "plays throughout his canon resist traditional generic limitations" (236). Andrew Gordon argues more expansively that "the extant textual forms of Middleton's oeuvre" are "representative" of "the diversity of early modern textual culture" (*Writing* 155), and Alison Chapman appreciates Middleton's ability to "inser[t] himself into the centre" of distinct textual forms, deploying their languages and conventions (247). To speak of the Middletonian style or worldview, in this reading of Middleton, seems misguided, in part because he clearly can write across wildly distinct forms for wildly diverse audiences depending on the demands of the moment.

Of course, many early modern professional writers share Middleton's range, but I am interested here in what this variety of modes of writing means for Middleton's capacious and dynamic sense of London's meanings and the character of the city's history. Specifically, I am concerned with the diversity of historical accounts of the city he musters when representing Cheapside, and in the import of this variety when reading the notoriously complex and critically divisive *Chaste Maid in Cheapside* (1614). Recognizing that Middleton could render the city and its history according to many different historiographical imperatives – from the humanistic to the providential – provides us with a useful tool for understanding the complex vision of London that he offers when recounting the story of Moll and Touchwood Junior, and it also offers us a useful lens through which we can explore the play's mimetic complexity. The play is ultimately characterized, I argue below, by its double vision, the sort of double vision that one might expect from a playwright who produces antiquarian and humanistic critical history while also creating idealizing, mythologizing civic pageantry. The distinction between these forms is ultimately, I argue, a structural tension that quickens *Chaste Maid*, a play characterized by ambivalence regarding the city and by a sensitivity to the heterogeneous temporalities that were thought to characterize city life. In Middleton's play, London is readily comprehensible by appeal to something like Jacques Le Goff's "merchant time," or a secular unfolding of linear temporality, disarticulated from seasonal cycles and yoked to the demands of money lending; at the same time, however, it remains comprehensible by appeal to the grand cosmological cyclicity that is central to so many of Middleton's civic pageants as well as his *Owl's Almanac* (1618).

This conflation of heterogeneous temporalities ultimately emerges from the play's preoccupation with Cheapside, a space that bears a variety of wildly contradictory readings, in ways that are largely unacknowledged in the criticism on the play. A centre of the gold trade, Cheapside was also a spiritual space, suffused with meanings starkly distinct from those associated with the practice of goldsmithing and selling. The neighbourhood's space was caught up both in the temporality of urban life and the temporality of civic spiritual redemption. This double temporality of city life is ultimately the source of an intractable interpretive crux surrounding the play's central lovers and their mock deaths. In light of this doubling, the faked deaths of Moll and Touchwood Junior are readable as neither signs of cynical theatrical wit nor as symbols of grand cosmic redemption of the city. Instead, the play traffics in the ambivalent meaning of Cheapside and forces its audience to experience – pointedly – that ambivalence. As an icon for England's growing economic power and a centrepiece in the city's grand mythic accounts of itself, Cheapside is best understood within a variety of conflicting historical discourses that Middleton brings to bear on the city he stages.

Middleton, "Realism," and the Meaning of London

City comedy was popular in the first decade of James' reign in part because of its innovative realism. Taking advantage of a growing theatre-going population in London, companies turned their gaze to their city, exploiting the pleasure of self-regard to attract audiences. Between the last years of Elizabeth's reign and the middle of the 1610s – the height of city comedy's vogue – theatre-going in London enabled a sort of generalized cultural introspection, staging the spaces and streets in which audience members spent their days. This theatrical self-observation would remain popular in some form or other until the 1640s, but the most popular form of city comedy, associated with Jonson, Marston, and Middleton, peaked and began to wane by the time Middleton completed *Chaste Maid* in 1614, replaced in subsequent decades by the more urbane and less London-centric comedies of manners associated with playwrights such as Massinger and Ford.

While audiences were apparently attracted to this realist turn, critics have struggled to describe both the precise character of city comedy's "realism" and the genre's relationship to London comedy more generally. When Brian Gibbons first identified the genre in his 1968 *Jacobean City Comedy*, for instance, he explored plays by Jonson, Marston, and Middleton, and he defined city comedy in terms of its tone and its sociological sensibility. Because they focused largely on urban vanities and vices, Gibbons argued, city comedies "may be distinguished from other kinds of Jacobean comedy by their critical and satiric design, their urban setting, their exclusion of material appropriate to romance, fairy tale, sentimental legend or patriotic chronicle" (11). To this list of formal and tonal characteristics associated with city comedy, Gibbons also adds the sort of Lukácsian realism, or a realism that imagines characters by appeal to the social and political world that establishes their conditions of possibility. City comedy, Gibbons claims, is fundamentally interested in social claims, drawing attention to the "deeper sources of conflict and change" of which the play's action and characters are symptomatic (17).

The terms through which Gibbons delimited the genre have remained largely unquestioned, providing the language through which critics have read city comedies in the subsequent decades. In the shadow of Gibbons' appeal to Lukács, scholars have often treated class antagonism as the ground of city comedy's realism, as in Alexander Leggatt's expansive *Citizen Comedy in the Age of Shakespeare*, where he explores "social relations in their most material form – sex and marriage, money and property," distinguishing as he proceeds between playwrights who are more or less critical of the city's gallants, citizens, and apprentices (151). This idea that city comedy is about social relations and class types fundamentally informs Theodore Leinwand's *City Staged*, in which he finds in city comedy a catalogue of character types that emerge from the social relations of the early seventeenth century. Frequently satirizing these social types, city comedies stage "merchants as the gentry thought of merchants ... gallants as citizens thought of gallants" (14). The social world imagined in these accounts of the genre is thus largely characterized by its cultural specificity: "gallants" and "citizens" are imagined as classes. But the critical accounts also allow for a surprising topical energy, wherein city comedies stage a "major social movement – the transference of land from the older gentry to the citizen middle class" (Knights 261–2). The power of this social movement is the ultimate "reality" to which the realism of city comedy apparently points, as in Lawrence Manley's nuanced reading of the genre that pits "realism" against "romance" as the opposed representational impulses. More than simply referring to aesthetic features, these generic distinctions are themselves based, for Manley, on historical class antagonisms, wherein "romance" stands for a sort of Empsonian pastoral ("the classes feel part of a larger unity or simply at home with each other") (*Literature* 436) and realism stands for the opposite of romance, or for a vision of the city attentive to political and economic conflicts. In Manley's and similar accounts, the "socioeconomic reality of Jacobean London fully saturates the content of the plays" (Frassinelli), and this reality is predicated largely on one's relation to the market, the "central urban institution of the preindustrial city" (Wells 37).

In those studies of city comedy that move beyond this Lukácsian genre- and class-based vision, critics tend to characterize the genre's realism in terms of geographical topicality and civic self-fashioning. Growing from scholarship by Ian Archer and other historians, the work of critics such as Jean Howard, Karen Newman, and James Mardock has read city comedy alongside historiographical writing, chorography, and maps, arguing that these forms all participate in a vast project of civic self-figuration. In such accounts, early modern dramatists operated as socially attuned surveyors of the urban scene, making the city's tumult somewhat comprehensible at a moment of profound social instability. As London's population grew (quadrupling in size from 50,000 to 200,000 in the years between 1550 and 1600), its infrastructure and social relationships transformed radically in ways that extended beyond transformations in class status: consider poor Rafe in Dekker's *The Shoemaker's Holiday*, unable to find his wife after returning from war in the Low Countries simply because the city's too large. Against the confusion and uncertainty inspired by such rapid change, Howard argues, city comedy and the less cynical "London comedy" answered calls for understanding rather than edification, attempting to "come to terms with a complicated and changing city." "I would argue," she adds, "that the theatre was popular in part because it was not a moralizing institution but an opportunistic one, making fictions from the arenas of life – gender and family life, commerce, encounters with foreignness – where change was most immediate and solutions least pre-scripted" (22). In this vision of London comedy, drama is a decidedly productive force, transforming an inchoate mass of bodies, infrastructure, and activity into a meaningful and comprehensible space.

In terms of this account of city comedy's "real-life" realism – a realism more capacious than the limited, economic realism of Gibbons' Lukácsian model – the genre's work seems to complement other forms of civic self-representation. Mardock makes a broad version of this claim when he situates city comedy in a "cultural and intellectual context" during which a "shift in spatial awareness" took place. In the wake of the major English mapping projects of the mid-sixteenth century, the epistemological work of London's dramatists, he argues, is best understood within the framework of the cartographic and chorographic sense of space, meaning we should understand their plays in the larger framework of "chorographic descriptions of local British natural and social landscapes." To understand city comedy, that is, we need to see them as an extension of such mappings as the *Britannia* of William Camden (1586) and William Lambarde's *Perambulation of Kent* (1576), which "carried out the cartographic process in descriptive prose" (11). Citing Howard here, Mardock ultimately claims that the playwrights of city comedy – like the chorographers Camden, Lambarde, and Stow – set out to render lived spaces comprehensible according to the imperatives of cartographic and chorographical logic.

This critical consensus on city comedy's realism has proved both tenacious and productive, persisting for decades and enabling rich critical discussions of the genre's ideological or cultural function. Reading city comedy as a fundamentally synchronic genre, however, which this approach entails, is ultimately partial, and is particularly problematic when we approach plays like Middleton's *Chaste Maid,* which struggles in various ways against this realist mimetic logic that thinks in terms of contemporaneous social relations. As I argue in the following pages, *Chaste Maid* exceeds the limits of this realist mode not in spite of its close attention to urban life and the city's infrastructure, but because of it. As Jonathan Gil Harris emphasizes, urban infrastructure – persisting over time and appearing perennially in new contexts – is fundamentally polychronic or, in his sense of the term, "untimely"; this untimeliness produces in Middleton's play a richness of semantic possibility that works against any simple sense of synchronic realist totality.[9] More than any other play in the period, *Chaste Maid* emphasizes the urban environment, referring to specific spaces with surprising regularity and even putting the city's central thoroughfare in the play's title; rather than anchoring it in the realist mode, however, the play's spatial references regularly point to myriad non-realist discourses through which these spaces were made meaningful. Cheapside, for instance, bore a variety of meanings in the period, and Middleton's play makes this polyvalence clear. On the one hand, it is the site of various corrupt, deformed, mercenary, libidinous characters who jockey for social position, as well as a space associated with the early modern trade in gold and luxury goods. On the other hand, however, the play regularly invokes the sense of spiritual redemption with which Cheapside was also associated in the period, as we see in civic pageants that Middleton wrote. Middleton draws attention to these overdeterminations of civic space, and by doing so, he produces a play that imagines London as both a synchronic totality – the realist city at the dawn of modern capitalism, characterized by new forms of class antagonism – but also within a larger and older history of spiritual growth and redemption.

By recognizing the polysemous character of the city, my argument draws tacitly on much recent scholarship on "urban palimpsests," as well as on the enormous selection of recent scholarship that borrows de Certeau's famous distinction between space and place, according to which place is space that has been has transformed and made meaningful by the practices of life, even while contradictory and subversive practices struggle to articulate alternative meanings to given spaces.[10] These contests over the city's meanings pit various interests against one another, producing a volatile semic mixture that, as I argue here, Middleton engages, regularly drawing attention to the various non-realist discourses through which civic life is meaningful. To read Middleton in terms of such semantic capaciousness is, as Gary Taylor and Trish Henley argue, to come to terms with the "Middleton system" (13); such a system, grounded on a potentially spurious vision of authorial integrity, makes visible something like a "Middletonian vision" of the city, or at least acknowledges how readily conflicting discourses of urban life might be incorporated into a single corpus.

The heterogeneity of Middleton's vision is clear when reading his civic pageants against the putative realism of his city comedy. Of the non-realist representations of the city in Middleton's oeuvre, civic pageants seem furthest away from the often satirical, gritty, bawdy accounts of London so central to city comedy's definition. Against the claims of a realism based on class antagonism, civic pageants, such as the annual Lord Mayor's show, framed the city in a way that was both grand and coherent. Purportedly designed to inaugurate a new mayor's term and to teach that new mayor how to reign virtuously, these processions through London's streets also invoked a vision of the city as an idealized and unified space in which all persons of the community – whether the guild members who participated in the procession or the Londoners who watched as the procession passed – have a place and a role. In the idealized London that these pageants stage, "distinctive segments and echelons of society" were, as Manley argues, implicated "in a ritual '*communitas*,' a quasi-sacred condition of solidarity expressing the deepest and most basic values of the collectivity" (*Literature* 214). The potential efficacy of these processions is perhaps best captured in a letter by Piero Contarini, chaplain to the Venetian ambassador Horatio Busino, in which he describes Middleton's *Triumphs of Honour and Industry*, the pageant designed for the inauguration of George Bowles in 1617. Along the route of the pageant, Contarini claims, "All Glasse windowes [were] taken downe, but in their places, sparkeled so many eyes, that had it not bene day, the light which reflected from them, was sufficient to have made one" (in Bergeron, *Pageants* 75). This vision of the city turns a familiar urban spectacle into a spiritual, cosmically resonant event, helping London readily echo the harmony of the spheres.

The ideological ends of civic pageants are clear in this image of thousands of eyes silently absorbing the pageant's spectacular displays, as it recalls a benevolent cosmos in which London features. Performed to a captive audience, mayoral pageants provided city dwellers with an idealized image of the city, and they would putatively offer lessons in virtuous supplication. Apart from exploiting the sheer power of spectacle, however, these pageants also engaged in the work of community building, in that they offered fantastical histories that associated civic life with broader, mythographic, and royal scales of historical meaning.[11] This conflation of orders is perhaps clearest in the first triumph of Middleton's *Sunne in Aries*, set in the courtyard of St Paul's. Written for the instalment of Mayor Barkham, a member of the Company of Drapers, the first "Tryumph by land ... attends his Lordships most wished arrival, in *Pauls* Church-yard, which is a Chariot most Artfully framed & adorned, bearing the Title of the Chariot of *Honour*." The triumph is expansive and hyperbolically laudatory. On the chariot, we are informed,

> many Worthies are plac'd, that have got Trophies of *Honour* by their Labours & Deserts, such as *Jason*, whose Illustration of Honour is the Golden Fleece, *Hercules* with his *Ne plus ultra*, upon Pilasters of Silver, a fayre Globe, for conquering *Alexander*; a Gilt Lawrell for triumphant *Cesar*, &C. (A3r–A3v).

The mix of hard-working worthies becomes explicitly topical when Middleton points out the importance of Jason to the Drapers. Jason, naturally, is "the Personage most proper (by his Manifestation) for the Societies Honour" (A3v). In a tortured analogy, Jason's adventures with the Argonauts echo the perilous "*Adventure*" of statesmanship on which Barkham is preparing to embark, just as Jason's seafaring echoes the adventure of international trade on which Barkham's career relied. In this fantasy of relation between Barkham and Jason, the golden fleece becomes a commodity like any other fabric and provides a potent symbol for Middleton's encomiastic mythography. A recognizable forebear of the Company of Drapers and a mythic antitype of Barkham, Jason is turned into "*One of the first* [guild] *Brothers on Record*," and the Drapers become his early modern inheritors, travelling and trading in fleece, hoping for "*Honour got by Danger*" (A3v).

Subsequent triumphs in *The Sunne in Aries* expand on such fantasies and similarly mix history with myth, blurring the chronicle of the Company of Drapers with a variety of grander narratives. The second triumph, the "*Tower of Vertue*" (B1r), features "Encouragement of after Ages" (B1v), or Drapers who had previously served as mayor, such as "Sir *Henry Fitz-Alwin* Draper, L[ord] Maior foure and Twenty yeeres together and Sir *John Norman*, the first that was rowed in Barge to *Westminster* with Silver Oares, at his owne coste" (B1v). These Drapers next appear in an expanding ring of historical figures that encompasses Sir Francis Drake and the Tudor monarchs, "*Two* Henryes, Edward, Mary, Eliza, James / (*That joy of honest Hearts*)." Like Barkham, the string of sovereigns have been forced to "*undergoe the weight of Degree*" or suffer the burdens of authority (B2v).

If the pageant loosely imagines a historical relationship between Jason, Caesar, Barkham, and James, between mythological, classical, civic, and royal histories, then its central metaphor – the sun's move between Pisces and Aries – locates these relationships in a temporality of cyclic historical renewal. As the preamble to the published pageant figures this overarching image,

> *Pisces*, being the last of the *signes*, and the Wayne of the Sunnes Glory; how fitly and desiredly now the Sunne enters into *Aries*, for the comfort and refreshing of the Creatures, and may bee properly called the *spring* time of Right and Justice; observed by the Shepheards Kalendar in the Mountaine, to prone a happy Yeare for poore mens causes, Widdowes, & Orphans Comforts; so much to make good the Sunnes Entrance into that Noble Signe. (A3)

By yoking Barkham's inauguration to an image of the spring and rebirth, the pageant adds another historical discourse to its already burdened frame: to understand the processes of urban history, suggests the pageant, one must understand the city as a microcosm of the astronomical and agrarian worlds, and one must recognize that the installation of a new mayor is analogous to springtime regeneration. Of course, imagining the city within both astrological and "Shepheards" calendars requires some rhetorical sleight of hand. The "renewal" of lambing and springtime is translated into the logic of the early modern *polis*: just as Colin Clout finds lambs to tend in the springtime, Barkham finds the "poore men," "Widdowes," and "Orphans" for whom to care. In *The Sunne in Aries*, the urban is not a human departure from the pastoral or "natural" but is instead a natural extension of it. As Middleton points out, for instance, the twelve guild crests, mounted on a triumph, correspond to the "12.Celestiall Signes" of the lunar calendar (B3r).[12]

These annual processions in honour of the mayoralty were as close as London's civic authorities ever came to establishing a political theology of civic life. Though theologically, mythologically, and rhetorically unsystematic, such rituals drew on a repository of familiar tropes as well as on a long history of thinking about community. The language of sacred authority, that is, was bound up with older traditions of the Midsummer Watch, for example, to produce a fantasy of community that embodied, and was authorized by, forces more impressive than the bureaucratic authority of civic institutions. Recounting the significance of such ceremonial "sites and rites," Manley suggests that pageants like *The Sunne in Aries* produced an "important corollary of the calendrical observance of a ritualized time in government" by transforming the city into "a sacred space, a physical embodiment of historic destiny and community spirit" ("Sites" 45). The institutional and bureaucratic temporalities of urban life might be made meaningful apart from the daily or annual grind of civic management, and Middleton worked carefully with the city to produce such meanings.

While early modern civic pageants provided London with a sense of "historic destiny and community spirit" (Paster, *Idea* 128), the pageants distributed such ideological freight unevenly across the city. St Paul's, for instance, was laden with substantial spiritual and political meaning, and this cultural significance was translated into pride of place in the staging of pageants along the ceremonial route. Dekker and Middleton's coronation pageant marking the entry of King James into London goes so far as to insist that St Paul's is the "privie chamber to this our Court royall," and the churchyard becomes the initial site for an elaborate Latin oration designed to flatter the king's learning and "prudence" (F3). Dekker and Middleton point out that the space, a location of obvious spiritual significance, is also central to the civic *polis* and the sovereign nation, superimposing various orders of meaning on the cathedral and its grounds.

Naturally, civic pageantry invested other important urban sites with spiritual and political significance – the gates into the city, for example, played a major role in civic pageants, as did Baynard's castle along the Thames – and yet few spaces were made to bear a more substantial semiotic burden than Cheapside. In the matrices of religious, mythic, civic, guild, and economic power around which mayoral and coronation pageants were organized, Cheapside took pride of place as the space in which various discourses of spiritual and civic value could be materialized, making it "the central core of the city's ceremonial space" (Manley, "Rites" 41). As Mary Erler argues, the importance of Cheapside stemmed in part from its relationship to St Paul's: "[f]rom the twelfth century St Paul's central role in London spectacle was well established, not only in religious procession within the cathedral and its precinct, but in the secular space to the north, in Cheapside, which became the principal route for royal entries and for reception of visitors from abroad" (x). And yet while its spiritual significance emerged in part from its proximity to the city's cathedral, Cheapside was also invested with an autonomous spiritual significance. Middleton underscores the importance of Cheapside in *Triumphs of Truth*, written to celebrate the 1613 inauguration of a mayor also named Thomas Middleton, by arranging for the mayoral procession to move down the street of Cheapside not once but twice.

Middleton's attention to Cheapside in *Triumphs of Truth* is, in part, topical: Mayor Middleton was from the Grocer's Company, and the company, whose shops lined much of the street, footed the pageant's exceptionally large bill of approximately £1300. While the attention lavished on Cheapside may have pleased Middleton's patrons, its focus is entirely conventional for civic pageants that had understood the cultural, spiritual, and political significance of Cheapside for at least the preceding two and a half centuries. Running between St Paul's churchyard in the west and St Thomas à Becket church in the east, Cheapside was central to most civic pageants because it made visible the spiritual authority in the larger urban scene, providing a quarter mile for pilgrimage. Making spiritual import palpable in urban infrastructure was a crucial task of civic pageantry since at least the thirteenth century, when, instead of water, wine flowed from Cheapside's Pissing Conduit during the 1274 coronation of Edward I and Queen Eleanor. The conduit also coursed with wine for the 1299 coronation entry of Margaret of France after she married Edward I; it filled again with wine in 1312 to celebrate the birth of Prince Edward, in 1377 for the coronation of Richard II, in 1392 after Richard had quarrelled and then reconciled with the city, and so on (Lancashire 44, 45). At these moments, pageants imagined the glory of Cheapside not in economic terms, as an important commercial centre, but as a space in which the divine was imagined to articulate approval of a certain historical event. As Anne Lancashire notes, the sudden switch in the conduit from water to wine "had obvious Christian suggestiveness" (49), and it seemed to mark Pissing Conduit as a strange oracle through which God spoke approvingly of a new era. A similar search for providential approval leads Jack Cade in *2 Henry VI* to insist, as his first official decree, that "Pissing Conduit run nothing but claret wine this first year of our reign" (4.6.1–3). Moments of imagined cultural rejuvenation, then, are marked in the city by a purportedly miraculous event that recurs in Cheapside, one that merges the sublimity of transubstantiation with the pleasure of collective drinking.

Despite Cheapside's inherited and inherent complexity and range of meaningfulness, recent critical responses to *Chaste Maid* are assiduously synchronic, often imagining London and Cheapside solely in terms laid out in Stow's chorographical account. In a passage that appears regularly throughout the criticism on Middleton's play, Stow describes the section of Cheapside just beyond the confines of St Paul's known as Goldsmiths' Row where stand "the most beautiful frame of fair houses and shops that be within the walls of London, or elsewhere in England ... It containeth in number ten fair dwelling-houses and fourteen shops, all in one frame, uniformly built four storeys high"; Cheapside in general "is worthily called the beauty of London" (1.345; cf. Newman, "A Chaste Maid and London" 267; J. Howard 136; Brissenden 1; Porter 107; Harding 83). Emerging from the association between Cheapside and the gold trade, most recent criticism sees the play as a satire of the conspicuous consumption that Stow records. Middleton is concerned with gold and the economic logic that the concentration of wealth inspires, we are told, and he probes the curious ways that exchange suffuses the world in which it is introduced. This reading takes the bite out of the play's opening scene and imagines it again and again throughout the play, consuming all that comes after. I want to read the play here differently as an interrogative text, discursively interrogative in ways that demonstrate the sorts of palimpsestic heterogeneity characteristic of Middleton's civic pageants. While city comedy certainly tarries, as Manley argues, with the tensions between pastoral and satire wherein pastoral is figured in Empsonian terms, *Chaste Maid*, I argue below, engages a broader tension between romance and satire wherein romance speaks to a sense of inevitable spiritual redemption and purification. Such a claim is ultimately a *historical* proposition, one that yokes London's civic life to grander patterns of recovery, just as Middleton's civic pageants conflated forms of historical representation and comprehension in order to make sense of the city in diverse ways. This attention to Cheapside's palimpsestic meanings, including *Chaste Maid*'s treatment of spiritual space and time, ultimately enables a more robust sense of the play's complex engagement with the city and its people than current criticism affords when it sees *Chaste Maid* as a thoroughgoing satire.

Plotting *A Chaste Maid in Cheapside*

If Cheapside was central to both spiritual and secular faces of early modern London's life, this doubleness is all but absent from criticism on Middleton's play, most of which finds Cheapside's meaning determined by the apparently vulgar role it played in the gold trade. To clarify the contrast of this approach with my own argument, it is worth detailing it more fully. A commonplace in criticism on *Chaste Maid* is that London – specifically Cheapside – is the "play's central character" (Newman, "Goldsmith's" 112). More than any other play in the period, *Chaste Maid* is concerned with specifying London, pointing immediately to particular places with which the audience might be familiar. The effect of this geographic focus is, according to many scholars, naturalistic, and it produces in audiences a frisson of recognition while ultimately limiting semantic possibilities to the realm of "realist" experience and the built environment. In Darryll Grantley's formulation, the staging of specific streets, wharves, and stairs "adduces a layer of experiential knowledge to [an audience's] judgment of what transpires within the scene" ("Comedy" 33).[13] Seeing the city on stage lets the audience know ahead of time what the play means – it is a play preoccupied with "experiential knowledge" where "experience" is synonymous with empirical facticity. Staging London adds an air of both "realism and theatrical intensity" (Grantley 34) and imparts "precision to the action" (Newman, "Goldsmith's" 112), ultimately producing a play best understood as quasi-naturalistic because its depictions are so precise.

From this understanding of Middleton's representational practice and the apparently straightforward deixis of his references to London, readings of the play ultimately imagine London without the possibility of something like transcendence. Perhaps the most rigorous and single-minded of these critical accounts is Linda Woodbridge's, which appears as an introduction to the play in the *Complete Middleton*. There, Woodbridge reads the play as "blistering" in its satire (907), identifying it not with the genial spirit of London comedies by Dekker, with whom Middleton collaborated, but with the caustic nihilism of *The Revenger's Tragedy*; she finds in Middleton's comedy the sort of "subversive black camp" that Jonathan Dollimore famously attributes to the tragedy (139). In Woodbridge's dark reading of the play, Middleton's satire "serves the cause of 'horror.'" She explains that "in a superficial world of materialism, sensuality, self-serving, and cheap intrigue, horror lies in recognizing that this ugly surface *is* the world: there is nothing underneath." Continuing her depiction of the play's inhumane horror, she asserts that "Life's farcicality, unlike its tragedy, is offset not even by human dignity; such recognitions are savage." She sees but one spark of humane life: "Yet *A Chaste Maid*'s very savagery crackles with vitality and a spirit of play" (907). With "nothing underneath" the surface of London's built environment, that is, the pleasures of the play for Woodbridge are ultimately the pleasures of Juvenalian satire. Furthermore, this satire is bound to the question of urbanity: "The play will have a stage future as long as audiences can respond to wit, trickery, brilliant plotting, infectious cynicism, and sheer vitality. It still bids us, in Maudline's words, 'Draw near and taste the welcome of the city'" (911). When we "taste the welcome of the city," however, "the city" implies both a specific content and an attitude towards life, which is horrifically sour and unwelcoming.

Woodbridge's account of the drama's satirical edge is common to criticism of the play, even among those who recognize that *A Chaste Maid* points to romantic or more genially comedic forms. Set at the end of Lent and consequently pointing up the comedy of paschal redemption corresponding with its own comedic conclusion, this potential of spiritual possibility looms in the play only ironically. Speaking in a uniform voice, each of the play's elaborately interwoven plots offers only critique: in the primary plot featuring Touchwood Junior and Moll – a typical New Comedy blocking plot, with Sir Walter as the constraining *senex,* abetted by Moll's parents – the protagonists eventually outwit the parents to marry and demonstrate the vital energies of love against the oppressive, worldly interests of an older generation. In the Kix and Allwit plots, "adultery is rewarded" in a city without "a moral centre" (Woodbridge 909); in the plot featuring Tim and the Welsh Whore (one of Sir Walter's mistresses), the feckless son of the Yellowhammers is too dumb to be anything other than satisfied with his marriage.[14] The promise of life-affirming cyclic renewal associated with Easter, surprisingly set in an urban rather than pastoral world, thus becomes a point of friction against which world-weary satire rubs. Tacitly invoking or anticipating Gibbons' idea that city comedies eliminate "material appropriate to romance, fairy tale, sentimental legend or patriotic chronicle" (25), such scholars read the play's satirical tone against its structure, and they identify the play's structure as ironic: there is no real romantic redemption in *A Chaste Maid,* they argue, because the play stages a world in which redemption is a fantasy. The most robust of these readings is, perhaps, Neill's, where he argues that Middleton's "comedy ultimately endorses the festive claims of the body." He explains: "In its satire of Lenten solemnity and celebration of the immortal flesh, it offers a profane version of the *Risus Paschalis,* the Easter Laughter with which the medieval church answered the grimness of Lent"

(Neill, *Issues* 60). In sum, we are expected to find something deeply ironizing in Middleton's play.[15]

Such readings of *A Chaste Maid* are ultimately partial, ignoring the play's tonal heterogeneity, its apparently sincere engagement with the conventions of romance, and the ultimate configuration of its ironic, satirical voice. The beyond of the play's irony is curiously tender and decidedly pious if not zealous. The play treats Sir Walter Whorehound as a risible cad, for instance, but it also stages his repentance using the resonant language of perdition. The broad comedy of the Kix's infertility plot is capped by a poignant and evocative celebration that inverts with a felicitous pregnancy the cruelty of the Yellowhammers ("I would not have my cruelty so talked on / To any child of mine for a monopoly," Kix notes [5.1.33–4]). Tim's marriage to a prostitute is characterized by a genial acceptance rather than the sort of dark regret that we find in comparable punitive marriages on the early modern stage. Touchwood Sr. may be a philanderer, but his love for his wife is marked in a clearly sincere parting scene as they separate because they are unable to afford their fecundity: "the tediousness Will be the most part mine, that understand / The blessings I have in thee" (2.1.3–5). The mix of tones and moods here corresponds with the play's fraught sense of romance and urban realism, and it seems to be a characteristic of Middleton's dramatic vision in general. One might consider here, for instance, the curious tonal contrasts in *The Revenger's Tragedy*, which moves from tragedy to farce and back, or the notorious double plotting of *The Changeling*, as the broad comedy of the madhouse jostles uncomfortably against the baroque tragedy of the main plot. Among city comedies, we might also consider the lament of the Country Wench's Father, who seeks his daughter – now a prostitute – in the "man-devouring city," also invoking the language of preterition in the acknowledgment that "One minute" of sin can lead one to be "eternally undone" (2.2.20, 30)

While the mix of tones is characteristically Middletonian, the tonal heterogeneity in *Chaste Maid* is ultimately an effect of the various visions of the city that the play offers, finding it at once a place of debased vulgarity and sacramental grandeur; this mix also reminds us of the various forms of narrative through which the plot is made to make sense. The critical tradition tends to ignore or marginalize this urban doubleness by focusing solely on the city's vulgarity, as when exploring the nature of Cheapside itself. Such readings often rely on a tautology centred on the presumed nature of Cheapside: Cheapside is bound to ideas of vulgar exchange, which is evident in the play's satire; we know the play is a satire because it is set in Cheapside, the epitome of vulgar exchange. In this account, the play's title contains an irony we're expected to detect: Cheapside is a particularly corrupt microcosm of a mostly corrupt city and that "chaste maids" are among the few commodities that are impossible to locate in the shops that line this street to the east of St Paul's. When pointing to the potential quibble in the title, however, the critical tradition fails to note that Cheapside was no stranger to chastity. This very virtue in fact makes an appearance at Pissing Conduit as part of Middleton's mayoral pageant, *Triumphs of Truth*. In 1613 – in the year that *Chaste Maid* was first performed at The Swan – Middleton allegorically located Chastity in Cheapside in the middle of a civic pageant. She appeared "wearing on her Head a Garland of white Roses, in her Hand a white Silke Banner, fild with Starres of Gold" (C3). The thoroughfare was busy with buying and selling, but it was also semantically busy, connoting a variety of incongruous readings.

Here, I want to take seriously the play's engagement with romance – specifically the sense of Christian redemption – that other critics tend to read as ironic. This acknowledgment of the play's sincerity, as I argue below, is ultimately clearest in Middleton's singular and surprising engagement with the convention of the mock death, but the doubleness of the play's thinking is obvious from its outset.In the opening scene in the Yellowhammer household, which sets the play's satirical tone, we witness Maudline Yellowhammer as she cajoles her daughter to marry well, suggesting that gold and daughters are fungibles. Marrying well for Maudline, that is, means establishing a fair exchange of gold for a daughter, and she worries that her daughter, unwilling to practise the skills of seduction necessary to win a husband, is unworthy of the gold filling her dowry. Her daughter, Moll, is "dull," she claims, and Moll "dance[s] like a plumber's daughter," consequently deserving "Two thousand pound in lead to your marriage, / And not in goldsmith's ware" (1.1.21–2). The traffic in women at this point in the play is the object of satire as we see the vulgar Maudline assume that all values can be measured in terms of precious metal. Moll's suitor, Sir Walter Whorehound, subsequently suggests as much when he attempts to marry his "Welsh whore" to Maudline's son, Tim; he explains to the Welsh woman with whom he travels that he brought her to London to "turn thee into gold, wench, / And make thy fortune shine like your bright trade" (1.1.107).

In Maudline and Walter's accounts of marriage, then, eligible daughters are reducible to Marx's "universal equivalent" where gold stands in for currency in general. The exchange of gold for love or marriage is clearly central to the scene's satirical critique of the status-hungry

Yellowhammers. But gold also means something else in the scene. Like the "Starres of gold" on Chastity's banner in *Triumphs of Truth*, gold also signals the wedding ring that Touchwood Junior seeks. He intends to marry Moll without Yellowhammer's knowledge and asks Yellowhammer to produce the ring. Here, the redemptive structure of New Comedy – celebrating youth over age, sincerity over cynicism – is buoyed by but not reducible to the cynical economy of gold that the Yellowhammers appreciate. Against the rhetoric of romantic fungibility, Touchwood Junior observes of his future father-in-law: "How strangely busy is the devil and riches!" He continues by noting the trouble his beloved faces because her mother, "being to" – or in favour of – Whorehound's courtship, treats Moll cruelly:

> Poor soul, kept in too hard, her mother's eye
> Is cruel toward her, being to him.
> 'Twere a good mirth now to set him a-work
> To make her wedding ring. I must about it.
> Rather than the game should fall to a stranger,
> 'Twas honesty in me to enrich my father. (1.1.166–72)

Against the vulgarity of the Yellowhammers, Touchwood Junior is keen to produce the sort of "mirth" that interests the financially depleted, roguish gentlemen of city comedy. Yes, he also wants to "enrich" his father. But his response is couched in sincere moralism and empathy – the devil's busy with his riches, he notes, and Moll's mother is cruel. The moralized affects he articulates in this passage are foreign to the world of city comedies with which *Chaste Maid* is often tied. In this distinction from others of its kind, *A Chaste Maid* declares itself to be tonally distinct from *The Puritan Widow*, say, where women are "meat and money, too" (4.1.99), just as most of Middleton's plays are evocatively distinct from the "snarling" satire associated with city comedies.[16] More specifically, the gold in the ring is different from the gold we find in city comedies where spendthrift gallants cynically woo wealthy widows.[17] Touchwood Junior wants a ring made from a "half-ounce" of gold, "sparked" with a diamond because "'twere pity to lose the least grace" (1.1.181–3). Even as the play establishes its satirical tone, it evokes a more genial and morally sincere counter-mode, establishing the uneconomic and symbolic resonance of gold in its assumed alchemical purity and even religious connotations with "grace." This doubleness of vision, producing a sort of sweet satire, suffuses the play, and it draws *Chaste Maid* away from the kind of cutting satire associated with playwrights such as Jonson and Webster.

If gold is partially redeemed in Middleton's *Chaste Maid*, the play's elemental interest in water is ambivalent and equally expansive, echoing the tension between sacred and secular that suffuses the play's thinking. The play is saturated with water, from that used at the Christening of Allwits' daughter, to that "made" by drunken gossips at the subsequent reception, to the Thames River into which Moll falls as she attempts to elope, to the virtuous watermen who comment on Maudline's cruelty, to the pleasure Allwit feels when living near the "waterhouse and the windmills" that improve access to this necessity, to Touchwood Senior's particularly potent "water" (2.1.180), to the water that Yellowhammer thinks is a "bane" to Moll (5.2.6). Even the first name of the play's penitent Whorehound, "Walter," might have been pronounced "Water" on the early modern stage. Just as gold operates polyvalently in the play, water is similarly elusive as it flows between registers of sacred and profane. Paster, famously, has unpacked the semantic valences of fluidity in *Chaste Maid*, explaining how water and semen and urine and blood make meaning while circulating through the city's streets (*Body* 57–63); my interest, however, is in the other, sacral, side of the play's fluid poetics. Water may be the foundation of the figural economy of the play's humoral thinking – the pure fluid subtending all the humours – and yet the imbrication of water in holy rites of baptism and purification also determines our sense of this precious fluid as it flows through *Chaste Maid*. In this vein, we might remember where Chastity appeared in *Triumphs of Truth*: allegorical and glorious, she comes into view at a public fountain called Pissing Conduit. Such a moment – with its combination of urine, chastity, continence, incontinence, and public utility – suggests the various and divergent ways that water works or might work in *A Chaste Maid*, and the diverse manners in which urban space might be asked to signify.

As often as water is "made" by drunken Puritan gossips, the play also points to water as part of the ritualized purifications at the centre of the play, tying it to the sense of redemption associated with the play's Lenten setting. The central plot device – that which brings Sir Walter to the city and that ties multiple plots together – is a christening. This baptism, occurring off stage, drives one of two scenes in *Chaste Maid* that feature characters from the play's many plots. The salvation that the baptism suggests comes to fruition only partially in the closing scene, but the baptismal promise haunting the play offers a potential redemptive fluidity alongside the coarser liquidity that interests Paster. This doubleness of water in the play is obscured by a preoccupation with humourality and the bawdy intrigue: "That the lovers' break for freedom leads naturally to the river is a hint that London mirrors the human body," Woodbridge observes. She adds that "The Thames is the city's 'master-vein' which 'shoots from the heart' (3.1.16): 'blood' (that is, lust) naturally seeks it" (909). The flattening of semantic possibility is clearest here, perhaps, where Woodbridge quickly reduces the "heart" and "blood" to "lust" in a play that regularly points to the polyvalence of such categories. The "master-vein" shooting from the heart is, in fact, not (or not only) lust, but the vein imagined to flow from the ring finger inward, unifying inner and outer, soul and sign. When we see the semantic polyvalence that characterizes Middleton's vision of London – his awareness that Puritan gossips make water and that baptisms require it – Moll's putatively fatal fall in the Thames comes to seem a perverse baptism of sorts, one that makes possible the ultimate redemption in the play's conclusion.

According to the imperatives of the multifarious representational and narrative strategies that characterize Middleton's work – from realism to mythography – the city appearing in his corpus is non-identical with itself, suffused in apparently contradictory ways with spiritual light and the forces of social life. In terms of narrative, this variety means that Middleton imagines civic life through contradictory temporalities: from pagan astrology to Christian providentialism to hard-nosed humanistic "politic history." Middleton was able to emplot in multiple ways the world he recorded. The possibility of narrative variety is crucial to our understanding of *Chaste Maid*, I argue, because it helps us to make sense of the play's conclusion. More specifically, it helps us to recognize that the conclusion refuses the conventions surrounding the mock death, and in the process fundamentally undermines the convention's generally cynical or satirical edge.

Chaste Maid ends as Moll and Touchwood Junior feign death only to emerge from their caskets during concurrent funeral processions that become a single wedding procession. By deploying the conventional mock death, *Chaste Maid* appears to follow generically satirical city comedies in which the convention features, and yet it seems to resist the conventions as well. While mock deaths appear frequently in city comedies such as Chapman's *The Widow's Tears*, Middleton and Dekker's *Honest Whore*, and Middleton's *Anything for a Quiet Life*, it appears always as a ruse in which the audience participates. When Young Franklin fakes his death in *Anything for a Quiet Life*, for instance, our pleasure is one of subterfuge, as a young man pretends to be dead, poses as his father's servingman, and quibbles as the father settles his son's "riotous debts" (5.2.55): as a creditor agrees to take 50 per cent of the debt owed, Young Franklin celebrates "hard bargains and dead commodities" (5.2.50–1). In *The Honest Whore*, the play's intrigue requires an audience to know that Infelice is alive while Hippolito thinks her dead. This same awareness of a death's falsity is crucially what Middleton withholds from the audience of his play.

Instead of the lightness associated with the conventional mock-death, the final scene of the play is characterized by a darkness of tone utterly distinct from the broad comedy, however hard-hitting, which so many critics see throughout the play. The stage direction describing the funeral processions for Moll and Touchwood Junior clearly captures this tonal shift:

> Recorders dolefully playing; enter at one door the coffin of the Gentleman, [Touchwood Junior], solemnly decked, his sword upon it, attended by many in black [including Sir Oliver Kix, Allwit, and a Parons,] his brother [Touchwood Senior] being the chief mourner; at the other door the coffin of the virgin [Moll], with a garland of flowers, with epitaphs pinned on't, attended by maids and women [including Lady Kix, Allwit's Wife, and Susan]. Then set them down one right over-against the other. While all the company seem to weep and mourn, there is a sad song in the music-room. (5.4.0.1–13)

The scene here militates against satire and irony, in part by way of its complexity, requiring specially made and complicated props, a pair of cues for doleful music, and well-designed stage action with coffins that cross paths before being set beside one another. The elaborately precise stage direction suggests that the scene operates in a decisively sentimental register. The darkness of tone here seems inevitable, and generically disruptive, because the audience, like the mourners on stage, is unaware that Moll and Touchwood Junior are, in fact, alive. The dramatic irony that would open the scene to city comedy – young lovers pull a fast one on their elders – is simply absent. Instead, the scene foregrounds the heterogeneity of tone that characterizes the concluding scenes more generally around questions of repentance and redemption. Sir Walter's repentance, for instance, has often perplexed critics for the apparent sincerity of its moralizing tone ("O how my offences wrestle with my repentance!" [5.1.73]).[18] We need to take this sudden turn to darkness seriously if we hope to understand the play's conclusion.

Almost alone in the tradition of mock deaths on the early modern stage, *A Chaste Maid* withholds the falsity of the mock death from the audience. In doing so, it engenders a narrative doubleness, one that provides the effect of romantic resurrection without necessarily abiding to the cosmology of Christian redemption. The only other play that works with the convention of mock deaths in a similar fashion is *The Winter's Tale*, a play marked by the sort of ambivalence around questions of romance and redemption that, I argue, characterizes *Chaste Maid*.[19] Equally concerned with penitence and redemption, *The Winter's Tale*, like *Chaste Maid*, both insists on the possibility that the audience witnesses a resurrection and exploits the affective resonances of the scene, even while also leaving open the possibility that the plot that has just unfolded is a plot in which, as Lupton argues of *The Winter's Tale*, "theological themes [remain] firmly grounded in this world" ("Judging" 642).

In its ambiguous cosmology, *Chaste Maid* challenges the distinction that Lupton draws between "theological themes" and "this world." The play is able to stage this doubled world in part because Middleton's play operates in a discursive field characterized by multiplicity. When explaining the world of early modern London, Middleton, as I have argued, could turn to several historiographical schema with which he was familiar. As in the *Annales* and the *Farrago*, Middleton was able to provide secular, sophisticated, socially sensitive analysis of institutions (as in the "realist" mode of city comedy), and yet he was also able to look at various institutions – the guilds, the civic government, the kingdom – in terms of broadly mythic or providential logic. When critics attempt to determine once and for all whether the resurrection at the end of the play points to a romantic sense of redemption or to the rise of shrewd young gallants in a new urban arrangement, they misperceive the play's studied ambiguity. To presume the mutual exclusivity of these forms of historical emplotment is ultimately to rely on an anachronism. *Untimely Deaths* works against this form of anachronism, attempting to establish a clearer sense of the methodological variety in the field of early modern historiography and within individual works of historiography, including drama.

Chapter Three

Epic Tragedies in Marlowe's *Dido, Queen of Carthage*

If the fields of literary and historical writing were more closely related in early modern England than historians of historiography usually suggest, then this proximity is clearest around the myths on which stories of grand British origins were founded, though such myths were first imagined well before the sixteenth century. Mythic histories of Britain were written in England as early as the twelfth century, and they emerged from an earlier continental tradition of universal chronology associated with Eusebius, St Jerome, Nennius, Isidore of Seville, and others. The derivative twelfth-century universal histories were particularly useful to anyone attempting to establish a sense of national glory or cultural legitimacy because they synchronized mythic and biblical timelines with more recent national histories, thus conflating the sublime and the mundane. Through these universal histories, a reader could learn how long Nebuchadnezzar antedated Daedalus and Cymbeline and Caesar, and could also identify the present in relation to grander schemes of teleological, universal development. The most influential and ideologically valuable thread in these English universal histories soon became the *translatio imperii* as it was imagined in Geoffrey of Monmouth's *Historia Regum Britanniae*, according to which England was founded by Brute, grandson of Aeneas, thus translating the imperial greatness of Troy, by way of Rome, into a British form.

Of course, we are often told, the problem of Geoffrey's method became obvious to any minimally competent writer of history by the late sixteenth century. As Polydore Vergil in *Anglia Historum* (1534) crankily attested, it was difficult to reconcile factual and fictitious timelines. After describing Gildas' ecclesiastical history, *De Excidio et Conquestu Britanniae*, a work he admires for its veracity, Polydore criticizes the falsity of the so-called *Prose Brut*, published by Caxton in 1482 as *Historia Anglica*:

> There exists a second little book (that I may issue the reader a timely warning about a wicked fraud), which is most falsely entitled *The Commentary of Gildas*, doubtless written by some rascal in order to corroborate the lie of a certain modern writer. But this villain, by far the most impudent since Man's creation, has summarized this modern writer's farrago, tricking it out with frequent mention of Brutus, a thing of which Gildas never dreamed, and so that he might do a more clever job of deceiving his readers, he has concocted his own invention that there were two men named Gildas, or at least that you can believe this little book is a summary of Gildas' earlier tract.

Replacing one triumphalist story with another, historians of historiography often point to Polydore and the ascent of antiquarianism, and they do so to mark the point at which reason displaced myth in the program of historiography. When historiographers such as Polydore and Leland modernized methodologically in the sixteenth century – when they became more sceptical of sources and more reliant on material history or documentary records – Aeneas and Brute were left to playwrights and poets. In his survey of English antiquarianism between 1586 and 1695, Graham Parry insists that mythic history had all but vanished by the turn of the seventeenth century and that this was a triumph of "clarity" over "fable": "The Reformation and the growing sense of national destiny that accompanied the improving fortunes of England in the sixteenth century caused scholars to try to form a clearer understanding of the origins of the nation, and to trace the verifiable course of English history through Saxon times, rather than rest content with old British fables deriving from Geoffrey of Monmouth, which described a colourful but undocumented association with princes from Troy" (2). Beginning his survey of early modern antiquarianism with the publication of Camden's 1586 *Britannia*, Parry agrees with Joseph Levine's description of historiographical modernization and with his account of Camden's singular achievement: humanist historiographers of the mid-sixteenth century were "soon ready to discard" the mythic history of Geoffrey, "and it was William Camden, finally, who set out all the evidence and politely disposed of it once and for all in the *Britannia*" (49). The story Parry, Levine, and others tell is one of straightforward supersession based on a model of intellectual modernization, and it grants an astonishing degree of intellectual influence to Camden. Modern historiography could only become modern, following Camden, once it refused to "rest content," deciding instead, in Donald Kelley's words, to "discard" or "overthrow ... various legends, including those of Roman and Carolingian as well as Trojan origins" ("Theory" 752).[1]

Though convincing in its broadest contours, this narrative of methodological supersession occludes a more complicated and stranger story in which historians of the sixteenth and seventeenth centuries could recognize the significance of "verifiable" history without abjuring the mythic foundations of British identity. Indeed, one of the first great English antiquarians in these stories of methodological modernization is Leland, who demonstrated his antiquarian *bona fides* in order, perversely, to prove Polydore wrong and the *Prose Brut* correct where it testified England's Trojan foundations.[2] At the end of the sixteenth century, then, one could be an antiquarian who paradoxically "verified" myth by turning to material history and certified documentation. John Stow, for instance, was at the cutting edge of antiquarian enquiry and was also invested in the truth of Britain's Trojan roots. After beginning his 1580 *Chronicles* with an account of Noah and the "universal floud," he moves to Geoffrey's story of the Brut myth, correcting it to note that Noah's son, Japheth, had been the island's "first discoverer" (15). Striking in this mythic account of origins, however, is the antiquarian rigour with which Stow negotiates the myths he recounts:

> it shall not be impertinent to note here that where as Pomponius Mela me[n]tioneth that one Hercules killed Albion a Giant aboute the mouth of Rhosne [Rhone?] in Fraunce, manye learned men have judged the said Albion to have ruled here, (sith the Greeke monume[n]ts do always call this Isle ALBION,) and after his deth that Hercules came hither, Lilius Giraldus writeth. An auntient aultar also conveyning the inscription of a vowe founed in the uttermost North part of Britaine 1500.yeares since, as Solinus reporteth, plainelie proued that Vlisses [i.e., Ulysses] the renoumed Gracian in his tenne yeares trauailes, after the sacking of Troy, arriued in this our Countrey. (15–16)

This account is different from the sort of story offered by Geoffrey, who claimed to find the Brut myth in an old British book that he subsequently lost. Instead, Stow assays and interprets material evidence – Greek monuments, an ancient altar – and uses them to ground a history involving English history, Greek heroes, and the Trojan War.

Stow's curious method – combining modern, critical, "verifiable" history with "mythic" or "fictive" elements – is embodied in the list of "Authours out of whom these Chronicles are collected," which opens his massive work. Included in Stow's bibliography are universal historians such as Eusebius, Nennius, St Jerome, and Ranulph Higden; mythographical sources such as the *Prose Brut* and Geoffrey's *History*; politically minded chronicles by Fabyan, Hall, and Froissart; classical sources including Caesar's *Commentaries*; and poetry and drama from Chaucer, Homer, and Robert Greene. The bibliography also demonstrates, however, a dedication to the archives that would characterize so much work by the rigorous, innovative Elizabethan Society of Antiquaries, of which Stow was a member. Not simply making histories from other histories, Stow synthesizes historical narrative from documentary records. While he includes "Old Records" as a vague catch-all in this bibliography, he can also be more precise, identifying records from the archives of Canterbury, Warwickshire, Gloucestershire, Norwich, Kenilworth, London, and other cities and towns, as well as the *Antiquitates* of St Paul's Cathedral in London, a work containing records of local medieval customs and parish rolls, and Bishop Parker's ecclesiastical *Antiquitates*, which includes notes on the material practices of the English church (*Chronicles* i). Antiquarian methods, then, failed to foreclose thinking about England in terms of its Trojan origins, and could ultimately be deployed in the name of a curiously antiquarian mythography.

The story of England's Trojan roots owes its surprising persistence in part to its practical and political utility, a fact that early modern historians recognized. Edmund Bolton, for instance, claims as much in *Hypercritica* (c. 1616), where he responds to ambient anti-Galfridian sentiment. Worried about the nation's historical roots, he first insists that Galfridian history is better than no history, so they might as well keep it: "If that Work be quite abolished, there is a vast Blanck upon the Times of our Country, from the Creation of the World till the coming of *Julius Caesar*, not *terra incognita* it self being less to be known than ours." More to the point, however, is the political significance of that history, regardless of its truthfulness:

> out of that very Story (let it be what it will) have Titles been framed in open Parliament, both in *England* and *Ireland* for the Rights of the Crown of England, even to entire Kingdoms. And though no Parliament can make that so be a Truth, which is not such in the proper Nature thereof, nor that much Authority is added thereby to that traditional Monument, because Parliament men are not always Antiquaries, yet are we somewhat the more, and rather ty'd so look with favour on the Case. (225–6)

Identifying the truth here as "mixed," Bolton recognizes the substantial intersection between the political present and historical accounts of the British past. Selden would also make room for the story of Brute in his gloss on Drayton's *Poly-Olbion* because history was valuable as a matter of "tradition" regardless of truth value. Though he might elsewhere critique Galfridian mythography,[3] Selden insists that readers of Drayton's poetic history "shall enough please *Saturne* and *Mercury*, presidents [sic] of antiquity and learning, if with the Author [they] foster this belief" in Britain's Trojan roots (19). As Reid Barbour notes on the passage, the history may be "suspected of egregious lies and mystifying fictions" but it seems "still valuable, as their 'highest learning,' true in its own way" (84).

The political value of this fictional history grew profoundly in the second half of the sixteenth century as England was attempting to establish its global, proto-imperial significance in the face of Spanish dominance. As Richard Waswo argues, Geoffrey's story, when put to work by Spenser and others, "enshrine[d] in the most prestigious literary tradition of the period aims, motives, methods and justifications of European colonialism as it had gotten well under way by the end of the sixteenth century ... The foundations that England in particular was attempting [were] inscribed in the story of England's foundation" (95).[4] Brute, then, provided the early modern nation with a plot and a trajectory, a teleological justification for national being and a fantasy of pastness that valorized the present by appeal to genealogy. The *translatio imperii* is in this sense a curiously transnational national biography, or the story through which the kernel of heroic identity can, by way of narrative, maintain itself over time and find itself flourishing in the present. Such logic is captured in Jasper Fisher's relentlessly jingoistic history of the Roman conquest of Britain, *Fuimus Troes* (1632), in which the title phrase ("we were the Trojans") is imagined to ennoble the British while yoking them inevitably to the glories of both Troy and Rome. The play's ambitious subtitle – *Aeneid 2* – renders transparent the ideological work to which the story of Trojan roots could be put.

I discuss this broad historiographical context because it is only within this wider setting that Marlowe's engagement with political fantasy in *Dido, Queen of Carthage* becomes clear. Of course, the relation between England's nascent imperial ambitions and Marlowe's play has long been recognized, most explicitly and convincingly in the work of Emily Bartels, Clare Kinney, Lisa Hopkins, and Margo Hendricks. What interests me here, however, is the fundamentally formal, historiographical character of Marlowe's response to fantasies of imperial teleology; this response, I argue, is of a piece with his characteristically ironic relation to the genres and narrative forms with which he worked. Specifically, Marlowe's play is shattering and "counter-Virgilian" not – as many critics have argued[5] – because it takes epic material and stages it as tragedy, but because it does the opposite, eliding the conspicuous tragic form and logic of the Dido episode in the *Aeneid* and replacing it with a vision of epic historical emplotment. Virgil writes a tragedy, and Marlowe transforms it into a staged epic. The epic historical logic of Marlowe's play takes nations, cultures, and peoples, rather than individuals, as the proper subjects of history, or as the media through which historical forces articulate themselves, and it leaves the tragic individual awash in the eddies of history's broader unfolding. In this sense, Marlowe's play sets two forms of historical understanding and explanation in conflict – epic history at the scale of nations and tragic biography at the level of individuals – and applies the former to a story that had widely been retold and staged in terms of the latter.

Marlowe's innovation in the Dido story was not, then, in treating it as tragedy – it had already been staged as such a number of times in the sixteenth century – but, as I argue below, in his insistence that her death *was not* a tragedy, at least in the Horatian terms through which tragedy was understood in the late sixteenth century. Reimagining the *translatio imperii* as a story of traumatic repetition,[6] Marlowe ironizes the triumphalist vision in cultural translation by exploring the repetition of catastrophe bound up with it. Where Virgil's history of the *translatio imperii* is decidedly supersessionary, adapted by the English so that London might supplant Rome and Troy as the centre of Western civilization, Marlowe's emplotment of catastrophic history transforms both the logic of the *translatio* and the character of the biographies caught within the imperial plot. In this re-emplotment of the Dido story, I argue, Dido becomes a victim of epic rather than a victim of her own *hamartia*, and her death, as her sister Anna suggests in the play, becomes "senseless" from the perspective of Dido's biography (5.1.328). This scuttling of tragic expectation sets the pattern for the plays in Marlowe's career that will follow *Dido*, all of which are similarly concerned with history,[7] and all of which refuse to heed the prevailing model of tragedy. From the beginning of his career – perhaps from as early as his time at Cambridge[8] – Marlowe's "tragic glass" never reflects the sorts of tragedy that early modern accounts of tragedy would have identified as tragic, always instead imagining the relationship between character and tragic catastrophe in oblique, counter-tragic forms. It is ultimately in his resistance to tragedy that Marlowe is most historiographically innovative, as characters such as Tamburlaine operate always in curious relation to the plots in which they dwell, never quite fitting any sort of narrative forms that might be familiar. This is the story of causeless, untimely death that Marlowe, as Graham Hammill points out, would ultimately theorize under the name of "massacre" throughout his corpus and most obviously in *Massacre at Paris*.

A Frieze and a Statue: Repetition and Replacement in Marlowe's *Dido*

After Aeneas is shipwrecked at Carthage in the first act of Marlowe's *Dido*, he offers the confused vision of historical supersession that the remainder of the play will stage. Bereft at the loss of Troy and the presumed loss of his Trojan fleet, he feigns a fatalistic confidence when addressing his troops, and he works to inspire them by providing a synoptic history of Trojan struggle and a future history of Trojan redemption:

> You sons of care, companions of my course,
> Priam's misfortune follows us by sea,
> And Helen's rape doth haunt ye at the heels.
> How many dangers have we overpassed!
> Both barking Scylla and the sounding rocks,
> The Cyclops' shelves and grim Ceraunia's seat
> Have you o'ergone, and yet remain alive!
> Pluck up your hearts, since fate still rests our friend,
> And changing heavens may those good days return
> Which Pergama did vaunt in all her pride. (1.1.142–51)

Both melancholically fearful and blithely optimistic, Aeneas tries here to situate himself and his troops not spatially but historically. While he opens the second act orienting himself in geographical terms – "Where am I now?" he asks in the second act's first line – he attempts in the first act to find himself within a broader temporal order, and he has trouble doing so. Describing the situation in which he and his soldiers find themselves, he claims that they are burdened by a past that, in some way, remains with them as they are followed by "Priam's misfortune" and "haunted" by Helen's rape. Though they have sailed from the fallen Troy, and though they have travelled an indeterminate distance around the Mediterranean, they remain trapped by a legacy that continues to determine their imperilled state as shipwrecked wanderers. For Aeneas, the primary problem that he and his companions face is one of historical inertia: they struggle to escape their past – they have fled the wreckage of Troy – but they are unable to do so. In a strange turn at the end of this speech, Aeneas suggests a paradoxical solution to this problem: though they are troubled by their inability to escape once and for all, their goal is to return to Troy and to the "good days ... Which Pergama [i.e., Troy] did vaunt in all her pride." Instead of positing forward momentum, a break from the past, a struggle towards a new future, Aeneas hopes that Pergama will "return." Aeneas's goal here is to overcome the past by returning to that past, or to move forwards into a lost past.

Aeneas is similarly confused about his historical position when he, Achates, and Ascanius, searching for Carthage, stumble across a statue of Priam that Dido has had erected outside the city's walls. As they wander, Aeneas is struck – he seems "amazed" according to Achates – because he sees the statue and thinks that it is Priam himself, unslain: "here's Priamus, / And when I know it is not, then I die" (2.1.8–9). Achates soon after suffers the same delusion, but he catches himself when struck by the limits of mimesis:

> I cannot choose but fall upon my knees
> And kiss this hand. O, where is Hecuba?
> Here she was wont to sit; but, saving air,
> Is nothing here, and what is this but stone? (11–15)

Despite Achates' attention to the stoniness of the statue with which they are faced, Aeneas remains strangely divided, both knowing that the statue is carved from stone and believing otherwise. It seems to Aeneas that "nothing now is left of Priamus" and that "Priamus is left, and this is he!" (20–1), and he succumbs to further delusions, rendered more pathetic by his own occasional self-consciousness:

> Achates, though mine eyes say this is stone,
> Yet thinks my mind that this is Priamus
> And when my grievèd heart signs and says no,
> Then would it leap out to give Priam life.
> O were I not at all, so thou mightst be!
> Achates, see, King Priam wags his hand!
> He is alive, Troy is not overcome! (23–9)

Within this confusion, we see not only the transubstantiation of stone into flesh, but also the sudden transformation of Carthage into Troy. Aeneas recognizes that the walls by which the statue of Priam have been built "should be Carthage walls," but he also thinks "that town there should be Troy, yon Ida's hill" (1, 7). This transformation repeats itself as a leitmotif in the play, superimposing the dead onto the living and the fallen city upon the upright. Everywhere on Aeneas's path, for Aeneas and for *Dido*, is Troy, a city of catastrophe translated across the Mediterranean.

Where Aeneas confuses past and present, imagining that everywhere is a new Troy, he offers a vision of history that the play bears out.[9] Aeneas's hallucinatory confusion, that is, marks the truth of history in the play because *Dido* repeatedly stages the past's rebirth in the present.[10] Just as Carthage's walls become Trojan walls for Aeneas, the dead are reanimated here and continue to dwell among the living. Dido's first husband, Sichaeus, murdered by her brother Pygmalion, reappears on stage in the guise of Aeneas: upon her marriage to Aeneas, Dido insists that "'Sichaeus', not 'Aeneas', be thou called" (3.3.58). Ascanius, too, after losing his mother Creusa in the fall of Troy, insists upon meeting Dido that "Madam, you shall be my mother" (2.1.96), and she agrees to bear this role. Where Virgil emphasizes a homology between Dido and Creusa – Aeneas leaves both behind and in flames (Smith 186) – Marlowe's play perversely literalizes the figural truth. In a space so haunted, it makes sense that Dido would ask Aeneas for a child to replace him: "Had I a son by thee, the grief were less, / That I might see Aeneas in his face" (5.1.148–9). Aeneas's delusion becomes something else here, a figure for human life and history that involves imitation across time. In a gesture of parodic literality, *translatio* has become *imitatio*.

The reincarnation of the dead in the living repeats at the level of city and space. The promised rebirth of Troy arrives early for Marlowe in the form of Carthage, which bears the pains that such an identification engenders. After deciding to remain in Carthage, for instance – contrary to Virgilian precedent and against the insistence of Mercury and Jove that he continue on his journey – Aeneas explains to Achates that

> here [in Carthage, rather than Rome] shall flourish Priam's race,
> And thou and I, Achates, for revenge
> For Troy, for Priam, for his fifty sons,
> Will lead an host against the hateful Greeks
> And fire proud Lacedaemon o'er their heads. (4.4.87–92)

Aeneas subsequently reiterates this point that Carthage must be regarded as a second Troy when he cajoles his soldiers, "Triumph, my mates, our travels are at end. / Here [again, in Carthage] will Aeneas build a statelier Troy / Than that which grim Atrides overthrew" (5.1.1–3). When asked by Ilioneus "But what shall it be called? 'Troy', as before?" Aeneas claims that "That I have not determined with myself" (18–19). Before Aeneas settles on Anchiseaeon as the name of the new Troy (after his father, Anchises), the analogy between Carthage and Troy has been drawn so clearly that the subsequent and recursive parallels are difficult to ignore. When Marlowe introduces this moment into the story of Dido, he departs significantly from Virgil, who neither includes such explicit descriptions of Carthage as the second Troy[11] nor suggests that Aeneas dallies after Mercury arrives. As with many of Marlowe's inventions that depart from his Virgilian model, this change emphasizes the parallel between Carthage and Troy and the logic of historical repetition.

Plausible conceptions of the play's original performance further suggest the repetition of catastrophe in Carthage, inscribing the play's vision of historical repetition on the space of the stage itself. Absent any substantial evidence regarding the play's first staging, textual evidence – rather than evidence about the nature of a specific performing space – suggests that the acting area featured a wall to which Aeneas gestures when referring to "Carthage walles" (Smith 178), or at least implies such a feature.[12] As Mary Smith points out, this emphasis on walls and their porosity implies a spatial pun on Troy, conspicuously evoking Troy's famous walls and reinforcing the powerful analogy that Marlowe repeatedly draws between the cities. Marlowe's staged space is particularly evocative when recalling the problem that the original Troy suffered: the city fell catastrophically after welcoming a dangerous foreign gift into its walls, just as Aeneas, whom Marjorie Garber identifies as a second Trojan horse (20), is welcomed through the gates of Carthage only to wreak havoc.[13] When the play ends in flames, when Aeneas leaves behind a second Creusa in wreckage and flame, and when Marlowe offers hasty mass deaths rather than the extended torture of Dido that Virgil provides, the relationship between Troy and Carthage comes to seem particularly pointed.

This vision of historical repetition that characterizes *Dido* is striking in its distinction from the Virgilian source, more obviously concerned with the future story of Rome rather than with a vision of Carthaginian Troy. The *Aeneid* regularly points up its curious temporality, which is both recursively knotted and insistently teleological. Written at the fruition of the historical processes it depicts, its famous scenes of prophecy foresee in Rome's past – Aeneas's future – a story of destiny and fruition or culmination. When Anchises promises that Aeneas's trip to the underworld will allow him to "hear of your whole race to come, / And what walled town is given you" (5.958–9), the journey bears out the promise in the form of Aeneas's shield. Taking this shield, made by Vulcan, Aeneas sees that

> the Lord of Fire,
> Knowing the prophets, knowing the age to come,
> Had wrought the future story of Italy,

The triumphs of the Romans: there one found
The generations of Ascanius' heirs,
The wars they fought, each one. (8.848–53)

Unlike Marlowe's Aeneas, who seems unable to escape the repetition of his past, Virgil's Aeneas distinctly functions within the world that his shield stages, in which there is a "future story of Italy" – an "age to come" – that makes his present meaningful within a forward-moving, future-oriented historical trajectory. For Virgil's Aeneas, this gift of a shield and a future history provides him with the distinct pleasure of historical meaningfulness that is proleptically retrospective: "Knowing nothing of the events" represented, Aeneas still "felt joy in their pictures, taking up / Upon his shoulder all the destined acts / And fame of his descendants" (9.985). Rather than imagining the present and future as mere repetition, Virgil's Aeneas imagines his present in terms of a future to come that he does not yet understand despite its apparent inevitability. This epic temporality of Virgil's poem seems unavailable in Marlowe's play: Virgil's history is pre-emptively complete, teleologically ordered, grand in scope, and supersessional.

In light of the contrast between Virgil's and Marlowe's visions of historical self-positioning, Marlowe's Aeneas comes to seem more like Virgil's Helenus than Virgil's Aeneas. Wandering en route to his inevitable founding of Rome, Virgil's Aeneas coincidentally stumbles across Priam's son Helenus, who is married to Andromachë, Hector's widow. Helenus and Andromachë's new encampment exists in stark juxtaposition with the sense of directed, future-oriented inevitability that characterizes Aeneas's travels around the Mediterranean: Helenus and Andromachë have not overcome their past, and they move nowhere historically, having built for themselves, in a disturbing and heart-rending gesture of mourning, a miniature version of Troy. As Aeneas describes a tour of the encampment that Helenus provides, the scene is pathetic and evocative, bleak and moving:

Walking along with him
I saw before me Troy in miniature
A slender copy of our massive tower,
A dry brooklet named Xanthus ... and I pressed
My body against a Scaean Gate. (3.476–81)

This rebuilt Troy – its sense of repetition, its bleak historical stasis, its mad entrapment in the past – serves in the *Aeneid* as a contrast to the very project that characterizes Aeneas's own travels. For Virgil's Aeneas "That day [with Helenus and Andromachë] passed, / And other days.

Then sailing weather came / When canvas bellied out, filled by a southwind" (3.485–7). For Marlowe's Aeneas, however, the present and future are experienced as a struggle to rebuild a Scaean gate against which to press: "sailing weather" never comes for Marlowe's Aeneas if we imagine that this sailing weather involves a strong wind to cast him once and for all from the shadows of a fallen Troy. Where Virgil offers Helenus as a pathetic icon of failure, the melancholic failure of history becomes the truth of Marlowe's epic hero.

Against Marlowe's sense of repetition within putative progress, his critique of the *translatio imperii* becomes visible in a new way. Modern scholars often point out that Marlowe's play serves to challenge the ideology of the *translatio imperii* on which England's nascent imperial aspirations were founded: he draws attention to the human cost of imperialism by identifying the moral claim of history's losers, as Bartels and Hendricks suggest, or he insists on a space for heroic human agency within the teleological unfolding of history, according to Kinney. Marlowe's intervention, however, seems more radical, undermining the very foundations of the *translatio* and its strategies of validation through repetition. What, the play asks, does it mean to "rebuild" the past in the present if the past is characterized by tragedy and destruction? If London is a new Troy, as Carthage, briefly, became a new Troy, should London fear catastrophe at its walls? Marlowe's play takes seriously the logic of repetition on which the *translatio imperii* relies and exposes the cost to life when one justifies and idealizes the present by appeal to the ghosts that haunt it.

Dido without Tragedy

But what does it feel like to live in this repetitive epic history? What does it feel like to be, inevitably, a second Creusa dying in a second conflagration in a second Troy? If Marlowe's play offers a critique of the *translatio imperii,* then it does so by forcing audiences to ask this question with respect to Dido, making them consider the unfolding of epic history without the expansive, justificatory narrative machinery of epic poetry. The play's answer to these questions: to die in epic feels like something other than tragedy. Early modern theories of tragedy uniformly insist that tragic catastrophe emerges from character, serving a mark of moral failure. Other poets and playwrights treating the Dido story in the period regularly follow this model of tragedy, expanding on the tragic contours of the Dido plot found in Virgil's poem. But Marlowe resists this model, refusing to locate Dido's fall in her character or in a moral lapse. Where the early modern tradition of Dido poetry and drama is a predictably dreary rehearsal of threatening female sexuality and its cost, Marlowe disassociates Dido from the desire that leads to her downfall. In this version of her story, Dido becomes the antithesis of Marlowe's other heroes. Typically, Marlovian heroes such as Tamburlaine, Faust, Edward II, and even Barabas are heroic in their grand desire and will. Their overreaching ennobles while it dooms. Dido, on the other hand, is burdened by a desire not her own in Marlowe's play. She becomes a figure for the loss of history, for the anti-heroic character of imperial fatalism that the *translatio imperii*, always moving westward, implies.

Sixteenth-century theories of tragedy in England and on the continent uniformly insisted that tragedy must be morally edifying. This notion grew primarily from the "rhetoricization" of aesthetics in Renaissance literary theory, and specifically from the rhetorical understanding that poetry was valuable only insofar as it was morally didactic.[14] In Brian Vickers' concise formulation, which owes considerable debt to the seminal work of Bernard Weinberg, "the Renaissance" – Italian, French, and English, from the fifteenth century on – "had a perfectly coherent theory of literature, covering the whole sequence of composition and consumption, which we might call ethical-rhetorical. The main justification for poetry and drama was that literature helped create a good society" (Vickers, *English Renaissance* 10). Of course, not all literary art in the sixteenth century was morally or ethically useful in the ways that theorists might insist, and not all literature in the sixteenth century could be understood as contributing to the good of society. This sense of poetry, nevertheless, was ubiquitous, and it determined how tragedy and tragic emplotment were imagined to operate.

The vision of art's didactic role manifested in a literal-minded sense that, in order to teach, tragedy must stage a plot in which punishment is a morally justified conclusion. The hegemonic force of the tragic model was so powerful that it could inspire profound misinterpretations of tragedies, as is clear in Alexander Neville's (1560) account of Seneca's *Oedipus*, a play that he translated for the influential *Seneca his Tenne Tragedies*. As a pedagogical aid, Neville claims, *Oedipus* is useful because the play's plot follows a satisfyingly moral arc, just as human lives conform to gratifyingly God-directed paths:

> The right high and immortal God will never leave such horrible and detestable crimes unpunished, as in this present tragedy, and so forth in the process of the whole history, thou mayst right well perceive, wherein thou

> shalt see a very express and lively image of the instant change of fickle fortune in the person of a Prince of passing fame and renown, midst whole floods of earthly bliss, by mere misfortune (nay rather by the deep hidden secret judgements of God) piteously plunged in most extreme miseries. ... Only wish I all men by this tragical history (for to that intent it was written) to beware of sin. (125–6)

With a flourish – "nay"! – Neville makes a move here that typifies early modern accounts of tragedy, foreclosing the possibility of amoral catastrophe ("mere misfortune") and pointing instead to the "deep hidden secret judgements of God" that actually determine tragic ruin. Neville finds in the terrible tragedy of *Oedipus* a lesson we can readily take away, and that lesson concerns sin and punishment as they manifest over the course of a plot. Such a reading of Seneca seems obviously problematic to modern readers who find in *Oedipus* a very different sort of tragedy. As Vickers notes, "Neville imposes a Christian scheme onto Seneca's version of Sophocles, in which Oedipus' murder of the man who assaulted him (his own father, as he cannot know) is a coincidence, to which no design attaches." That is, in Neville's (re)-interpretation, "The fact that Oedipus acknowledges his responsibility for the deed by blinding himself is, rather, a triumphant demonstration of human ethics" (*English Renaissance* 126 n.1). While Vickers' reading may be similarly partial, his sense of Neville's account captures the force of the idea that tragedy should moralize, and that it should moralize through its plot: there is no tragic plot "to which no design attaches" for Neville and for other such theorists on early modern tragedy, because tragedy, as tragedy, is a plot about the punitive design of the world. To make such a claim is not to say that other, more humane, more conflicted, more secular senses of tragedy were unthinkable in the middle of the sixteenth century, but to point out that they were largely unthought, especially among men such as Neville, who was formally educated in the traditions of Renaissance rhetoric.

The most influential and subsequently best-known English accounts of tragedy from the sixteenth century make explicit the moralized character of the tragic plot. Sidney, for instance, famously praises tragedy over history precisely because it guarantees the sorts of morally edifying punishments that Neville identifies in *Oedipus*: if evil men appear on the stage "they ever go out – as the tragedy writer answered to one that misliked the show of such persons – so manacled as they little animate folks to follow them" (24). The moralized plot and the moralizing character of drama are so central to Puttenham's *Arte of English Poesy* that he uses them to found a history of theatrical and literary development: satire was the first genre because, when tyrants died, satirists mocked them and showed "the just punishment of God in revenge of a vicious and evil life" (123). Tragedy emerged only later in the art of plotted morality when styles became "higher and more lofty" as mockery was done away with (123). This sense of tragic elevation and tragic punishment appears frequently in the antitheatrical debates, and is a point on which both sides curiously agree. Heywood's *Apology for Actors*, for instance, insists on theatre's didactic value and it does so in part by insisting that tragedy represents terrifying, just punishments: "If we present a Tragedy, we include the fatal and abortive ends of such as commit notorious murders" (F3r). Even Stephen Gosson, to whom both Heywood and Sidney are tacitly responding in their *apologia*, insists that the tragic plot is morally edifying, just so long as one reads the tragedy rather than seeing it performed. The theatre may corrupt by teaching the world to lie, he insists, but a reader could behold in *John Baptist*, for instance, "the practice of Parasits in *Herods* court, The Tyranny of *Herod* powred out upon the messenger of the Lord, and the punishment that followed: He might learne to governe his owne house, and beware what entreaty he gives to the Prophettes of God" (E4ii). Gosson might not be concerned with delighting readers, and he may distrust theatre because it teaches dissimulation, but the rhetorical justification of aesthetics – art teaches – remains true. And art teaches, for Gosson, through plots that traverse a punitive arc.

Among late medieval and early modern poets and translators who thought of plot in these moralizing ways, the details of the Dido episode in the *Aeneid* lent themselves to a variety of predictably misogynistic interpretations.[15] In the first English translation of the *Aeneid* (1513), Gavin Douglas readily explains in his argument to Book 4 that Dido "wroucht her own undoing ... throw fuliche lust" (Y1r); Stanyhurst's translation of *Aeneid* 1–4 would similarly identify "carnal leacherye" as the cause of her death (65). In a less scolding account of Dido's moral failing, Chaucer's *Legend of Good Women* (c. 1386) probes her sexuality as a fault without spelling out the punitive logic of her fall from "gentil-woman and a queen" to "wyf thus foule fleen" (III.1306–7). The poetic popularity of Dido in the period – Surrey, like Stanyhurst, would also translate *Aeneid* 4 – suggests an ambient desire for stories of female debasement, but also an eagerness to engage with plots that could lend themselves to ready moralization. Dido was widely treated as an icon or an emblem, a figure who might remind readers about the danger of female desire and sexual licence.

This moralized story dealing with female sexuality, sovereignty, foreign suitors, and political stability made the Dido plot particularly evocative during Elizabeth's reign, and it was twice transformed into drama pointedly aimed at the queen by scholars aiming to be helpful, once in 1564 by Edward Halliwell at King's College, Cambridge – a performance that Elizabeth attended – and once in 1583 by William Gager at Christ Church, Oxford. Though Halliwell's *Dido* is lost, Gager's play makes clear that the stage was to be treated as a scene of pedagogy and that drama produced lessons through its plotting. Gager's play insists, for instance, that its primary ends are didactic rather than aesthetic, and it does so by including an extensive epilogue listing truisms that explain the plot's motivating forces, key lessons that the plot makes clear, and the policy failures that led to Dido's downfall. Gager informs his audience specifically that

> Love forbids us trust an ancient foe. Though an enemy may favour, he is always planning schemes; though Juno may be kind to the Trojans, she is actually preparing plots against them. It is royal to give trust and help to the wretched, and great hospitality ennobles a distinguished house. But whosoever remains bound by an obligation is diminished in status, and ceases to be free. Though he may be ever so grateful, he will be considered an ingrate. The storm, formed by Juno with evil intent, demonstrates what faith should be placed henceforth in Prometheuses, and that no one can imitate the thunderbolt of Jove. It is right to obey the admonitions of the gods, and any delay, even if it be brief, is too much. Women are soft and can be moved by tears, but a man staying strong ought to barricade his ears. If personal obligations are holding back the greater good, then whatever they may have been, they hold nobody bound. Foreign marriages rarely turn out well; the power of Love is great; the heavier passion tends to seize hold of women, the lighter one kindles the men ...

Striking in Gager's litany here is the relative absence of erotic low-mindedness – no "fuliche lust," no "carnal lecherie" – and yet the list demonstrates the fundamental ideas of the rhetorical tradition where tragic plots produce knowledge through their catastrophes.

The widespread moralization and eventual theatricalization of the Dido plot make sense ultimately because the plot was already didactic and quasi-theatrical in the Virgilian source text. Though the *Aeneid* is mostly uninterested in sexual morality, the Dido episode is, as David Quint argues, clearly concerned with the threat of female desire, drawing out the danger of uncontrolled female passion, and juxtaposing the dignity of Roman *pietas* with the erotic "monstrosity that characterized Carthage itself, the great barbarian foe of Rome" (183). The ramifications of the plot seem particularly pronounced also because they operate in a protracted narrative hiatus. A stand-alone story – "the one major digression in Aeneas' epic quest" (Pugh 84) – the Dido episode is marked off from the epic machinery of the *Aeneid* and is also designed as a semiautonomous tragedy. When Halliwell, Gager, and Marlowe put the play on stage, then, they were following Virgil's cues and his own formal debts: Virgil conspicuously frames the episode within a *scaena* between towers and before a woods as Aeneas approaches Carthage (Pugh 84), and the episode's formal features point to Euripides more than Homer.[16] In the Dido plot, as Mary Gamel, Susannah Braund, and others have pointed out, Virgil introduces theatrically agonistic speeches, a sister who operates as a female *nutrix* to a queen, and a series of comparisons in which Dido becomes Pentheus, Orestes, Medea, and Atreus. Conventionally theatrical even in verse, the story of Dido, Gamel concludes, "raises the possibility that the poem will metamorphose from epic to tragedy" (613).

To see the Dido plot in this way means rethinking Marlowe's engagement with Virgil, his characteristic "anti-Virgilian" attitude, and the nature of *Dido*'s relation to the traditions of epic imperialism. The translation from the relative grandeur of epic to stagey tragedy has frequently been read as a more or less successful critique of the ideology associated with epic, but Marlowe's engagement with Virgil and with the tradition he inherits is altogether different and altogether differently critical.[17] Although he inherits a tradition that sees Dido as a tragic figure, emplottable in a tragedy apart from the epic energies in which her story is told, Marlowe produces a figure who seems unable to achieve tragic consistency, or seems unable to fit within a plot that emerges from her character and apart from the broader unfolding of epic. In the process he actually diverges from Virgil as well as the traditional literary and dramatic representations of Dido. The tragic plot that Virgil offers Dido may be distinct from the moralistic plots provided in the Dido tradition, but his Dido plot clearly situates the queen in a causal relation to the death that she suffers, figuring the end of her life as a natural result of her character and her actions. The unity of action is thus guaranteed by the plausibility of the character's consistency over time in the world that sustains her. Marlowe resists this fantasy, however, and in refusing to make Dido's death fitting or timely, he refuses to participate in a tradition that imagines history operating in an orderly way at two distinct scales: one human and the other imperial. Scuttling tragic unity and diffusing agency, Marlowe opens his theatrical career with a gesture of defiance that characterizes his art's generic ambivalence. This defiance of tragedy is not simply a matter of ideas – "overreaching may be heroic" – but a matter of form, wherein

Marlowe rebelliously fashions plots that rarely produce any easy sort of knowledge.

To read Virgil's and Marlowe's accounts of the Dido episode next to each other is to see clearly what being "un-Virgilian" or "counter-Virgilian" or "anti-Virgilian" means to Marlowe. Many of Marlowe's revisions to Virgil's poem are, as scholars such as Patrick Cheney recognize, typically Ovidian: Marlowe treats the gods irreverently, he clearly sympathizes with Dido, and he figures Aeneas as an oath-breaker. But Marlowe's refiguration of the Dido story is more radical than the revaluation of character and reattribution of guilt that Ovid offers in the *Heroides*. For Marlowe, the plot of Dido's story is the plot of epic history rather than a plot of necessary individual downfall, and his play regularly and consistently figures Dido as the victim of a fate not determined by her character. The imperial ambitions of Virgil's poem in this sense run aground on Marlowe's own ambitions to produce a more complicated, messier storyline that attends carefully to character, to experience, to affect, and to the occasionally gruesome demands of piety or providence.

To see the tragic contours of Virgil's Dido, it helps to recognize that the *Aeneid*'s Carthage emerges from a field of desire and pleasure, carefully distinguished from the austere privation of Aeneas and the heroic self-abnegation of Roman piety that opens the poem. When Aeneas lands, Dido compels him to "linger ... with her blandishments" (1.917), and the episode is built from a language of erotic rather than epic verse. When the story of Troy is told in the *Aeneid* Books II and III, the details ultimately jar against the framing device: *Aeneid* II and III transcribe the story recounted by Aeneas at a feast held by Dido in his honour. The sober fall of Troy is told in the sort of scene that led to Troy's fall; then Dido appears here "amid magnificence / Of tapestries, where she had placed herself / In the very center, on a golden couch" (1.952–4). Aeneas finds here "finger bowls," "bread in baskets," "boards with meat," "wine cups," and Tyrians "crowding through the radiant doors, all bidden / To take their ease on figured cushioning" (1.955, 956, 963, 964, 966–7). Against the vision of hunger with which Book I opens – Aeneas sets out to kill a deer to feed his soldiers – such delicacy and excess establish the meaning of Carthage. Its aesthetics and hedonistic ethics distinguish it from the main story of the *Aeneid*, which is a grand narrative of heroic sobriety. As framed by the rest of the poem, the Dido episode thus seems less like a diversion from history than a heterodox space to be destroyed by epic Roman *pietas*. Inevitably "luckless," Virgil insists, Dido was "already given over to ruin" before the energies of epic could arrive at Carthage in the form of a disguised god (1.973).

This festive excess figures often in the Dido tradition, as in the elaborate confectionary model of Troy that featured in the original staging of Gager's play, and it clings metonymically to Dido. Her court is, for Surrey, "sweet" (repeated three times, lines 5, 6) and is characterized by "marveylous" abundance (6); for Douglas, the court is "rich" (repeated four times 1.11.8, 13, 31, 67), and it seems out of place in the least indulgent of epics. But Marlowe omits this traditional characterizing context, a fact more striking when measured against his capacity for rendering luxury, as in Gaveston's fantasy that opens *Edward II*, or Faustus' promised gifts to the scholars of Germany. Rather than engaging in the typical description of excess, Marlowe has his Dido meet and welcome Aeneas, and then hear from him the story of Troy's fall in a more banal and practical setting: on the streets of Carthage, the city she rules. Dido's feast and its pleasures are ultimately crushed in Virgil's poem for aesthetic and ethical reasons, and the frame of epic guarantees the catastrophe's internal integrity: luxury is doomed by an aesthetic world that rewards solemn *pietas*. But the framing narrative in Marlowe's play – where venal, vulgar gods argue about sex – fails to charge the episode with the same order of values, and instead highlights Dido's sobriety by contrast. In Marlowe's play, that is, we find a cosmological inversion: the gods, rendered in terms of luxury and caprice, frame a Dido associated with sobriety and sovereign competence.

The relationship between Dido's character and the delicate, indulgent feast grows clear in Virgil's poem when Dido responds to the story of Troy's fall. For Virgil's Dido, Aeneas's account is an entertainment that logically follows Iopas' music-making. After Iopas makes "the room echo with his golden lyre" (1.1012),

> Dido, fated queen, drew out the night
> With talk of various matters, while she drank
> Long draughts of love ...
>
> ....
>
> "Come, rather," then she said, "dear guest, and tell us
> From the beginning the Greek stratagems,
> The ruin of your town and your sea-faring ..." (1.1021–3, 1027–9)

Between "long draughts of love," and talk on various matters, the story becomes fatuous to the queen who fails to recognize the sense of the tale, the danger of strangers, the peril of ease. The first lines of Book IV remind us immediately that Dido is oblivious to the sense of political peril that Aeneas's tale might engender for herself and her kingdom. She is preoccupied instead by an all-consuming desire:

> The queen, for her part, all that evening ached
> With longing that her heart's blood fed, a wound
> Or inward fire eating her away.
> The manhood of the man, his pride of birth,
> Came home to her time and again; his looks,
> His words remained with her to haunt her mind,
> And desire for him gave her no rest. (4.1–7)

Described by Virgil within the claustrophobic space of a chamber in which only Dido and Anna converse, the "manhood of the man" (or the "prowesse of the man" [Surrey]; or the "wights doughtie manhood" [Stanyhurst]; or the "great prowess of Aenee" [Douglas]) penetrates with the register of the erotic, and the "words" that haunt Dido drift apart from a story of urban catastrophe. Troy's destruction becomes a love song, and once again Virgil's scenic ironies and narrative reframing point to Dido's lightness.

But Marlowe's Dido hears something other than a love song in the story of Troy's fall. When Virgil's two books describing Troy's fall become a long set speech on Marlowe's stage, Dido listens correctly here, and hears what she needs to hear, reacting as queens, one presumes, should react: "O Hector," she cries, "who weeps not to hear thy name!" (2.1.209). Aeneas worries his account is too grisly, that there are too many "Young infants swimming in their parents' blood" and "Headless carcases [sic] piled up in heaps" (2.1.193–4); Dido implores him to continue. Most pointed here, however, is that Dido hears in the story of Troy a moral about the dangers of "uncontrolled female passion," and curses Helen: "O had that ticing strumpet ne'er been born!" (2.1.300). Virgil's Dido is haunted by Circe – Dido's feast stands in for Circe's bower – and they share the same fate.[18] Marlowe erases the homology, extracting Dido from a tradition of Circe's "daughters"[19] and providing her with sovereign majesty untainted by erotic female monstrosity.

Only by recognizing Marlowe's recharacterization of Dido does the import of 3.1 and its otherwise bizarre action come to make sense. The scene – an argument between Dido and Iarbas, as Dido carries Cupid-as-Ascanius – registers the friction between epic and tragedy, or between two narrative forms that imagine agency on different scales.

Marlowe's Dido again is essentially different from Virgil's Dido, who is "already given over to ruin." Marlowe's Dido instead appears onstage in 3.1 as a savvy political calculator, able to sustain Iarbas' courtship – the courtship of a foreign prince – without ever offering "enjoyment" or the fruition of wooing. At the opening of 3.1, however, Cupid appears on stage disguised as Ascanius prior to an exchange between Iarbas and Dido, and he recounts the plan that Venus devised at the end of the previous scene:

> Now, Cupid, cause the Carthaginian Queen
> To be enamour'd of thy brother's [i.e., Aeneas's] looks;
> Convey this golden arrow in thy sleeve,
> Lest she imagine thou art Venus' son;
> And when she strokes thee softly on the head,
> Then shall I touch her breast and conquer her. (3.1.1–6)

In the action that follows, the dialogue appears confused, in part because the 1594 quarto lacks a stage direction for the moment of pricking and in part because Dido's astute political negotiation jostles with uncharacteristic desire. Iarbas enters with Dido and asks about the status of his courtship:

> How long, fair Dido, shall I pine for thee?
> 'Tis not enough that thou dost grant me love,
> But that I may enjoy what I desire:
> That love is childish which consists only in words. (7–10)

The question and its assumptions presume an earlier narrative in which Dido grants love without enjoyment, and then offers only more language, sustaining good will without ceding political power. Dido assures Iarbas that, "of all [her] wooers," he has "the greatest favours [she] could give":

> I fear me Dido hath been counted light
> In being too familiar with Iarbas,
> Albeit the Gods do know no wanton thought
> Had ever residence in Dido's breast.
> ....
> Fear not, Iarbas; Dido may be thine. (11–17)

When Dido says "Dido may be thine," she operates in the sphere of realpolitik, where desire and authority are forced to mix. In this, she appears, famously, like Elizabeth. And yet the dialogue here changes. With Cupid sitting on Dido's knee, the audience witnesses Dido's bizarre fickleness:

> Iarbas: Come, Dido, leave Ascanius; let us walk.
> Dido: Go thou away; Ascanius shall stay.
> Iarbas: Ungentle Queen, is this thy love to me?
> Dido: O stay, Iarbas, and I'll go with thee.
> Cupid: And if my mother go, I'll follow her.
> Dido: [*To Iarbas*] Why stay'st thou here? thou art no love of mine.
> Iarbas: Iarbas, die, seeing she abandons thee!
> Dido: No, live Iarbas; what hast thou deserv'd,
> That I should say thou art no love of mine? (34–42)

Dido's fickleness is uncharacteristic here. Without a stage direction, it remains unclear at what point she was pricked by Cupid's arrow, though multiple pricks prove to be necessary: repeatedly stabbed, she wavers in her sudden devotion to Aeneas before Cupid gives a second, third, and fourth poke until she finally insists that Iarbas "never look on" her again (53). Rather than succumbing to her own desire and a predisposition for sensual pleasure, that is, Dido resists – repeatedly, energetically, and conscientiously – the prompting of divine devices, something that more robust stage directions would make clear.

The problem here is ultimately a narrative problem, or a problem for tragic emplotment. More specifically, it is a problem of the uncharacteristic character: when behaviour is uncharacteristic, the relation between character and plot dissolves. When Marlowe's Dido undergoes a radical refiguration under the weight of the god's power – when action is no longer bound to the agent of that action, or when agency itself becomes an inadequate category – then moralistic emplotment no longer seems plausible. Playing up the gaps between Dido and her subsequent action, the play points to this fact of transformation: Dido loathes the "ticing" Helen and yet, according to Achates, she has become "ticing" (2.1.330, 4.1.30); Anna implores Dido, "Sweet sister, cease; remember who you are!" (5.1.263); Dido's speech, according to Aeneas, becomes "doubtful" (3.4.30). Where the critical tradition finds Aeneas risible when he seems unable to recognize Dido's seductive speech – it is "doubtful," he claims – it is the tradition that misreads Dido, Aeneas, and the play: her speech, attempting to seduce Aeneas, *is* doubtful, voicing desires that alienate Dido from herself.

Dido's doubtful speech becomes the trope through which the play emphasizes her self-alienation as she moves closer to tragedy. From the incoherence of her speech as she vacillates with Iarbas, to the curious nature of her speech as she seduces Aeneas, Dido ultimately becomes alienated from language as she grows alienated from her own plot. Once Aeneas is finally fixed on leaving Dido behind in Carthage, he explains his plan to Dido and she responds in a direct transcription of Virgil's Latin:

> By this right hand, and by our spousal rites,
> [Dido] Desires Aeneas to remain with her:
> *Si bene quid de te merui, fuit aut tibi quidquam*
> *Dulce meum, Miserere domus labentis: istam*
> *Oro, si quis adhuc precibus locus, exue mentem.* (5.1.134–9)

["If ever I have deserved well from you and if anything relating to me has ever pleased you, take pity on a falling house, and, I pray you – if there is still place for prayers – abandon this present plan"; Oliver's translation.]

This Virgilian interpolation ultimately, ironically, operates to un-Virgilian ends, pointing out Dido's imbrication in the epic machinery of the *Aeneid* rather than allowing her the integrity of tragic action. To speak a foreign tongue in this instance is to indicate the counter-tragic character of Dido's speech, to mark the various ways in which she has ceased to be herself, and the various ways that her plot has ceased to traverse an arc powered by her character. So far are her words from her own desire that she can only desire in words from elsewhere, words that – like history in *Dido* – seem to repeat earlier catastrophes.

Characteristically uncharacteristic, Dido's death at the end of the play fails as tragedy in either early modern or classical forms. Virgil's poem accepts the fundamental convention of Attic drama where catastrophe reveals the character of the character who suffers. The catastrophe of Attic tragedy is, in this sense, necessarily yoked to *anagnorisis*, where suffering serves as a device of self-revelation, or a tool for exposing the self to the self. Highlighting that this feature is absent from Marlowe's *Dido*, Adriana Cavarero explains the relation between *anagnorisis*, character, and catastrophe in her reading of *Oedipus Tyrannus*:

> [b]y being ignorant of the factual truth of his birth, [Oedipus] has been able to believe himself to be another; but he was never able to become another. He became exactly who he was and is – in the very times that his uniqueness lived through, perhaps under a false genealogy, but not under a false *daimon*. (11–12)

Oedipus becomes "exactly who he was and is," just as Virgil's Dido arrives at the catastrophe to which she was "already given over." But in Marlowe's play, Dido's catastrophe refuses to be revelatory, demonstrating instead only that she no longer has her own language and that epic has interceded in the temporality of biography. Planning her death by suicide, Dido's knotty relation to herself becomes clear in the curious nature of her suicidal formulations: "I must be the murderer of myself" (5.1.270); only through death, she declares, can she "rid me of these thoughts of lunacy" (5.1.273), a formulation that recognizes her disidentification with her own innermost voice. But even in dying – welcoming a death that eases suffering – her most intimate pain is voiced with someone else's words: "Sic, sic, iuvat ire sub umbras" (5.1.313). The recognition of *anagnorisis* here is a recognition of something within oneself that is foreign to, rather than the absolute truth of, oneself. When catastrophe is no longer linked to character, there is nothing, in fact, to "recognize," no relearning the truth of the self, no finally comprehending one's true genealogy.

The disarticulation of character and catastrophe in *Dido* ultimately engenders the play's notoriously ugly conclusion. When Dido's death is narratively unsatisfying – when it ruptures what is known about character and action – it erupts into Carthage as trauma. And as trauma, its effects are unpredictable and expansive. With a disunity of action, the play seems not to know how to end itself, featuring a surprising flurry of deaths, each of which emerges from impulse or contingency rather than manifesting some sort of inner truth or punitive, providential principle. Iarbas follows Dido for love, and Anna follows Iarbas. The cascade of death here comes to make a parody of the mouth of hell that appears on stage. Bodies that fall from a stage, through a trapdoor, and into fire should be doing so in a morality play, biding the imperatives of divine will and moral order. Here, however, that order vanishes. The stage instead reproduces the sort of scene that Aeneas recounts when first speaking to Dido about Troy, a *Massacre at Carthage* rather than a *Tragedy of Dido*. This messy conclusion ultimately embodies the vision of impersonal, repetitive history that *Dido* instantiates in various ways. Dido is alienated from herself at her death, and in this moment she becomes a second Creusa left behind by Aeneas in a blazing city, just as Aeneas has become a second Sychaeus, or just as Carthage here conspicuously echoes the fall of Troy. Castastrophe; untimely death; flame; disaster; repeat.

The catastrophic suffering that the play stages complicates attempts to treat the play as a farce. Inaugurating this critical tradition in a famous marginal note, Anthony Trollope insisted that Marlowe wrote a "burlesque" (Oliver xix, n.1). The tradition has often fixated on the deflating irony of the final scene: by juxtaposing Dido's death with the deaths of Iarbas and Anna, it seems Marlowe either undermines the scene's *pathos* or demonstrates the clumsiness of a young playwright. In Oliver's reading of the scene, for instance, the "deaths of Anna and Iarbas ... probably unintentionally ... weaken rather than heighten the tragedy" (xxxvi). According to Hendricks, "the scene tends to trivialize the tragic implications of what has befallen Dido. What are we (the audience) supposed to think of this sovereign whose death is framed by the ridiculous?" (170). Thinking along the same lines, Dawson argues that following Dido's suicide

> comes the anti-climactic, almost casual and certainly inconsequential suicide of Iarbas, Aeneas's rival ... to which is added in an almost absurd gesture of mourning lost love, the suicide of Anna, Dido's sister, whose unrequited love for Iarbas has been a glancing subplot throughout. (70)

The aesthetic claims here are apposite: "tragedy" has been "weakened"; the "tragic implications" of Dido's death are "trivialized"; the plot has been disrupted by an "anti-clima[x]" and a "certainly inconsequential suicide." But as the play has been operating throughout as a sustained critique of tragedy and the vision of biographical wholeness that tragedy assumes, the aesthetic claims seem also to miss the mark.[20] The play is not an aesthetic failure or a burlesque where it features an indecorous conclusion; the ending – so horrific and austere with its Latin interpolations from Virgil – is ill-fitting because the play refuses to believe in the cosmological order in which catastrophe could be anything but ill-fitting. The world of epic history that Marlowe stages is stripped of tragic possibility because it operates at a scale broader than the tragic. Instead of tragedy, the world appears contingent at the level of the individual while operating in orderly, if capricious, ways at the scale of nations and empires. Tragic dignity becomes impossible in Marlowe's vision, but its absence provides a conclusion more horrifyingly contingent than the ideas of "burlesque" or "farce" allow.

The play's refusal of tragedy is ultimately, in this sense, a feature of its sustained historical vision, just as the question of tragedy in the early modern context is always a question of history. As Neville suggests, the claims of tragic punishment are often yoked, as in *The Mirror for Magistrates*, to truth claims about history: "The right high and immortal God will never leave such horrible and detestable crimes unpunished, as in this present tragedy, and so forth in the process of the whole history, thou mayst right well perceive" (126). The absurdity of the claim – that detestable crimes are punished through "the whole history" – is outweighed only by its necessity in the didactic scheme of early modern tragedy. If tragic plots teach audiences to do good by showing them what happens when one does ill, then the tragic plot can only be effective by insisting on its truth status. Moralizing plots make claims about the nature of history, its ultimate justice, and its utmost fairness, which is why the *Mirror for Magistrates* was considered both a tragedy and a work of history in the sixteenth century and why it remained popular in the seventeenth century, when it was regularly revised and reissued, adding the tales of even more princes who had fallen by their sins.

Working within this discursive space that bound history and poetry both intellectually and politically, Marlowe's engagement with tragedy is ultimately an engagement with historical forms of knowledge and the political work that they are expected to perform. When Marlowe produces a tragedy that fails to fit the ideal of the tragic plot, he makes claims about the nature of justice and providence that are familiar from his work in *Faustus* and *Tamburlaine*, plays that challenge, ironize, or re-value the fantasies of justice built into the form of moralizing tragedy.[21] When this critique of tragedy appears in an account of Dido, however, Marlowe's critical work is redoubled. Just as Shakespeare would demonstrate the incompatibility of historical forms of emplotment in *Richard II*, Marlowe draws attention to the conflict between forms of emplotment around the question of the *translatio imperii*. At stake in the specific historical account is the foundation of England and the very meaning of such an identity when yoked to the fantasies of historical repetition on which the *translatio imperii* fundamentally relies. While the critical tradition has long acknowledged the place of Marlowe's play in ironic relation to the stories of quasi-imperial, national value that circulated in England, it has yet to recognize that this ironic relation is fundamentally mediated by historical forms of imagining the past. To imagine a history in which "we were Trojans" is to conceive of a history filled with catastrophe, in which individual deaths are doomed to be untimely as lives wind up in the wake of epic historical action.

Chapter Four

Military Catastrophe and Elegiac History in *The Atheist's Tragedy*

Buy, ye who want to learn and many marvels know!
They happened in the siege: he watched, his heart sunk low.
Never has like been heard nor seen nor yet was written!
Where such great numbers choked and grievously were smitten!

—From Philippe Fleming,
Oostende: Vermaerde, gheweldigea (trans. Anna Simoni)

By ignoring the tragic plotting of the Dido story that he found in Virgil and Ovid, Marlowe ultimately explains Dido's death by appeal to history at an epic or imperial scale rather than by appeal to biography: her death seems necessary in Marlowe's play not because of *hamartia* but because of the *translatio imperii*. Considering Marlowe's narrative intervention in the tradition of Dido stories, we need to rethink the genre of tragedy if we hope to believe the title of his play. Marlowe may have written a play called *The Tragedy of Dido, Queen of Carthage*, but Dido's death refuses to be "tragic" in any way that is familiar within the classical or early modern traditions, traditions that make the relationship between death and character their hallmark. Where Kinney, agreeing with Suzuki, argues that "the Marlovian text not only reemphasizes human agency but also allows Dido to lay claim to a transcendent power to order her destiny" (Kinney 264), he misinterprets both Virgil's and Marlowe's versions of the story and misreads the tradition within which Marlowe was working. If Marlowe's play offers a troubling view of historical progress, then it does so by erasing the tragic shape and narrative motivation of the Dido plot that he inherited, a plot that was always of a piece with, but eccentric to, the story of Augustan *fatuum*.

These tensions between broadly historiographical and narrowly biographical strategies of emplotment are treated quite differently in Cyril

Tourneur's *Atheist's Tragedy* (c. 1609).[1] Like Marlowe's play, it wrestles with the relationship between broadly historical and narrowly biographical scales of meaningfulness, but it offers the inverse vision of history's unfolding. If Marlowe deploys stories of imperial progress in order to undermine the logic of tragedy that he inherited, then Tourneur relies on the formal logic of tragedy to complicate the limited historiographical accounts of international politics that were circulating as he wrote, and in particular accounts about the Siege of Ostend. The siege that Tourneur features in his play – briefly but crucially – was a "long carnival of death" in the "cockpit of Europe" that saw the Spanish forces of the Infanta Isabella and her husband, Archduke Albert of Austria, in battle against Anglo-Dutch forces at Ostend (Motley IV.63). Ostend interested English audiences particularly because it was a "cautionary town" in the Low Countries, under English control as collateral for English contributions to the United Provinces' war effort. Notoriously bloody, the three-year-long siege produced close to 100,000 casualties before Ostend finally fell to the Spanish in 1604. I argue here that Tourneur deploys and explicitly thematizes a tragic, biographically sensitive view of the historical world in which English military forces operated, and in doing so he intervenes provocatively in contemporaneous historiographical discussions of the siege.

The Atheist's Tragedy is centrally concerned with *hamartia,* or what I have described as the fantasy of a biographically determined, narratively proper death, defined in moralizing terms. This generically determined preoccupation with the biographical propriety of death is key to understanding the play's engagement with history. As the epigraph to this chapter from Philippe Fleming's *Oostende* suggests, the Siege of Ostend was considered stunning in the early seventeenth century because it featured a sort of combat that was unprecedented in its violence: "great numbers choked and grievously were smitten" during the siege because military innovations related to the use of gunpowder were proving brutally effective in the Low Countries (Fleming in Simoni 108). Fleming's claim that "Never has like been heard nor seen nor yet was written" is correct only because the improved gunpowder technology was transforming the battlefield.[2] Though gunpowder appeared in Europe as early as 1480, the revolution continued to transform battle at a surprising rate as technology and strategy improved. Tourneur seems unconcerned, however, with history and combat at the scale of such "great numbers." Instead, as his genre and his medium demand, he focuses on the singular lives of combatants, as if the story of national history made sense at the granular level of individual human lives.

By staging the Siege of Ostend in his revenge tragedy – a genre concerned with punitive justice at a personal level – Tourneur swims against the tide of contemporaneous English writing on the military operation. A matter of considerable interest in London, the siege was featured in at least five English pamphlets between 1601 and 1605, all of which dealt with the operation through the language of an emergent "military science" that was interested in the impersonal strategies of military combat rather than in the abilities or character of individual fighters. Mostly written by gentlemen observers of the battle, who were in Ostend to learn how to lead armies or battalions, the focus on strategic, military-scientific concerns seems a matter of necessity or habit rather than a self-consciously chosen rhetorical gesture, though it fundamentally shaped the discursive climate in which Tourneur's play was first written and staged. As declared outright in the anonymous *Newes from Ostend* (1601), writers in England who covered the siege focused on the "new deuices and warlike stratagems" that were employed on the field in the Low Countries (B2). The devices of combat used at Ostend were "new" in 1601 because gunpowder technologies were rapidly changing the field of battle as their efficiency increased. As the author of *Newes from Ostend* suggests when describing the technological innovations inspired or made necessary by the siege, both sides were "earnestly busied ... the one, nor the other sparing any cost or labor to annoy their enemy, and to defend themselues, and that thing which to day is not thought upon, is the next day put in practice" (B2). The armies were innovating in an arms race during Ostend: they could think of a stratagem or defensive architecture one day and would put it into practice the next, only to face a novel countermeasure on the other side.

The most extensive and elaborate account of the combat published in England in the early seventeenth century, Edward Grimeston's *True Historie of the Memorable Siege of Ostend* (1604), emphasizes this interest in the technology of war by exclusively discussing the novel "deuises ... for the well assayling & defending of the Towne" (A3). At the outset of his book, the rest of which is translated from a French source, Grimeston specifically explains why he undertook the translation and why *The True Historie* may seem dry: the book's concern with military technology and strategy "frees" its author and translator "from giuing any censure" of a moral kind, enabling instead a rigorous study of weapons and tactics that were new to Ostend. The siege, he insists, was called by "Some not vnproperly ... an *Academie* and an excellent Schoole, for Gouernours, Captains, Souldiers, Ingeneurs, Phisitions, Surgions, Pilots and Mariners" (A3). Certainly Grimeston and the Ostend pamphleteers produced "news-writing" for an interested market at home (Schrickx

315), but they did so with a surprising degree of interest in the armaments used to attack a town, in the fortifications employed to defend a town against cannon shot, and in the history of military innovation. Emerging from this preoccupation, Grimeston's *Historie* focuses on "Ramperes, Bulworkes, Spurres, Counterscarses, Rauelins, Trauerses, Parapets, halfe Mooes, Reduites, or Block houses and such like" (A3v), rather than paying attention to the religious and political contours of the battle. The relative silence in Grimeston's *Historie* and in contemporaneous pamphlets about the political stakes of the siege may speak to King James' tacit censorship of any such discussions, at least in those published after 1603. Largely isolationist in military matters, James' foreign policy would have made any discussion of the moral value of continental intervention seem dangerously provocative.

When gunpowder ultimately transformed siege and trench combat, making it "tedious, dangerous, [and] murderously unhealthy" (M. Howard 36), the early modern stage attempted to make sense of the increasingly traumatic warfare. Dramatists performed this sense-making, counter-traumatic labour in part by turning to the strategic and professionalized language of the military revolution, which writers such as Grimeston were making more widely available to English audiences. As engineers provided armies with increasingly potent weaponry, military strategists and the writers of military manuals began to reconsider martial discipline by appeal to the "massifying practices" characteristic of modern military science or a nascent biopolitics: they came to think of combatants, as Patricia Cahill argues, through the lens of the "era's new discourses of measurement" that organize "bodies in a spatial grid," compare them "on a horizontal axis," and reproduce them "as a socially engineered population" (18). This vision of the relationship between the stage and early modern military traumas echoes Steven Mullaney's description of the Elizabethan theatre as a "critical affective arena in which significant cultural traumas and highly ambivalent events – cultural fault lines – could be directly or indirectly addressed, symbolically enacted, and brought to partial and imaginary resolution" (82). The stage, that is, attempted to bring the eruption of gunpowder terror to some sort of symbolic close.

But the epistemic and technological transformation at the level of military theory and discipline, however, might also be mitigated by a turn to the stage and its familiar practices. If combat depersonalized death, that is, moving it into the realm of chance, chaos, and impersonal menace, the stage might also, as we see in the case of Tourneur's *Atheist's Tragedy*, attempt to provide sense by turning to forms that the impersonality of gunpowder combat seems to supersede. While Cahill may suggest that a modern, biopolitical "turn to social abstraction" may have served a counter-traumatic function when featured in military handbooks or even when invoked rhetorically in plays, it is a turn that could never be adequately or fully made on the stage, which traffics in individuated human bodies and consequently thinks about warfare differently.[3] When theatre companies were usually working with casts smaller than sixteen players, and when individual actors were recognizable to savvy audiences (Lopez, "Imagining the Actor's Body" 189, *passim*), this personalization seems even more pronounced: if combat is staged by individual actors rather than thousands of soldiers, the scale of early modern dramatic practice works against any sense of biopolitical scale.

This conflict of representational scale is clearly treated as a problem in the opening of *Henry V*, a play first performed with a cast of fourteen to sixteen men and boys. As the opening Chorus insists, the theatre stages persons rather than populations, and it replaces the "vasty fields of France" with a dozen or so men whose faces are distinguishable as they battle one another and die (12). The virtuosity of combat on stage – many actors were able or master fencers[4] – further suggests that battle was staged at the level of the individual rather than at the level of massed bodies. Robert Weimann's reading of the opening chorus of *Henry V* can, in this sense, be generalized to early modern theatrical practice, even though Shakespeare seems unique in his explicit thematization of the matter: the chorus to *Henry V*, Weimann argues, "shows how deeply the business of *mise-en-scène* is implicated" in the "gap between imaginary representation and the imperfect site of its staging" (*Author's* 70). Attempts to represent the world on stage are, in Weimann's account of stage practice, always self-consciously non-mimetic, where the *platea* of the performance space exists in tension with the locus of the fictive world.

This formally necessary interest in individuals determined the scale at which the early modern stage understood and represented history. As Weimann, Brian Walsh, and Phyllis Rackin each point out when discussing history plays, a play's "*dramaturgy* inflects its sense of historical knowledge" (Walsh, *Shakespeare* 160, italics in original), meaning that the constraints and demands of the stage inform the sorts of historiographical work that theatrical performance might undertake. In the case of military history, such an insight suggests that the outcome of a given battle remains – theatrically speaking – a matter of individual prowess and corporal talents, even if the broad discourse on warfare was coming to be measured impersonally at the scale of corporate bodies. When Shakespeare's *Richard III* stages Richard's defeat at Bosworth

Field, for instance, the result of the battle is determined on stage not by the size or organization of the forces (Richard reminds the audience that he has three times the forces of his rival [5.3.11]), but by hand-to-hand combat when Richard loses a mute duel with Henry Tudor. Contrary to the historical record that Shakespeare found in Holinshed, More, and others, his Richard dies in silent combat with the future king, and the historical world is subsequently reduced to a story of combat between individuals and the political programs that they synecdochally make present in performance.

To make the same point about the personalization of combat by way of negative example: no character in any early modern play dies on stage as the result of an un-aimed cannonball, even though capricious cannonballs are everywhere in the accounts of combat provided by authors such as Grimeston and the Ostend pamphleteers. Non-dramatic writers on the Siege of Ostend, for instance, would often describe as shocking the volume of cannon shot and its haphazard violence, as when Grimeston describes a particularly violent battle on 17 August 1601, during which the Spanish "discharged 35000. cannon shot," so much shot that the bulwark around Ostend "seemed to be a wall of Yron, and they might heare the Bullets strike one against another" (B4).[5] Recognizing the danger that this gunpowder violence posed, the *True Historie of the Memorable Siege* often describes unpredictable deaths made more shocking by the document's refusal (as a chronicle) to provide narrative context or details, as in the entry on 26 August 1601 that describes "four corporals marching with a woman which had a childe in her armes, [who] were all slaine with one shot" (C1v). As he later explains, "[t]hese be the ordinarie accidents in warre" (D1v). Such "ordinarie accidents" never appear on the early modern stage.

Just as the early modern stage seems formally unable to represent combat at the scale of populations or battalions, the demands of genre also locate historical explanation at the level of the individual, as performed at the scale of the early modern stage, with distinctive narrative forms and internal logics inherited from properly theatrical and literary traditions. Here, I pay attention to the generic conventionality of Tourneur's play in order to suggest that if playwrights might look forward to modern rationalities and modern military science when considering the catastrophe of warfare during the age of gunpowder, they might also work in the mode of retrospection: military catastrophe is made comprehensible in *The Atheist's Tragedy* not by appeal to emergent, extra-dramatic language, but through the play's old-fashioned, moralistic structure. In this sense, Tourneur's revenge tragedy – as revenge tragedy – owes more to the residual morality tradition and its offshoots than to an emergent "modern rationality," and its vision of historical unfolding consequently speaks to this generic focus on individuals, consistent with early modern stage practice. Though bodies during the siege piled up so rapidly that they were used as fill when new bulwarks were built (Simoni 141 n.11), and though cannons inspired capricious fatalities at an alarming rate, Tourneur wrestles with Ostend, while also following the logic of tragedy and insisting on biography as a viable chronotope. In abiding the contours of tragedy, Tourneur's play thus stages a world in which casualties at Ostend might look like deaths in morality inflected tragedies such as *Respublica* (1553)[6] or in saint plays and the *de casibus* tradition that many critics identify as Tourneur's influences.[7] This formal inheritance ultimately militates against the vision of history that makes Marlowe's *Dido* seem so bleak. In Marlowe's play, an audience faces the horrors of historical impersonality *as* horrors only because Marlowe's stage traffics in bodies with recognizable faces while insisting on the impersonality of history; in Tourneur's play, however, the face of history remains fully human.

By relying on the revenge tragedy to make sense of the deaths at Ostend, Tourneur in effect ennobles and validates war on the continent against the Spanish. In doing so, his play demonstrates early modern drama's properly historiographical work, as well as the political valences of such work. England's role in the war against Spain was a particularly volatile issue around 1610, and it was an issue about which Tourneur had strong opinions. Allied with a faction associated with Prince Henry that hoped for an English return to the "cockpit" after the end of James I's "pacific reign," Tourneur insists on the providential virtue of English bellicosity on the continent. Using properly dramatic forms to mediate history is, in this sense, both a political and historiographical intervention: it makes claims about the unfolding of history in order to speak about English involvement on the continent against the Spanish. The battlefield on the continent is a matter of heroic virtue for Tourneur rather than one of broadly political manoeuvring or strategic capacity, and such a vision is demonstrated by the dramatic form in which Tourneur stages war. In this sense, Tourneur's historical engagement may not appear as rigorous, clearly theorized or developed as contemporaneous antiquarian histories, yet his rendering of the historical world certainly participates in early modern historical culture, or what Woolf identifies as the "perceptual and cognitive matrix" through which the present, the past, and their relationship is best understood in something like a historical *mentalité,* or, as Woolf further explains, the "habits of thought, languages, and media of communication, and patterns of social convention that embrace elite and popular narrative and nonnarrative modes of discourse" ("Little Crosby" 94).

Despite the capacious vision of historical culture that Woolf outlines, his argument has been taken up conservatively by scholars of early modern drama who work to find "proper" historiography at work in the theatrical archive. Such scholars track the ways that drama, in its performative necessities or generic formulae for emplotment, participates in its historical culture as a form of humanist historiography.[8] To some extent, *Untimely Deaths* repeats this conservative appropriation of Woolf's arguments when it reads *A Chaste Maid in Cheapside* through the logic of antiquarian civic history or when it describes the humanistic habits at work in *Richard II* or sees histories of imperial "world progress" at the centre of *Dido*. Tourneur's play, however, absolutely refuses to appropriate extra-dramatic methods when addressing history. Instead, it explains history through the forms that it inherits from dramatic sources. If the so-called modernization of historical thought at the end of the sixteenth century is marked by the institutionalization of history as a discipline and its concomitant distinction from literature and drama, Tourneur's play operates in the field of "historical culture" in the term's most capacious sense, paying little heed to contemporaneous historiographical writing that treats the same topic. If we want to understand the Siege of Ostend, Tourneur's play insists, then we need to do so through the moral universe and conventions of revenge tragedy, rather than through the work of humanist historiographers or the technological preoccupations of antiquarianism and military science. In its self-conscious thematization of its form, Tourneur's play ultimately compels us to read Woolf's description of the social circulation of the past more straightforwardly than scholars interested in theatre history usually read it. The play draws attention to the historiographical work that dramatic forms – *as aesthetic narrative forms treating the past* – undertake.

In its engagement with historiography, politics, and the moral shape of biography, *The Atheist's Tragedy* as drama is thus part of a larger intellectual, historical, and political project. As I argue in the conclusion to this chapter, the play's intermixture of ideological, political, aesthetic, and moral concerns is at the centre of Tourneur's oeuvre and it speaks to the distinctly elegiac character of his creative and political imagination. Apart from *The Atheist's Tragedy*, all of Tourneur's extant works are elegies that combine the politics of bellicose Protestantism with a fantasy of life's morally measured narrative fullness in order to make polemical points about virtue, vice, and foreign policy. Perhaps unsurprising, the one-time soldier in the Low Countries maps politics most clearly and carefully onto moralized biography in an elegy for Sir Francis Vere, the commander with whom Tourneur likely served in the 1596 Cádiz attack and who designed the military strategy at Ostend described at length in *The Atheist's Tragedy*.

Why Ostend?

The Atheist's Tragedy engages most explicitly and extensively with Ostend in its longest speech, which needs to be quoted at length to give it due consideration. In this protracted set piece, Borachio, the villainous D'Amville's lackey, appears on stage disguised as a soldier returned from Ostend. He arrives at court during a wedding feast and lies at D'Amville's behest, claiming that the play's hero, Charlemont, has died. Interrupting the wedding between Rousard and Castabella, and pretending for nefarious reasons that Charlemont is among Ostend's many dead, Borachio describes the scene of carnage. D'Amville, who will benefit from the lie, and Montferrers, Charlemont's bereft father, interject. Borachio begins:

> The enemy, defeated of a fair
> Advantage by a flattering stratagem,
> Plants all th'artillery against the town,
> Whose thunder and lightning made our bulwarks shake,
> And threatened in that terrible report
> The storm wherewith they meant to second it.
> Th'assault was general, but for the place
> That promised most advantage to be forced,
> The pride of all their army was drawn forth
> And equally divided into front
> And rear. They marched, and coming to a stand,
> Ready to pass our channel at an ebb,
> W'advised it for our safest course to draw
> Our sluices up and make't unpassable.
> Our governor opposed and suffered 'em
> To charge us home e'en to the rampier's foot,
> But when their front was forcing up our breach
> At push o'pike, then did his policy
> Let go the sluices and tripped up the heels
> Of the whole body of their troop that stood
> Within the violent current of the stream.
> Their front, beleaguered 'twixt the water and
> The town, seeing the flood was grown too deep

To promise them a safe retreat, exposed
The force of all their spirits, like the last
Expiring gasp of a strong-hearted man,
Upon the hazard of one charge, but were
Oppressed and fell. The rest that could not swim
Were only drowned, but those that thought to 'scape
By swimming were by murderers that flanked
The level of the flood both drowned and slain.
D'AMVILLE:
Now by my soul, soldier, a brave service.
MONTFERRERS:
O what became of my dear Charlemont?
BORACHIO:
Walking next day upon the fatal shore,
Among the slaughtered bodies of their men
Which the full-stomached sea had cast upon
The sands, it was m'unhappy chance to light
Upon a face, whose favour when it lived
My astonished mind informed me I had seen.
He lay in's armour as if that had been
His coffin, and the weeping sea, like on
Whose milder temper doth lament the death
Of him whom in his rage he slew, runs up
The shore, embraces him, kisses his cheek,
Goes back again, and forces up the sands
To bury him, and every time it parts
Sheds tears upon him, till at last, as if
It could no longer endure to see the man
Whom it had slain, yet loath to leave him,
With a kind of unresolved unwilling pace,
Winding her waves one in another, like
A man that folds his arms or wrings his hands
For grief, ebbed from the body and descends
As if it would sink down into the earth
And hid itself for shame of such a deed. (2.1.39–93)

Borachio's speech is remarkable for a number of reasons, not the least of which is its length. Often mannered and presentational, *The Atheist's Tragedy* features a number of long speeches, but a single speech of fifty-two lines – interrupted only once by brief interjections – is exceptional. Where Borachio needs for the sake of the plot to deliver a short, dishonest message – "Charlemont died in battle" – he delivers instead a mournful encomium on the themes of Ostend, mourning, mass death, and the horrors of war. Also remarkable here is the elegance of Borachio's speech, contradicting the general critical sentiment that *The Atheist's Tragedy* "is not a vehicle for the passionate display of poetry and the assembled arts of language" (Morris and Gill x). When Borachio transforms armour into a coffin and imagines the ocean's personified waves washing anxiously over the corpse, the verse is measured, and its imagery is both coherently sustained and efficient.

Beyond simply its size and style, Borachio's speech is remarkable for its accuracy: it uses the language of a soldier to describe a real scene from the siege that took place in 1602. Drawing heavily from the vocabulary of military science without sounding foreign to the biographically minded logic of tragedy, Borachio refers to "stratagems," "bulwarks," and "advantage" on the field; he describes the Spanish army "coming to a stand" as they "charge"; and he points out the defensive "rampiers" that have been "breached" only to be defended by the "push o' pike." He demonstrates significant knowledge of the battle and its setting when he describes the sluiceways around Ostend being used as defensive weapons. Drawing his account from Philippe Fleming's contemporary diary, John Motley describes the flood that, according to Borachio, has taken Charlemont's life – a flood that Fleming himself designed to drown Spanish soldiers:[9]

> It was obvious, [Fleming] observed, that the fury of the [Spanish] attack was over, and that the enemy would soon be effecting a retreat before the water [in the sluice] should have risen too high. He even pointed out many stragglers attempting to escape through the already deepening shallows. Vere's consent was at once given the flood-gate was opened, and the assailants – such as still survived – panic-struck in a moment, rushed wildly back through the old harbour towards their camp. It was too late. The waters were out, and the contending currents whirled the fugitives up and down through the submerged land, and beyond the broken dyke. (4.85)

From this detailed report of the town's geography, a military strategy, and a specific tactical push, Borachio's speech further recalls the pikemen looming over the sluiceway to kill those Spanish soldiers who were able to swim, and it describes the mass of bodies dumped in the sea. As a possible sign of Tourneur's intimate knowledge of the battle, this detail of waterlogged corpses washing up on shore is absent in any extant contemporaneous accounts, even though it seems plausible considering the town's geography and the battle's unfolding.[10]

The accurate description of battle also invokes a topic that had been, in 1601 and 1602, politically volatile where it alludes to Sir Francis Vere's "flatt'ring stratagem," an often discussed, ethically dubious "false parley," which led to Vere's recall from the Low Countries (Schrickx 321). When describing it as "flattering," Borachio touches lightly on a strategy that was widely considered scandalous. Vere – a hero to Tourneur (Schrickx 322) – was waiting for reinforcements to buttress the town's beleaguered defences on 21 December 1601. He then decided to call a parley, "cunningly feeding [the Spanish] with Hopes of a Surrender" (Camden, *Britannia* 633); in fact before calling the parley, Vere was "not doubting but to draw it so out in length, vntill the succors which he expected were arriued" (Grimeston M4v). After calling the parley, Vere proceeded to march the Spanish ambassadors around the flooded town in muck up to their knees to exhaust them before any conference could take place (Motley 75); on the next day, "[m]uch time was ingeniously consumed in ... utterly superfluous discussion," and then Vere plied them with a heroic amount of alcohol. As recounted in one pamphlet, the Spanish ambassador to Ostend drank "for his share about fiftie twoo glasses of wine, besides Beere, answering euery man in the cuppe" (Anon., *Extremities* B2). In such a milieu, they would have been unable to discuss the implied surrender or renegotiation of terms that a parley implied. On the third day, once Dutch reinforcements had arrived at Ostend, Vere sent the ambassadors back to the Spanish camp without a truce or a meaningful discussion of surrender.

While the accuracy of Borachio's monologue is striking, its internal narrative arc speaks most strongly to the play's interest in biography and history. Borachio opens with a vision of armies as they operated through the logic of a corporal and corporeal whole: "the whole body of" the Spanish army exhausts itself in the sluiceways around Ostend before falling collectively dead with "like the last / Expiring gasp of a strong-hearted man." On the Anglo-Dutch side, a similar sense of shared trauma collectivizes the horror of combat through a meteorological trope that figures the Spanish attack on Ostend as a "storm" in which the "thunder and lightning" of cannon shot make "bulwarks shake." But the massive corpse of the Spanish army and the shared experience of the military disaster resolve, in Borachio's account of this battle, on a single face. The speech traverses a scalar arc, from armies and towns through to the the protagonist of Tourneur's play. After recounting an army personified as a single soldier and an embattled town, Charlemont's face comes to the fore in a gesture conspicuous for its human specificity in a field of carnage. His singular face sticks out in this scene of mass disaster as one that the sea knows should be living rather than dead. While the criminal Borachio is lying here, he speaks to the truth of the play's historical vision when he marks the sense of individual tragedy that even the sea – an icon of impersonal sublimity in the period[11] – might recognize.

Because the speech is so dramatically compelling and dramaturgically disruptive, its general omission from the critical literature on Tourneur's tragedy suggests that the scholarly tradition has ignored one of the play's more sophisticated cultural interventions. The critical focus instead has been on "renaissance naturalism" (Ornstein, "Renaissance Naturalism"), atheism (Ornstein, *Moral Vision*), the punitive work of providence (Ribner), and the theology of commemoration (Rist). In their edition of the play, Brian Morris and Roma Gill go so far as to insist that readers should *avoid* paying attention to the siege and its place in the play, imagining the drama's reference to Ostend as a throwaway:

> [Grimeston's] *True Historie of the Memorable Siege of Ostend* was published in 1604, and Francis Vere's memoirs, although not printed as *The Commentaries of Sir Francis Vere* until 1657, would have been accessible in manuscript had the dramatist made use of them. But the siege itself, except as a means of removing Charlemont temporarily from the scene, is of no major importance, and there are no signs of verbal borrowing form either of these sources. (x)

The claim here is curious and perverse, suggesting that Tourneur's engagement with Ostend is unimportant because too original. If, however, the play is interested in the martial valour of its hero, Charlemont, then the extensive novelty of the passage suggests that we take its attention to Ostend seriously. Why not focus on a battle involving French and English forces in the Low Countries, such as the equally well known but far more successful Battle of Nieuwpoort? If the play is interested in providential retribution and in the wages of sin, then why not think of the "great numbers choked and grievously ... smitten" at Ostend?

By so conspicuously negotiating the matter of England's engagement in the Low Countries, the play necessarily becomes history writing. Thomas Rist is right to point out that Borachio's speech recalls early modern confusions about the theological value of proper burial (109–10), but Borachio also raises here a question about biographical fulfilment, and it does so in terms of mass military casualties to which early modern audiences would have been attuned. As Nick de Somogyi argues, the five extant pamphlets treating the siege suggest that it "increasingly commanded the attention of London's populus [sic]" (32), and Andrew Gurr more generally points out that similarly topical drama about warfare dominated the theatres in the last decade of the sixteenth century (136). Warfare was a popular topic on the early modern stage because audiences were interested in the nation's engagements in Ireland and on the continent. They were aware in the early seventeenth century that potential fronts could reappear on the continent if political sentiment turned, and the Spanish threat loomed large in the popular imagination even if the first decade of James' reign was marked by relative calm in Anglo-Spanish relations.[12] A variety of contemporary plays suggest that the Siege of Ostend was meaningful as a cultural touchstone in the first decade of the seventeenth century because they refer to it offhandedly. In *The Return From Parnassus* (1606), Ostend is figured as a proverbial site of great danger, and *Westward Ho!* (1604) invokes the combat as a figure for stubborn resistance: "How long will you hold out, think you?" asks Birdlime, a bawd, of Mistress Justiniano as he tries to push her into erotic service "Not so long as Ostend" (1.1.96–7). Dekker and Middleton's *Honest Whore* also invokes the military operation as the icon of impossible labour when Hippolito asks his servant to deliver "the constancy of a woman" and his servant insists that a constant woman is "harder to come by than ever was Ostend" (4.1.29, 30). The siege might be treated casually and proverbially in these plays only because it was so profoundly evocative when treated elsewhere in a more serious tone, and it might be referred to widely because discussion of England's wars was a considerable part of London's nascent public sphere.

In this climate, the topical potency of a siege story would also have resonated in the court of James and in the court-within-the-court of Prince Henry as it grew quickly after his instalment as Prince of Wales in 1610. Distinctions between these courts are often made in hyperbolically stark terms, but they point to real tensions surrounding England's position in the religio-political world of continental Europe. To put these distinctions schematically and in a way that elides overlap in personnel and belief, the court of James was characterized by a loosely cosmopolitan acceptance of crypto-Catholicism, a taste for grandeur, and a reluctance to participate in continental wars; Henry's reactionary quasi-court was characterized by a "[f]iercely Protestant ... muscular Christianity" embodied in a prince who was the "epitome of militant Protestant chivalry" (Strong 13, 14). Frances Yates recognizes the distinction between these courts in terms of opposing attitudes to pacifism, a category which seems particularly useful when considering *The Atheist's Tragedy*'s concern with the bloody siege that ended within months of James' coronation:

> Jacobean peace – and James forever emphasized himself as a peacebringer and peacemaker – was an avoidance of conflict. It carried with it no mission of universal reform or support of European Protestantism ... Prince Henry

> wanted to end "jars in religion" by breaking the intolerant Hapsburg powers by military intervention. This would be a different attitude from James' policy of peace through appeasement. (10)

On the one hand, then, is the king's determinedly pacifist court, centred at Whitehall, which insists on English isolationism because of the economic cost of war and a loose religious sympathy with the plausibly Catholic (in 1608) Queen Anne. On the other hand, is Prince Henry's bellicose Protestant court, 500 feet away, centred at the palace of St James, which hoped for a return to Elizabethan policies vis-à-vis Spain, while dreaming of an English military presence on the continent to support the United Provinces against the Spanish. Yates' identification of a "different attitude" understates the enormous stakes of the divergence, stakes that expanded the semantic and political range of any reference to Ostend and continental engagement.

While the instalment of Henry as Prince of Wales in 1610 makes such a political distinction palpable, his court tapped an ambient taste for Anglo-Protestant interventionism that existed before he was granted his arms and title, even during the early years of James' "pacific reign." Men eager to join Henry's court and support its ideals were ready to hand at the time of his instalment, even if they had previously been excluded from James' inner circle. Such men included Sir Arthur Gorges, whose mother was Sir Walter Raleigh's cousin. After Raleigh's imprisonment for alleged participation in a plot against James, Gorges was suspected and then cleared, but the taint of suspicion around him lingered; this left him without meaningful position at court until he became a close ally of Henry. Even men who held some favour in James' court, such as John Harington, 2nd Baron Harington of Exton, were powerfully attracted to Henry's militant Protestantism. Harington's father had been guardian of James' daughter Elizabeth, but his keen interest in the continent led him to Henry's court, where he became close friends with the prince. When Tourneur wrote his play in the year or two prior to Henry's instalment, an allusion to Ostend would have spoken to the sentiments that drew men like Gorges and Harington quickly to Henry and his belligerent, if pious, dreams of Protestant hegemony on the continent.

If this was the political world in which *The Atheist's Tragedy* was first performed, then Tourneur's engagement with the siege is as provocative as it is curious: he engages with contemporaneous political matter by rewriting history in a revenge tragedy that deals more obviously with questions of atheism, Renaissance naturalism, moral degeneracy, and divine retribution. Tourneur appears only obliquely to touch on a volatile set of issues when the noble Charlemont leaves the comfort of his home to volunteer in Ostend, when Borachio delivers his speech, and when the ghost of Montferrers appears to Charlemont on the walls of the besieged Dutch town. But such an oblique approach tactically worked within and capitalized on the play's genre. While Tourneur might invoke the siege because it was topical, to negotiate the play's politico-historiographical intervention in this cultural environment required attention to its generic narrative logic. Participating in the tradition of revenge tragedy, specifically that strain of revenge tragedy which owes a considerable debt to morality plays, furthermore required that dramatic references to the military operation of Ostend run counter to the siege's representation elsewhere in the period. Tourneur supplants the military-scientific concerns of the pamphlets and he refuses to think of the siege as a straightforwardly political, topical, or military matter; instead, the siege and the bodies that pile up during the siege come to fit within the tacitly valorizing meanings that revenge drama is able to offer.

Mourning and the Narrative Satisfactions of Revenge

Though I argue here that *The Atheist's Tragedy* transforms history through the logic of revenge tragedy, the play is a strange example of the genre. As Lily Campbell first pointed out in 1931, to the agreement of all subsequent critics, Tourneur's play is a curious revenge tragedy in that it refuses to recognize the pleasure of revenge (286): it invokes the genre's tropes inherited from Seneca, including paternal ghosts, hyperbolically evil crimes, and long disquisitions on retribution, but it seems fundamentally averse to the affective and narrative satisfactions of personal revenge from which revenge tragedies produce theatrical pleasures.[13] Where the genre is generally assumed to take its early modern form with the ur-*Hamlet* and its paternal ghost's cry, "Hamlet, revenge," *The Atheist's Tragedy* features a paternal ghost in Montferrers who insists that his son Charlemont "leave revenge unto the King of kings" (2.6.23). Montferrers' demand implies a promise on which the play makes good: a providential order determines – according to the logic of retributive justice – the end of criminal lives, and "the King of kings" underwrites this promise. This fantasy of equalizing justice is rendered explicit in one of Charlemont's final lines, where he insists that "*Patience is the honest man's revenge*" (5.2.276), a line italicized in the play's quarto publication to suggest its status as a reliable apothegm.[14] Patience is the honest man's revenge because, in the world that the play stages, deaths are either criminal or punitive; if they are the result of a crime, then they become traumatically disruptive, and God subsequently takes action to remedy the injustice. This providential interest in the shape of human lives is central to the play's thematic concerns, and they inform its vision of history and Ostend.

Revenge tragedies all engage, whether in the mode of affirmation or scepticism, with this interest in the temporal propriety of death, and they usually do so through the same, equalizing, tit-for-tat model of justice. But *The Atheist's Tragedy* is unique in its preoccupation with the matter. The general interest in the temporal propriety of deaths is obvious in plays such as Middleton's *Revenger's Tragedy*, Kyd's *Spanish Tragedy*, Chapman's *Revenge of Bussy D'Ambois*, and Shakespeare's *Hamlet*, all of which feature elaborate dialogues or set speeches on the divine ordination of individual criminal deaths. Tourneur's play seems singular, however, because it deals with the timeliness of death whenever it stages a fatality. While, as Michael Higgins suggests, such a vision of fatal propriety may seem to speak to Calvinistic ideas of predestination (255), Rist demonstrates that the play is theologically confused, either unable or unwilling to situate itself vis-à-vis contemporary doctrine. Because it is ambiguous in regard to theology, its preoccupation with fatal ends ultimately makes more sense when read in terms of genre than in terms of contemporaneous and arcane doctrinal debates about special providence.

The play's extensive thematic engagement with revenge and a broadly conceived providence begins in its opening dialogue between D'Amville and Borachio. The Socratic set piece opening the play points up the fantasies of biographical propriety and wholeness, leading to the sort of death that works as punishment. After sending a servant to find his nephew, Charlemont, D'Amville asks:

> Borachio, thou art read
> In Nature and her large philosophy.
> Observ'st thou not the very self same course
> Of revolution both in man and beast? (1.1.3–6)

The obtuse formulation here – the question of "revolution" in both "man and beast" – is heard correctly by Borachio as a question of human lives and their apparent biographical homology with the lives of "beasts": "The same," he responds,

> For birth, growth, state, decay and death
> Only a man's beholding to his Nature
> For the better composition o' the two. (7–9)

The distinction between humans and animals, ambiguously predicated on the "better composition" of human nature, grows subsequently muddy where D'Amville insists that a human might be "as little-knowing as a beast" and Borachio agrees: "there's nothing in man above" the nature that humankind shares with animals, for "if there were" the human being's "excellency, 'twould not yield / To Nature's weakness" (12, 13, 14–15).

The opening scene, then, begins with a story about the plot of human biography. But if, as most critics insist, *The Atheist's Tragedy* is about Renaissance naturalism and the dangerous atheism implied by natural philosophy, then why start with *this* set piece on the "revolution" of "man and beast," an opening that Morris and Gill identify as "undramatic and anti-theatrical" (xi)? These editors suggest that the speech is theatrically surprising because it seems relatively distant from the concerns of the play's staged action; to remedy what they recognize as an aesthetic problem posed by the play's introductory gambit, they struggle to find comparable, similarly styled openings, including the first scenes of *Henry V*, *Faustus*, and *Bussy D'Ambois*, before finally concluding that the "enunciation of a theme" is "a dramatic event" in and of itself (xi). The observation seems generally correct, but the theme that they find enunciated in the dialogue between D'Amville and Borachio is problematically broad and general: they say that it "lays out the basic tenets of [the] philosophical position" called atheism (xi). Their reading of the opening speech falters as they fail to recognize that the "philosophical position" D'Amville articulates is more specific than a generic declaration of faithlessness. An atheist could discuss any number of more obviously sensational issues to mark his atheism: he could wrestle blasphemously with the Bible as the perversely faithful Faustus does, or he could speak shockingly about morality as the characters in *Antonio's Revenge* do. But D'Amville dwells at length on the brute biology of human lifespans, finding at the level of the species a truth about the trajectory of human lives. Despite the narrative awkwardness of this opening gambit, which tells us little about what the plot will offer, its philosophical matter ramifies throughout the play. Specifically, the opening dialogue becomes the philosophical occasion for the play's action. While D'Amville refuses to recognize the extra-biological meaningfulness of death, the play proceeds to stage deaths that militate against his philosophical position, as do the final speeches of the characters who die.

D'Amville may begin the play by insisting on the biological foundations of the human lifespan, but the play repeatedly insists that he misreads the world. Its resistance to D'Amville's vision of human life is obvious in the conspicuous gestures of "narrative overdetermination"[15] that accompany the deaths of many of its characters. In *The Atheist's Tragedy*, characters who die deliver set speeches that gloss their catastrophes and identify their deaths as the anchor that provides fundamental truths about their lives. In these formal declarations, death ultimately provides the archê to the archive that the characters plumb when writing their own elegies as they collapse in heaps, and their deaths offer them information about the meaningfulness of their biographies. In these moments of autobiographical exegesis, characters make available biographies that read death through antecedent actions, predilections, and failures that are profoundly moralized. If to philosophize is to learn how to die, because philosophy helps us live lives outside the shadow of relatively capricious or meaningless deaths – "let death take me planting my cabbages" – Tourneur inverts this sense, insisting in *The Atheist's Tragedy* that to die is to learn how to philosophize. To learn how to think about one's life is possible only by appeal to the death that one dies, a death that spells out the truth of the preceding life in moralizing ways.

This fantasy that death offers the truth of a life is clear in Tourneur's play when Levidulcia insists that her death transforms her into a moral *exemplum*. Immediately prior to her suicide, she invokes the distinctions that D'Amville erases when he considers human lives, and she does so by unpacking her suicide for the play's audience and for an undefined future audience that she imagines as interpreters of her death. The adulterous Levidulcia delivers her final lines over the bodies of her husband Belforest and her lover Sebastian. In a theatrically efficient scene, Belforest has just told Sebastian to stand aside as he pursues the fleeing Levidulcia, threatening to "make passage through [Sebastian's] blood"; glibly, Sebastian insists that his blood would be "slippery" and that "'Twere better you would take another way. / You may hap fall else" (4.5.55–8). They fight; both are fatally wounded; Levidulcia returns to face their corpses and deliver a set speech:

> O God! My husband! My Sebastian! Husband!
> Neither can speak; yet both report my shame.
> Is this the saving of my honour, when
> Their blood runs out in rivers, and my lust
> The fountain whence it flows? Dear husband, let
> Not thy departed spirit be displeased
> If with adulterate lips I kiss thy cheek.
> Here I behold the hatefulness of lust,
> Which brings me kneeling to embrace him dead,
> Whose body living I did loathe to touch.
> ………………………………………………………………
> Shall I outlive my honour? Must my life
> Be made the world's example? Since it must,
> Then thus in detestation of my deed,

To make th'example more forcibly
To virtue, thus I seal it with a death
As full of horror as my life of sin. [*Stabs herself*] (4.5.60–9, 80–5)

Ignoring the theatrical possibility of a duel between a cuckold and his wife's lover, Tourneur dwells instead on Levidulcia's explanation of her consequent suicide. Levidulcia's unquestioned sense that her death is matter for the "world's example" and edification is both striking and typical in the play, which often treats its dying characters as types of which they are examples. Here, to kill oneself is rhetorical, making "th'example more forcibly." Clarifying the logic of the scene, she asks a crucial question at a turn in the speech, wondering whether she "must" die for her sins: "Must my life / Be made the world's example?" To this knotty question, Levidulcia answers succinctly, yes, "it must." "Since it must" be an example for the world, Levidulcia kills herself. She kills herself for shame, as she has outlived her honour, but she does so in a gesture of didactic generosity. The site of her death ultimately produces a truth about life for two sets of observers – Tourneur's audience and a future "world" – and it does so by noting a relationship between catastrophe and the life that precedes it.

When the play suggests that the moment of death provides narrative coherence to a life, it proposes that divining a death's aetiology is crucial in broadly existential terms at the level of character, and in narrative or theatrical terms as an explication of a plot's motive forces. This presumption and description of such fatal determinations is clear in the case of Levidulcia's death, and it also characterizes the maudlin catastrophe of D'Amville's sons, Rousard and Sebastian. Peter Murray points out what he considers a dramatic flaw in the play when he argues that the "accidental" deaths of Rousard and Sebastian cause "the frail structure of the drama to collapse" (139): the sons die, but their deaths seem too haphazard, he claims, to fit within the providentially ordered world that the play struggles to render. This observation is troubled, however, because it seems rooted in an aesthetic disdain for the play's persistent bloodiness and because it fails to pay serious attention to the play's conspicuous habit of narrative overdetermination: the deaths are dramatically clumsy, perhaps, if one hopes to find a neoclassically decorous five-act play, but they fit felicitously within the drama's preoccupation with the narrative and moral satisfactions of death.

This absorption with morality and death is paradoxically clearest in the apparent contingency of Sebastian's death. Sudden and theatrically underexplored – the duel between Sebastian and Belforest begins and ends with little fanfare – Sebastian's death nevertheless remains potently emblematic: Sebastian is licentious, he dies during a duel over Levidulcia and – as if now serving as a corporeal sign of lust – his corpse lies beside Levidulcia as she delivers a speech about the wages of erotic sin. Sebastian dies "properly" (if not theatrically well), according to Levidulcia's sense of fatal propriety, because his death, at Levidulcia's foot and Belforest's hand, "makes the example forcibly." Any flaw here is "merely" aesthetic rather than narratively disruptive. The play's structure, surprisingly consistent rather than "frail," remains intact, despite the curious brevity of Sebastian's death scene.

Rousard's death similarly abides the play's rules of death and life, even if it does so in a curious way. More than simply supporting this internally defined and generically familiar set of rules, Rousard responds proleptically to Murray's criticism of the play as he struggles to make sense of his death and to diagnose its moral cause. After marrying Castabella against her will, Rousard declares on his deathbed that his non-consensual marriage – identified as rape by Sebastian (1.4.128) – inspires his death: "A general weakness did surprise my health / The very day I married Castabella / As if my sickness were a punishment / That did arrest me for some injury / I then committed" (3.4.63–7). The clumsiness of plotting here suggests most clearly the rigour of Tourneur's moral vision. Rousard was ill when first introduced, prior to the moment that he knew he would marry Castabella; but he rewrites his history to make sense of his biography. A stage direction in the first act claims that Rousard enters "sickly" (1.2.190sd), and D'Amville only introduces the forced marriage after this inauspicious entrance: D'Amville then tells him, "Rousard, I send you [as] a suitor to Castabella" (1.2.191). Though ill before his sin, Rousard ultimately echoes the self-diagnoses offered by Levidulcia and subsequently by D'Amville when emphasizing the general point that the play seems eager to make about the moral aetiology of biographical catastrophe. In Tourneur's play, it seems, one can be pre-emptively punished for the sins that one will inevitably commit, meaning that a narrative gaffe ultimately reinforces the play's commitment to biographical consistency rather than undermining it.

Where it "assaults modern sensibilities" with its moralism (Diehl 52), D'Amville's death in the play's final scene in fact ratifies the moral logic of biography that the play has attempted to establish all along. As *The Atheist's Tragedy* concludes, D'Amville raves because his sons have died, and he presents a case before a panel of judges, successfully if dishonestly arguing that Charlemont deserves to die because he has murdered Borachio and that Castabella deserves to die because she has committed adultery with Charlemont. As D'Amville raises the axe to execute the innocent Charlemont and Castabella, he hits himself on the head. The stage direction: "As he raises up the axe [he] strikes out his own brains, [and then] staggers off the scaff[old]" (5.2.241.a–b). Here, the executioner observes: "I think he has knocked / His brains out" (5.2.242–3). After stumbling from the executioner's scaffold, D'Amville delivers – brainless – a speech about justice and about the narrative propriety of his own death and of death generally. In its dramatic implausibility, the scene's theatrics reminds audiences that the play operates in a world between allegory and naturalism: on the stage, judges sit next to the executioner's scaffold and D'Amville – against any historical precedent – is allowed to perform the execution. As its dramaturgy and plot suggest, the play operates according to the representational logic of a loosely allegorical stage practice rather than a realist or proto-realist code. In this mimetic frame, the brained D'Amville is able to castigate the very judges who found Charlemont and Castabella guilty: they "didst want discretion ... but yond' power that struck me knew / The judgement I deserved, and gave it. O, / The lust of death commits a rape upon me" (5.2.264, 265–7). At the moment of his death, D'Amville is able to recognize that "yond' power" has passed proper judgment on a scene that human judges failed to comprehend. He is dying a properly punitive death because a higher force operates actively even when human judges fail to see the truth. By insisting on providence, D'Amville makes his "example" more "forcibly," just as Levidulcia made her example more forcibly, and just as the play insists that a death provides the truth of a human life.

These autobiographical accounts of individual lives correspond in the play with the biographical vision that D'Amville provides when reading the epitaphs on the tombs of Montferrers and Charlemont. Written by D'Amville, the epitaphs are dramatically ironic: when reading at a joint funeral the inscriptions on the tombs of Montferrers and Charlemont, D'Amville knows that what he says about the two characters is a lie. Despite the ironic mire, however, D'Amville's sentiment remains "true" according to the vision of human lives that the play stages, and it reminds audiences that *The Atheist's Tragedy* is primarily interested in the consistency and coherence of a life's trajectory. D'Amville accidentally declares the play's truth in his lie. In this dramatic space characterized by ironies, D'Amville eulogizes the brother he has had murdered when reading an epitaph:

> Here lie the ashes of that earth and fire
> Whose heat and fruit did feed and warm the poor;
> And they, as if they would in sighs expire

And into tears dissolve, his death deplore.
He did that good freely, for goodness' sake,
Unforced, for gen'rousness he held so dear
That he feared none but Him that did make,
And yet he served Him more for love than fear
So's life provided that though he did die
A sudden death, yet died not suddenly. (3.1.15–24)

D'Amville's measure of Montferrers' life is curious because it conflates the moralistic vision of human life that the play puts on stage with the materialistic vision that he offers in the play's opening scene: he invokes the sense of narrative biographical satisfaction while also recalling the rhetoric of "atheistic" biological life by invoking the language of ashes, earth, fire, heat, and fruit in the opening lines. Despite the materialist rhetoric with which it begins, though, the epitaph that he offers to Montferrers closes with a claim for the temporal propriety of Montferrers' death: his sudden death was not sudden because it was morally satisfactory. Even if an audience recognizes that D'Amville is lying here about the circumstances of Montferrers' death (Montferrers was beaten to death by a rock at D'Amville's behest), the vision of biographical life that D'Amville offers is true to the play's cosmology, and it ironically explains the ghost of Montferrers that returns twice in the play. Montferrers dies in a way that refuses to correspond with the sense of proper death; thus his ghost returns as so many ghosts do in early modern revenge tragedies, to find a proper conclusion to lives characterized by what Michael Neill calls "narrative abruption" (*Issues* 216).

D'Amville's epitaph to Charlemont offers a similar vision of the biographically appropriate death, and it does so while speaking to the meaningfulness of deaths that occur in battle. If a death is imagined to be proper in *The Atheist's Tragedy*, when it helps one to understand the truth of the life that led to it – if a proper death is narratively as conclusive – then a death during combat might provide narrative satisfactions. According to the epitaph that D'Amville writes for Charlemont's false tomb, Charlemont's

body lies interred within this mould,
Who died a young man, yet departed old,
And in all strength of youth that man can have
Was ready still to drop into his grave.
For aged in virtue, with a youthful eye
He welcomed it, being still prepared to die;
And living so, though young deprived of breath,

He did not suffer an untimely death,
But we may say of his blest decease:
He died in war, and yet he died in peace. (3.1.25–34)

If the death of Montferrers allows Tourneur to explain the death of virtuous old men according the imperatives of providential rectitude, then his reading of Charlemont's death allows him to justify the deaths of young men in the name of a presumably just cause: they are "properly" aged according to the imperatives of a moralized, military life. The paradoxes in the epitaph remind audiences (ironically) that the materialist vision of D'Amville's opening speech is unable to comprehend the nature of human life that the play offers. The relative youth of Charlemont refuses to bear on the timeliness of his death because it results from a presumably proper cause: "He did not suffer an untimely death," the epitaph reads, because "He died in war, and yet he died in peace." By recognizing that the biographical propriety of a death fails to correspond with biological age, the epitaph to Charlemont reconciles what might seem like providential punishment with the topically potent fact that young men died regularly in battle at Ostend and in other English military engagements. Charlemont was "prepared to die" in virtue rather than in vice, and the play measures preparedness by appeal to the terms that D'Amville offers in his epitaphs rather than according to the conditions he provides in his "naturalist" excursus on biography that opens the play. Even if an audience might identify dramatic irony when D'Amville reads the epitaphs, the epitaphs serve a metatheatrical purpose where they explain the narrative truth of the play; they also serve a historiographical purpose where they fit mass casualties in a distinct narrative frame. Grimeston and his contemporaries might write about military strategy and politics on the continent, but Tourneur inscribes providence and biographical coherence onto the corpses that accumulated rapidly during wartime.

History and Tourneur's Elegiac Imagination

Woolf's vision of early modern historical culture would suggest that the intersection between *The Atheist's Tragedy*'s biographically focused generic concern and the historical matter of Ostend produces meaningful claims about history and about the relationship between the past and the present. Certainly, early modern dramatists were influenced by contemporaneous historiographical practice, but Tourneur's play points towards a meaningful dialogue between these apparently discrete realms, enabling dramatists to comment meaningfully on the historical world by way of the generic habits of the theatre. As historiography was "modernizing" in the late sixteenth and early seventeenth centuries, growing into a discipline distinct from poetry, drama, and the other arts, the ambiguously defined object that Woolf calls historical culture continued to exist as a site of discursive production in which dramatists could deal with historical topics in a way that made their historical claims comparable with those made by historiographical proto-professionals such as the Elizabethan Society of Antiquaries, the writers of popular historical-minded pamphlets, and historians who were finding places at the universities. Audience members who knew about Ostend through the widely disseminated pamphlets and through other plays would also have been in the audience at Tourneur's play, and they would have recognized that it staked a claim in the discussions surrounding English engagement in the Low Countries. To make a more concrete claim: *The Atheist's Tragedy* imagines a sympathetic relationship between biography and history; in doing so, it echoes the work that Tourneur also undertook as a popular elegist for contemporaneous historical figures, work in which he made more obviously historical claims about the world in which he lived.

The imagined relationship between providentially shaped human lives and the history of international warfare suffuses Tourneur's elegies for Prince Henry, Edmund Spenser, Sir Robert Cecil, and Sir Francis Vere. His popularity as an elegist of great men suggests that this fantasy of a moralized, biographically meaningful historical world spoke to widely held beliefs or hopes, well beyond the play that he wrote. By reading these elegies against the play, one can see Tourneur's fantasies of moralized death and revenge in *The Atheist's Tragedy* as more redolent, moving beyond the generic demands of revenge tragedy into something like a worldview. In response to the trauma inspired by mass casualties after the gunpowder revolution, then, Tourneur's fantasies of an intersection between providential biography and military history would be evocative to early modern audiences and readers in the mode of reaction; similarly, this yoking of dramatic logic and historical chaos comes to seem a crucial feature of his oeuvre. In quantitative terms, Tourneur's extant oeuvre suggests that he was first and foremost an elegist. Besides *The Atheist's Tragedy*, only four of Tourneur's works remain, three of them were published, and all of them are elegies: in 1600 he published *The Transformed Metamorphosis*, a bizarre, allegorical elegy to Edmund Spenser; in 1609 he brought forth a *Funerall Poeme on Sir Francis Vere*; and in 1613 he had printed *A Griefe on the Death of Prince Henrie*. Tourneur's elegiac *Character of Robert Cecil* for the Earl of Salisbury began circulating in manuscript in 1612 or 1613, and, as

Pauline Croft claims, it was likely commissioned by Cecil's family in response to a variety of contemporaneous libels that questioned Cecil's spiritual allegiance, his moral strength, and his perceived lechery (59–60).[16] That Cecil's family commissioned Tourneur to write his "Character" suggests that Tourneur had a reputation as an elegist by 1612, or it indicates at least that in 1612 one might plausibly turn to Tourneur to perform with considerable dexterity an encomiastic, biographical summary of a dead nobleman whose reputation was under attack.

Read alongside *The Atheist's Tragedy*, these elegies suggest that Tourneur's reference to the Siege of Ostend was part of a larger political concern. Because Ostend was a Cautionary Town, battles that took place there spoke powerfully to supporters of a particularly bellicose Protestantism; consequently, it would have seemed a compelling subject for a playwright who also wrote elegies for men like Henry, Spenser, and Vere. Besides the commissioned elegy for Cecil, all of Tourneur's elegies are written emphatically for supporters of aggressively militant Anglo-Protestant expansion. Henry, as we have seen, established a staunchly militaristic and pious "court within the court," and in *The Transformed Metamorphosis*, Spenser becomes a valiant warrior against the forces of Catholicism in "Delta," a pastoralized allegory of Elizabethan England. Vere led English forces at Ostend during the siege, which further suggests that Tourneur's interest in Ostend was persistent, no matter how curiously out of place Borachio's long speech on the siege seems at first.

Like *The Atheist's Tragedy*, Tourneur's elegies are preoccupied with the biographical justification of deaths that occur in the name of a martially oriented Protestant expansion. In undertaking such work, they correspond with a modern vision of elegiac labour, but they do so while making broadly theological and political claims, valorizing and explicating deaths associated with a presumably just cause in the name of a providential plan. I say that Tourneur's elegies correspond to a modern vision of elegy not because modern or modernist elegies are fundamentally the same as early modern elegies (modernists tend to insist on a fundamental difference in their ethos), but because modern criticism on the elegy tends to think of the genre in terms of its biographical sense-making function: even if the cosmology is different, the elegy is still imagined to provide a psychic, cultural, or historiographical benefit. Characterizing the work of elegy by appeal to its psychic work rather than its form, Jahan Ramazani insists on reading elegy in terms of its generic characteristics while also refusing to "reduce all elegiac feeling to trope, code, and convention" (28). By considering its effects rather than its form, he transforms elegy into a genre that is best characterized as a "mimesis of mourning" (28), or as a genre that works to mitigate loss by providing narrative closure to a life. In formal terms that bear considerable affective weight, the elegy is expected to be summative and closural: it produces stories that mourn the dead by making narrative sense of their lives, and in doing so, it puts the dead in their place. As Peter Sacks claims in a similar vein, the presumed "psychic function" of the elegy makes it part of "the actual project of mourning" (22). Such extra-formal preoccupations complicating the discussion of genre speak to the overdetermination of "narrative," a category meaningful to both psychoanalysis and literary criticism; they also transform elegy into a subcategory of a psychoanalytically determined genre called "trauma writing." Just as the narrativization of trauma might make sense of that which is historically nonsensical in an attempt to provide counter-traumatic psychic benefits, the elegy's formal characteristics draw a line between the living and the elegiacally interred dead: elegies, that is, produce a world in which the living can dwell unhaunted because the dead have been moved to the past as well as the ground. Tourneur is clearly sensitive in *The Atheist's Tragedy* to this sense-making function of elegy, where one's death might be treated as the culmination of one's life. Levidulcia, for instance, is for Tourneur no more and no less than an adulteress, whose death stabilizes her life's meaning. This sensitivity to the biographical work associated with elegy is central to his elegies to great men, in which he invokes their religious and political interests to produce a characterological core that is dialectically related to the narrative emplotment of their life.

The summative and closural work of elegy is clear in Tourneur's poems for Vere and Spenser, where he fudges the historical record to produce neatly coherent, narrativized lives to which he pays tribute. In his conspicuous manipulation of the historical record in these elegies, Tourneur's preoccupation with the narrative meaningfulness of lives becomes obvious, just as it is in *The Atheist's Tragedy*. Throughout his dramatic and elegiac writing, that is, Tourneur generally erases any nonsensical biographical matter that he finds, insisting instead on the meaningful closure of deaths that seem to arrive at the right time according to the character that he engages with as a storyteller. As Rousard in *The Atheist's Tragedy* may ignore the actual facts of his illness to make his death seem a proper conclusion to a life of wrongdoing, so Tourneur manipulates the historical record to make the deaths of Vere and Spenser seem similarly conclusive, as if they were the effect of a life's activity.

The struggle to make Vere's biography and death narratively satisfying is clearest in Tourneur's aggressive reply to Vere's critics. Vere's reputation had suffered at the Siege of Ostend because he contravened the laws of war with his notorious false parley. In addition, his "arbitrary" leadership style (Belleroche 449) and "inordinate self-esteem" were considered "a frequent source of trouble and danger to the republic" of the United Provinces when he governed there (Motley 69; see also Schrickx 318). Such critiques disappear in Tourneur's *Funerall Poeme*, however, which burnishes Vere's reputation as a hero of a specific vision of the Protestant cause, while also addressing ambient concerns about his performance in the Low Countries.[17] According to Tourneur, "He that detracts / The *dead* Mans good" by questioning Vere's capacities "defames his own intent" (157). Vere was a tremendous leader according to Tourneur, and any second-guessing of Vere bespeaks confusion: his methods were "yet not vnderstood" by those who question his leadership or ethics. In this properly elegiac vein, the *Funerall Poeme* transforms the story of Vere's life, making it "vnderstood" as a story of heroism and military genius followed by a scholastic retirement. Historically, Vere's biography was a story of military success tainted by uncompromising leadership and at least one serious ethical lapse before a forced retirement, during which he wrote his *Commentaries*, but Tourneur's Vere was a misunderstood leader who "*Retir'd* with *Honour*" before he "*expir'd* in *peace*" after the "GLORY of the *Warre* did *cease*" (B2). In such a reading of Vere's life, his death seems satisfying according to the arc of a professional *cursus*: he led troops well, he retired, and he used his retirement to transform his experience into knowledge to be used by subsequent military leaders. After lionizing Vere and making his life abide the smooth arc of an idealized military biography, Tourneur insists that he has fixed Vere in the past with a "*Monument*" that "Shall neuer be forgotten or defac'd" (B2). Monumentalizing here serves a political point as well, transforming bellicose Protestantism into a divinely sanctioned politics of heroism.

Tourneur makes similar sense of Spenser's death in his bizarre *Transformed Metamorphosis*, an allegorical elegy that also smooths over much of the historical record. In *The Transformed Metamorphosis*, Tourneur ignores the political, literary, and biographical awkwardness of Spenser's failures in Ireland, his non-completion of *The Faerie Queene*, and his possibly penurious last days.[18] For Tourneur, Spenser died as a successful hero who kept England safe from a Catholic threat before dying triumphant once his earthly work was complete. In this account, Spenser – allegorized as the "Muses dearest," Mavortio – heroically battles against a monstrous Catholic beast as it spews its spawn and poisonous bile. The battle is closely modelled on Redcrosse's battle against Error in Spenser's *Faerie Queene*,[19] though Mavortio succumbs where Redcrosse survives, and his name is subsequently "aeternized" in a gesture of elegiac apotheosis (D1). Conspicuous here is Tourneur's sense that Mavortio's death was preordained by heaven: Spenser's death is temporally appropriate because the "heau'ns high trinary was not contented, / That in the world [his] spirit be contained / But there shuld dwel where *Ioue* himself remained" (D1r). Although Spenser's time in Ireland was far from successful, however "success" might look when measured from the perspective of a notoriously brutal colonial program, and although *The Faerie Queene* remained incomplete when Spenser died, and although his death might have been preceded by a professional excess of life, we find in Tourneur's poem a biography in which death comes at the correct time: like Vere, Spenser had finished his work battling the Catholic beast, and was brought to heaven at the apposite moment.

Tourneur's elegy for Henry in a different way self-consciously draws attention to an imagined coincidence between genre, narrative, character, and the psychic work of elegy when it insists on its failure as an elegy and as a work of mourning. The poem is, in one sense, a readily recognizable elegy: written after Henry's early death from typhoid fever at the age of eighteen, it praises his life while lamenting his loss, and it includes a generically appropriate apotheosis when the speaker describes Henry's "*spirit* turn'd into a *starre*" (B4r). On the other hand, however, the poem refuses to be an elegy and it refuses to identify itself as such: the poem is *A Griefe on the Death of Prince Henrie Expressed in a Broken Elegie According to the Nature of Such a Sorrow.* This new genre of "The Grief" refuses to draw a distinction between its formal character and its troubling content when it defines itself. The "nature of such a sorrow" – the sudden death of a beloved prince who promised future combat on the continent – engenders a new genre because the affective weight of Henry's death seems too great for the work of elegy.

Henry's death breaks the elegy. But the new genre is barely a genre, or is the shadow of a genre, existing liminally only by appeal to its "brokenness," or by its failure to be elegiac. Though it fulfils all the formal requirements inherited from the tradition of elegy, and though its verse seems far from fragmented, the poem ultimately suggests its elegiac failure when it closes on a speaker who "*liue[s] fore euer, weeping o'er* HIS *Herse*" (B4r). If Tourneur can provide a "*Monument*" to Spenser, he seems unable to monumentalize Henry because Henry's life provided a promise of military Protestantism that was never fulfilled since he died too soon. To end his poem, that is, Tourneur provides a scene of perpetual or failed mourning. If, as Ramazani, Sacks, and others suggest, the essential elegiac gesture is embodied in the final line of Catullus' elegy for his brother – "and for eternity, brother, a tribute, and farewell" [atque in perpetuum, frāter, avē atque valē] (101.10) – then we can find the brokenness of Tourneur's elegy only in the scene of a differently conceived "eternity," or an eternity "forever" filled with weeping over a "*Herse*" that refuses to inter its cargo, rather than an eternity filled with the lives lived by the living. The poem for Tourneur is a broken elegy precisely because it refuses to perform successful mourning; it fails to provide the simultaneously formal and psychic closure that are generically crucial to elegy.

If the elegy to Henry fails, however, the desire of elegy – the desire to round off lives and to imagine their fulfilment – proves too powerful when Tourneur deploys it against the capricious horror of combat in the age of gunpowder. In this sense, *The Atheist's Tragedy* inverts the sort of historiographical moves that appear in *Richard II*, *A Chaste Maid in Cheapside*, and *Dido, Queen of Carthage*. Where those plays exploit the tools of typically extra-dramatic historiographical forms to trouble the properly dramatic genres in which they participate, Tourneur attempts to consume historical material fully and completely into the logic of the genre he adopts so rigorously, even though the genre had already past its heyday. In this sense, Tourneur's play tests and exemplifies one of this book's key assumptions: that dramatic form often worked in the period against prevailing kinds of historiography and that, simultaneously, it stakes claims to historiographical legitimacy, at least where we imagine historiography as a type of writing that implies (fantastically) a mimetic fidelity with respect to the past, and where we imagine that it does so prior to the dawn of history as a discipline. According to our accounts of Tourneur, we know at least that he was a politically committed and intellectually serious writer who operated in close proximity to the centre of religious state politics during the seventeenth century. As such, he would have been able to write an account of Ostend like *The Extremities*, or even something like the much later history in Belleroche. If, as seems plausible, he or a relative had been at Ostend, the possibility for verisimilitude and careful scorekeeping would quite possibly have been tempting unless, of course, the elegiac fantasies of revenge ultimately tell the truth of history.

Conclusion

"Making Good the Conclusion": Ben Jonson and Bathetic Overliving

Untimely Deaths has traced the often conflicting methodologies that shaped English historical culture between 1574 and 1623 and has argued that playwrights were in a particularly strong position to recognize and articulate the nature of these methodological conflicts. Specifically, the historiographically sophisticated dramatists I have focused on have each dealt with the competing imperatives of historiographical and dramatic form as these kinds of writing run up against the contingencies of real or imagined history. Shakespeare, for instance, recognizes the various modes of historical explanation through which Richard II's biography had been plotted – as a secular humanist historiography, or as a moralized *de casibus* tragedy – and his ultimately interrogative play stages a conflict among these different sorts of historical explanation. In *Dido*, Marlowe similarly recognizes the frictions between epic or nationalist forms of history and the biographical focus of tragedy, just as Middleton explores the opposed types of historical thought through which early modern writers of history frequently represented London. Resisting the sense of narrative indeterminacy or overdetermination that quickens these other plays, Tourneur turns to the already outmoded revenge tragedy to produce a fantasy of historical order in the face of military catastrophe.

These playwrights, as I have argued, ultimately speak to the fraught character of historical thought at the moment when "Hystories" were becoming "History" (to use D.R. Woolf's distinction), and they did so by emphasizing moments of narrative disruption or conflict. When narrative forms fail on the early modern stage – especially when a death arrives too soon – we can see the mark left on early modern historical thought by the uneven "modernization" of historiography and by the methodological heterogeneity at the centre of early modern historical culture. The untimely death brings us close to the period's historiographical habits by drawing attention to their limitations, or by recognizing that available means of historical explanation often contradict one another, or fail to capture accurately the events that one might attempt to render. If, as we have often been told, narrative accounts of history are always structured as fictions, then the fictionality of these fictions becomes clearest when they end at the "wrong" time and demonstrate their inadequacy.

In each of the cases I have explored in *Untimely Deaths*, a death is untimely because, according to available forms of historical narrative, as we have seen, the death arrives traumatically too soon. Of course, as Emily Wilson observes, untimeliness may be a matter of dying too late rather than too early, and may draw attention to a different sort of limitation in the field of narrative historical understanding. Tracing a tradition of dramatic tragedy from Sophocles through Shakespeare and Milton, Wilson recognizes the possibility of tragic "overliving." "Lives do not always end at the expected time," she argues:

> Prolonged old age is one way in which life may seem to go on too long. But even young people may feel that they ought already to have died ... The sense that the central character "should" have died generates an uneasy feeling in the audience or reader that the text itself "should" have ended. These texts therefore challenge Aristotelian notions of tragic structure, in that they go on after the expected moment of ending ... [Such] tragedies of overliving encourage feelings of despair and longing for death that are never completely eliminated. (1, 11)

Crucial to Wilson's thesis is that tragedy is both a narrative form and a genre that operates in a particular affective register, producing and staging what Philip Fisher identifies as "vehement passions."[1] While *Lear* and *Samson Agonistes* may provoke this sense of affective extremity through narrative protraction, however, there are other ways of living too long, or there are ways of living too long that provoke less vehement feelings. In the case of Ben Jonson, for instance, both modern and early modern biographical accounts – responding to Jonson's own cues – tend to treat him as a figure who overlived bathetically rather than tragically, dying somehow after his career came to fruition rather than maturing gradually over time along a familiar literary-professional *cursus*. I want ultimately to argue that this biographical complexity is an issue to which Jonson pays particular attention in his late plays. There he recognizes both the narrative problems posed by pre-emptively memorialized life and also attempts to make sense of the career that has befuddled biographers who were searching for a plot. After outlining the various ways that Jonson's career has troubled biographers, I argue that Jonson pre-emptively challenges many familiar biographical readings of his life, and that he does so within his larger project of authorial self-presentation. In doing so, he produces for himself a well-plotted life, imagining his career according to the imperatives of dramatic plotting that he outlines most explicitly in *Discoveries* and in his final play – his crowning achievement? – *The Magnetic Lady*.

We can best understand Jonson's literary-professional self-understanding in the later plays if we consider the critical work that a literary biography is often expected to perform. In a recent volume of *Shakespeare Quarterly* dedicated to literary biography, Andrew Hadfield, Margreta DeGrazia, and Brian Cummings disagree on the origins of the genre, but they seem to agree on the ways that literary biography has been valued since the nineteenth century. For these scholars, literary biography is necessarily tied to the critical labours of "John Aubrey and others" who recorded literary gossip (Hadfield 373); Edmund Malone, who first attempted to determine the chronology of Shakespeare's plays (DeGrazia 384); or Samuel Johnson, who first established the literary biography "as an art form" (Cummings 482). Where the origins of the genre are various, however, the ends are the same: literary biography ultimately serves a hermeneutic purpose, tying life to art in an explanatory nexus and establishing the relation between the "life and corpus linearly over time, in dated sequence" before the "knowledge of the life gives rise to an explanation of the works" (DeGrazia 384; Cummings 487). Working within a language of organic poetic development that these scholars find somewhat problematic, the modern literary biography combines the literary life with the chronology of works to show readers "how the genius" of a poet "gradually expanded itself" (Malone in DeGrazia 396), recognizing an aesthetic development corresponding to a story of biographical maturation.

Whether or not this particular form of literary biography is distinctly modern as a critical project, its intellectual foundations are clear among early modern writers who attempted to establish their status as laureate poets by building a specific sort of poetic life. This literary-biographical self-fashioning is pronounced, as Patrick Cheney suggests, in the cases of Spenser and Marlowe, each of whom modelled his authorial *cursus* on a Virgilian or Ovidian model. The Virgilian Spenser, Cheney argues, moved in the course of his career from pastoral to georgic to epic, while the Ovidian Marlowe proceeded from amatory poetry to tragedy and, with his translation of *Pharsalia*, towards epic (10, *passim*). Jonson, too, as many modern critics claim, seems to have worked through the first half of his life as author – from circa 1597 to 1616 – according to a distinct *cursus*, but one that seems more Horatian or humanistic than Ovidian or Virgilian. Richard Helgerson, for instance, treats Jonson as a poet who focuses on the critical face of poetry, using "scholarship and labor to fill the place that in the previous generation had been occupied by inspiration" (*Self-Crowned Laureates* 27). As we see Jonson's career develop, he moves from satire on the public stage to the epigrammatic and panegyric, serving as a voice of humane judgment and providing intellectual service to elite patrons who, in his mind, require the learning of a scholar-poet. Douglas A. Brooks sees a comparable arc in Jonson's biography as the poet turns away from the public theatre and towards court appointments in the second decade of the seventeenth century; he notes that Jonson claims greater authority for himself in this later period by associating his art with elite circles via masques, entertainments, and patronage (111–13).[2] Rather than moving through genres that were thought to be more aesthetically sophisticated, that is, Jonson worked in those that were more politically influential and cerebral.

But Jonson's literary biography is troubled by narrative cul-de-sacs, sudden returns, and the outsized significance of the 1616 folio *Workes*. This latter monumental publication is often treated as the ultimate testament to Jonson's genius, even though he continued to write long after its publication. As a poet who famously renounces the theatre, returns to the theatre, renounces the theatre again, and returns to the theatre again, Jonson's ambivalence towards the stage makes it difficult to discern the "gradual expansion" of his theatrical or literary "genius." His changing fortunes at court also make it difficult to extend Brooks' account of his early career: Jonson's masques, given pride of place at the close of his *Workes*, would largely disappear from annual Christmas festivities at court after Charles I took the throne, featured only in the 1631 season. And the "monumentality" of the *Workes* would fix Jonson's authorial identity but would fix it twenty years before his death. As Joseph Lowenstein argues in his extensive study of Jonson's "bibliographical biography," the *Workes* testifies to "a kind of feedback between commercial and artistic practice" to produce a model of "editorial authorship," one in which the author, intervening in the publication of his own work, produces himself as the source and object of an oeuvre (*Possessive* 135). The folio project that emerged from this "feedback" loop is ultimately "totalizing" and "canonizing" as other critics have noted (see Connor 223)[3] and its monumental ambitions are marked in its large folio form and its impressive frontispiece.[4] Lynn Meskill makes this point explicitly in arguing that Jonson "used all the [publishing] alchemy at his disposal to hasten the process and induce the birth of his literary immortality" ("Folio"). Problematically, this apotheosis took place at mid-life, leaving Jonson to live and write in the shadow of the oeuvre that was framed as the sum total of his literary ambition and legacy. An inverted Tithonus, Jonson is immortalized as eternally youthful – or at least eternally middle aged – but is forced to endure through his old age and death. His aim to establish himself as a laureate poet ultimately seems problematically too successful, because he monumentalized himself too early and too effectively, excluding the recognition of his later work.

This vision of the *Workes'* monumentality is not unique to modern critics and scholars. As is clear in *Jonsonus Virbius,* an encomiastic celebration of Jonson's life published the year after his 1637 death, his early modern heirs and admirers treated the *Workes* as the *sine qua non* of his writing life. In an admiring, if often laboured, account that attempts to rehabilitate Jonson's legacy against his critics, Richard Weston directs "shallow sirs" who fail to appreciate Jonson's poetic gifts to look upon the "majestic splendor of thy book" (H4r), apparently forgetting that the book had been published more than two decades before Jonson finished writing. Joseph Rutter similarly insists on the monumentality of the folio when he claims that Jonson's heirs draw their poetic tools from the "inventory in thy Book" (H4v), and Dudley Diggs claims that the only way to "redeem" Jonson from the grave is to "look / Into thy papers, to read o'er thy book," thus conflating all of Jonson's poetic output with the folio (D3v). Jonson, it seems, died an untimely death because he lived too long after his interment. Buried in life by the monumental folio, Jonson was forced to spend the final third of his life beneath his own tombstone.

The folio's self-consciously crafted monolithic character has produced at least two distinct distortions in stories of Jonsonian literary biography. I argue below that these are deformations that Jonson himself worked to minimize in his late works, where he attempts to establish himself as a "mature" poet. As Martin Butler argues, Jonson's biographers and editors, most notably Herford and Simpson, distort Jonson's career when they follow the fantasies of authorial coherence that the holistic folio implies. When they find in Jonson's biography the story of a "laureate poet whose *Workes* unfold almost mystically as a coherent and self-sustaining body of *opera*" they abide the folio's logic but ignore the vicissitudes of Jonson's life and career (11). To attend to Jonson's self-fashioning in the folio is to ignore what Jonson actually accomplished over the course of his life, denying him the possibility of maturation or "lateness" allowed to Shakespeare, for instance. Scholarship that considers Jonson's vision of authorship often follows this model, as we see in Helgerson's seminal *Self-Crowned Laureates,* where he considers Jonson's authorial ambitions while attending exclusively to the work of the early career. Though stating an interest in the "tradition of the great poetic career diachronically" (17), Helgerson ultimately emphasizes only the first half of Jonson's work, explaining that "[f]or in those crossings of the threshold" to public recognition from obscurity, wherein "the author first appears before his audience, the pressure on self-presentation is greatest" (13). We might also think here of Richard Dutton's *Ben Jonson: To the First Folio*, a work that assays Jonson's status as a laureate poet by appeal only to the first half of the author's trajectory. When we read the folio within histories of authorship and copyright, Dutton ironically claims, its "historical significance seems in some perverse way to have obscured its intrinsic value as a statement by Jonson himself about *the nature of his career*" (4; emphasis added). Crucial to recognize here, however, is that the folio is unable to make visible "the nature of his career" – no matter how we read it – in part because it only speaks to its first half.

The folio's perception as peak and endpoint also often elides the vicissitudes of Jonson's post-folio career by leading to an overly hasty rejection of his later work, as if everything published after the folio – when he was still only forty-four years old – is best understood as a work of dotage. Often borrowing from comments made by Jonson's antagonistic contemporaries such as Alexander Gil and Nicholas Oldisworth, such readings of his authorial arc point up Jonson's "immodestly prolonged life," seeing the "downgrade spiral of Jonson's career" after publication of the folio (Brady 192, 199). When reading post-folio plays, we are often told, we should recognize (I would add, based on scant evidence) that Jonson returns to the public stage with *The New Inn* and *The Magnetic Lady* "most probably because he needed the money" (Dutton, *Authority* 12). Such readings of Jonson's later career have become heavily qualified since the publication of Anne Barton's even-handed account of the later work in *Ben Jonson, Dramatist*, and yet such a vision persists in more sophisticated ways, as in Meskill's *Ben Jonson and Envy*, where Jonson lives "in the shadow of his own sepulchre" after 1616 (41): once he has "enfolioed himself as a dead classical author," his subsequent work is mere "self-cannibalization" and self-citation, a perennial commentary on early glories at a moment of aesthetic failure and senescence (187–8). Even a sympathetic account of Jonson's final years such as Ian Donaldson's biography – which emphasizes both the aesthetic successes of Jonson's later work as well as the relative happiness of his later life – continues to reflect on this sense of Jonsonian overliving. The penultimate chapter of Donaldson's biography and the final chapter to reflect on Jonson's life is titled "Dying Late" (399).

Apparently aware of the "tradition of the great poetic career" well after publishing the folio *Workes*, Jonson in his later plays pre-emptively responds to such criticisms. While it seems clear that Jonson – more than most early modern playwrights – was concerned with his reputation after his death,[5] he prompts readers of his late plays to recognize the shape of his literary biography according to relatively novel biographical formulae. He had wanted his career to follow a more traditional *cursus*; he claims in his conversations with Drummond that "he had an intention to perfect an epic poem entitled *Heroologia*, of the worthies of his country" (5.343). When that intent failed to materialize, he needed to produce a new formula. Rather than look for a story that we might find familiar, then – a story of "late style" or "self-cannibalization" or "atrophy" – we are potentially better served if we follow Jonson's new self-imagining of his poetic trajectory. When we do so, we find in his later works a gradual distillation of thought, a return, and a resolution of material from earlier in his career.

Such genial stories of Jonson's career have previously been told by critics, who refuse the idea of Jonson's early dotage. But these sympathetic relations have worked against Jonson's own account of his career, considering his return to earlier forms and issues as a matter of nostalgia rather than fruition. They continue the general thinking of "overliving"; they just minimize the sense that Jonson's late works are aesthetic failures that fall outside the "canon" established by the folio. Barton, for instance, sees Jonson's late works in terms of a late mid-life melancholic reflection, associating them with the exercise of biographical self-understanding in the face of death. By 1632, while Jonson was probably writing *The Magnetic Lady* after the failure of *The New Inn*, Barton finds the playwright situated

> at that time of life when men are naturally tempted to embark on what psychologists call "the life review", the compulsion in late middle age to evaluate and re-possess the world of one's youth. In Jonson's case, this impulse can only have been strengthened by the long hours spent, of necessity [because infirm], alone. In doing this, he was also led to re-examine the writers, most of them now dead, who surrounded him as a young man. (*Ben Jonson* 286)

Where Meskill finds self-cannibalization an aesthetic problem, then, Barton finds self-reflection a psychological solution, one that allows Jonson to make good on his earlier life by returning to it in a mode of re-evaluation. This sense of retrospective self-consolation corresponds with Peter Happé's account of Jonson's late plays and their vision of memory. Suffused with nostalgia, Jonson becomes more genial than he had been in his earlier urban satires. The late plays – *The Magnetic Lady, The New Inn*, and *A Tale of a Tub* – retire from critique, from the present, and from the city. In an ultimate turn to nostalgia as an operating principle, Happé argues, Jonson's late plays echo medieval morality plays (¶30). Retrospection becomes pre-eminent in the late plays, then, as an aesthetic principle, and we can see how literary biography is operating in such critical visions: as DeGrazia, Hadfield, and Cummings each suggest, the biography offers a language for understanding the work. Old men become nostalgic and write with the past in front of them.

However, what is more pressing to Jonson in his later career, I would argue, is revision rather than retrospection. He regularly treats earlier work not as something to be repeated – either cannibalistically or nostalgically – but as something to be fulfilled or improved upon. The late plays, that is, become a conclusion to a career, or the apotheosis of early work. *A Tale of a Tub* is not only nostalgic in the sense that Happé suggests, for instance, recalling "earlier and apparently more innocent times, and ... [containing] glimpses of Queen Mary and Elizabeth I" (¶11); it is also nostalgic in the sense that it is a return to, and refashioning of, material he started to work on decades earlier. As Hugh Craig argues, Jonson revisits material from his early career in a mode of invention rather than reversion, and a mode of fruition rather than self-cannibalization. Critics have long recognized diverse "chronological strata" in *A Tale of a Tub*, for instance, suggesting that the play was rewritten or returned to several times before it was "finished" late in Jonson's career. When we recognize this chronological strangeness of Jonson's late work, Craig further argues, we get a better sense of Jonson as a writer because chronology, "like authorship," is a crucial context for understanding authorial identity. Turning specifically to the dating of *A Tale of a Tub*, he explains:

> it makes a difference if the student of Jonson's drama begins within a city comedy and a well-wrought display of humors or with a romance of disguised identity and concealed riches like *The Case Is Altered*, or with a rustic farce with some later satiric editions. It makes all the difference to *A Tale of a Tub* itself if it is a late work of pastiche or is in origins an early, naively conventional one. (230–1)

Whether Craig is right or not when he offers the strong argument for the ends of literary biography, he certainly seems correct if we hope to understand the final arc of Jonson's career and revisit the claims of melancholic nostalgia and self-cannibalization. What do we make of a career that ends with renewed energy being applied to early material? What does that biographical plot look like? Is this a story of Jonsonian lateness of the sort we might find about Shakespeare?

Craig's account of Jonson's rewriting is perhaps most convincing because it matches Jonson's own description of his late career. In his final play, *The Magnetic Lady*, the playwright describes his retrospection as a matter of fruition rather than nostalgia, and he offers a long commentary on the character of narrative. Allusively, his relation on narrative offers a rejoinder to those who might read his career as pre-emptively over at the publication of the folio. He voices this position through the Boy in the Induction to *The Magnetic Lady*, who explains that Jonson's retrospection here is both driven by psychology and the need to return to earlier work:

> beginning his studies of this kind with *Every Man In His Humour* and after, *Every Man Out of His Humour*, and since, continuing in all his plays, especially those of the comic thread whereof *The New Inn* was the last, some recent humors still, or manners of men, that went along with the times, finding himself now near the close or shutting up of his circle, hath fancied himself in idea this magnetic mistress ... And this he hath called *Humours Reconciled*. (Ind. 75–85)

To treat art-making as a program of study seems apt for Jonson who often thinks of writing in terms of its intellectual and critical energy, and yet more significant here is his sense that his play is both retrospective and contemporary: the humours comedy is familiar yet new, it is "with the times" and something from the "beginning of his studies" as well. Jonson here establishes a double story for *The Magnetic Lady* in the images of the "circle" and the "thread," and he develops these images in the intermeans interspersed throughout the play. The return is more than self-cannibalization for Jonson; it is a matter of reconciliation – tying up a thread or closing a circle – and the story he tells here about his career is, like his play, decidedly comic in structure despite its sudden turns and reversions.

While it may overstate the case to say that Jonson's meditation on narrative in the intermeans is a self-reflective commentary on the shape of his career, the account he offers through Damplay, Probee, and the Boy develops the issues of narrative unfurling that he raises when describing his career in the prologue. The intermeans ultimately offer the most sophisticated account of narrative in the period, one that develops classical thinking on storylines (probably via Scaliger) in a dialectical direction. Expanding on the image of the thread and the sense of redemptive circularity that we find in the prologue, the foolish Damplay, Probee, and the savvy Boy reflect on the narrative trajectory of the play and conclude that its apparent conclusion is in fact a false ending. Only a fool would see the end of a plot when the plot was in the middle. Insisting that the audience continue through the fifth act, Probee develops the thread trope, claiming that their inter-scene conversation distracts them from the play's action: "No, let us mark and not lose the business [or plot] on foot by talking. Follow the right thread, or find it" (Intermean 4.14–16). Damplay thinks that this fifth act is a waste of their time ("Why, here his play might have ended" [5.1.21]). But it is only by waiting through the fifth act that we can see the play's action finally resolve, as the mistaken identities of Placentia and Pleasance are revealed and the likeable heroes are betrothed to their appropriate loves. To pre-emptively presume the end of the story is to miss the final movement in which that story is resolved. Here again we get the image of the thread, with Damplay sure how to negotiate action: the play, he worries, "is almost puckered and pulled into that knot by your poet, which I cannot easily, with all the strength of my imagination, untie" (Chorus 4.1–3).

Damplay, the fool in these intermeans, is ultimately marked as a clown by his failure to recognize the proper conclusion of an action. To be foolish, specifically, is to imagine a conclusion in the middle of a plot or to fail to see that an action has yet to conclude. But Jonson, as the Boy reminds us, is always one step ahead of any conventional or hackneyed plot, and he is able to produce a conclusion that is both apt and surprising. The Chorus is in accord: "Stay and see his last act," it urges, "his *catastrophe,* how he will perplex that, or spring some fresh cheat, to entertain the spectators with a convenient delight, till some unexpected and new encounter break out to rectify all and make good the conclusion" (Chorus 4.21–4). The "reconciliation" the Boy describes in the prologue becomes a "rectification" by the fourth act, which "makes good the conclusion." Most important is the mixture of narrative propriety and surprise that the Boy celebrates. On the one hand, the narrative includes a proper catastrophe arriving at the right time, bringing the action to a conclusion; on the other hand, however, the catastrophe is utterly novel, unpredictable, and surprising. In aesthetic terms, this climactic moment for Jonson's metadramatic choric figures is best because it is both unpredictable and apposite.

Such a surprising but fully appropriate account of the narrative action makes sense differently when read in terms of Jonson's vision of his career. The biographical plot we might have expected – a literary biography moving towards epic, for instance – is supplanted by a storyline that ends with a surprising twist: a return to the early humours comedies that "rectifies" and "makes good the conclusion" of a life lived differently. The subtly dialectical account of narrative that Jonson here offers – an account of plot that responds to dramatic action rather than determining dramatic action – speaks to the artist's own paradoxical preference for both innovation and classical forms. To think that Jonson dies too late, that is, means that one misunderstands how to plot a life at all. A life, characterized by vicissitudes and complications, must always be re-narrated, responding to events, reimagined as it continues to grow beyond the shape of a familiar plot. Jonson concludes, and we might agree, that such return and rewriting is necessary if we hope to write a life well.

Jonson's sophisticated account of the relationship between catastrophe and plot means that he has an exceptional place in *Untimely Death*. Jonson would seem to naturally fit here, as perhaps the most sophisticated historical thinker to also write for the stage in early modern England. Like Middleton, he was Chronologer for the City of London, and yet he was more radically imbricated in the world of historical thought than Middleton or any of the other playwrights in the period. Jonson's familiarity with the period's historiographical innovation is perhaps clearest in an anecdote that opens Blair Worden's story of Jonson and the two English historians most frequently associated with early modern historiographical innovation, John Selden and William Camden. As Worden recounts, these two historians, along with Jonson's mother, were the only guests to join him as he celebrated his 1605 release from prison after the *Eastward Ho!* fiasco. Jonson's awareness of early modern historiographical innovation extended to his plays, as is clear in his philologically sophisticated marginalia for *Sejanus*, or in the learning about Deuteronomy, gleaned from exchanges with Selden, that suffuses *Bartholomew Fair*.[6] That Jonson lost a history of Henry V he'd written in his library fire only cements his status as a sophisticated historian in his own right, one who, as Worden says, conceived of history, like drama, "as an exercise of the imagination, in which historians, in sympathy with dramatists, asked themselves what a given character would have said or done in a given situation" ("Ben Jonson" 68).

And yet Jonson fails to fit neatly in *Untimely Deaths* despite his considerable historiographical acumen and his interest in historical drama. He fails to fit here in part because his sense of narrative propriety, clear in *The Magnetic Lady*, was too central to his poetic project. Just as he refuses to see his life as anything other than well plotted, and just as the Boy in *The Magnetic Lady* reminds us that Jonson is serious about the necessary resolution of his dramatic action, Jonson insists on the timeliness of his catastrophes in *Discoveries.* In *Discoveries*, Jonson claims that narrative abruption of the sort I treat in *Untimely Deaths* is a mark of aesthetic failure rather than historiographical seriousness or critique. Writing on the "magnitude and compass of any fable, epic or dramatic," Jonson insists – tautologically – 1) that a plot is well constructed only when it treats a complete action; and 2) that we know a "complete action" because it fits well within a well-constructed plot. He elaborates: "In such a 'perfect' plot, that is, the 'fable' is called the imitation of one entire and perfect action, whose parts are so joined and knit together [like threads?], as nothing in the structure can be changed, or taken away, without impairing or troubling the whole, of which there is a proportionable magnitude in the members" (7.482). Sounding more like Aristotle than Scaliger here,[7] Jonson makes the coherent imitation of a coherent action the ultimate end of dramatic art:

> As to a tragedy or a comedy, the action may be convenient and perfect that would not fit an epic poem in magnitude. So a lion is a perfect creature in himself, though it be less than that of a buffalo or a rhinocerote. They differ but in specie: either in the kind is absolute; both have their parts, and either the whole. (7.483)

Jonson's strict insistence on narrative propriety suggests that he ultimately views history and drama as different forms: history is rarely so "convenient and perfect" that it can be readily recounted, as his antiquarian friends would have known. Such a sense that epic, tragedy, and comedy all treat perfect actions with apposite narratives also intimates why Jonson would treat the history of Henry V in prose and why the *Heroologia* was never written. Henry's life, as I discuss in the introduction to this book, was narratively unsatisfying, and if Jonson had an intention "to perfect ane Epick Poeme intitled Heroologia, of the Worthies of his Country," the strict accounting of emplotment that he offers around epic, tragedy, or "fables" in general would fail to operate for the story of all worthies. Jonson, then, seems to be a limit case to the story that *Untimely Deaths* offers, appearing both central to the world of early modern historical thought and yet decidedly resistant to the frictions and conflicts that quickened and troubled it.

Notes

Introduction

1 In the "Authorship Companion" to the *New Oxford Shakespeare*, Gary Taylor and Rory Loughnane offer a comprehensive survey of the literature on *1 Henry VI*'s authorship and ultimately claim – convincingly – that "[a]lthough we cannot be certain that Nashe wrote every line, scene, or sub-scene of Act 1, he is clearly the primary author of Act 1" (514).

2 On the "motif of the interrupted ceremony" in *1 Henry VI*, see Hereward T. Price, *Construction in Shakespeare*, 28.

3 See also Hodgdon: "In that it functions as a betrothal, the playtext's final scene pays homage to the generic expectations of comedy, but its formal dissatisfactions and the series of replacements it dramatizes render it transgressive" (58).

4 In the 2012 Globe-to-Globe production by the National Theatre Belgrade, the throne sits almost empty at the rear of the stage for all five acts, holding only a mysterious silver box. In a final wordless scene added at the play's end, the silver box is opened and the ashes of Henry V spill onto the stage; the clowns who had been fiddling with the urn attempt and fail to gather up the dusty mess.

5 On *1 Henry VI* as *The Tragedy of Joan*, see Rackin and Howard, *Engendering a Nation*, 113.

6 On the conventionality of the *topos*, see Bevington, *Shakespeare: The Seven Ages of Human Experience*, 3.

7 For the seven ages of woman, one might look to Hans Baldung's "Allegory of Beauty and Death" (c. 1509). Note that Baldung excludes signs of career milestones and social roles, focusing solely on changing bodies.

8 See Anne Barton, "Shakespeare and the Idea of Play," where she notes that "[c]omparisons between the world and stage were so common [in early

modern Europe] as to become, in many instances, almost automatic, an unconscious trick of speech" (76).

9 For Grossman, the hysteric is a comparable figure: after repressing an event and, consequently, disrupting the coherent unfolding of biographical life, the hysteric occupies a space of varied identities. See *The Story of All Things*, 118–27.

10 Blixen published this story as Isak Dinesen in *Out of Africa*, 186–8.

11 For a sense of the broad phenomenological roots of this argument, see David Couzens Hoy, *The Time of Our Lives*, and Todd May, *Death*; both Hoy and May turn to Heidegger's *Being and Time* to find a phenomenological source for the argument that death "bring[s] together the threads of one's life" (May 29). For a critique of this model of human life, see Adorno's *Metaphysics: Concept and Problems*, 72, where he treats this vision of biographical wholeness as an illusion.

12 See Womersley's "Teleology of Technique," where he argues that Fussner's volume marks a turning point in the history of historiography, after which critics assume that modern historiography emerges in the sixteenth, rather than the eighteenth, century. See esp. 92–4.

13 On this point about More, see Helgerson "Weeping for Jane Shore," 451–76.

14 See also Grant and Ravelhofer, who emphasize Foxe's historical seriousness and rigour: he was "much concerned when writing the histories of the Protestant martyrdoms of the sixteenth century to gather together the corroborating evidence of as many witnesses as he could. We have a number of the letters sent to Foxe containing martyrdom narratives and it has become apparent to scholars that he spent considerable energy cross-checking these to try to arrive at the 'true' story, and altered later editions of the *Acts and Monuments* when the reliability of an account became questionable" (11).

15 On the "great man" form of humanist historiography, see Arthur Ferguson, *Clio Unbound*.

16 Kamps makes similar points on Blundeville in *Historiography and Ideology in Stuart Drama* and in his essay on history writing in the *A Companion to Shakespeare's Works: The Histories*, where he argues that "What is remarkable" about Blundeville, is not that he "appears to believe that providence illuminates history and that history illuminates providence ... but that he identifies two radically different ways of conceiving of the past but fails to recognize the profound methodological and epistemological differences" (17).

17 As Nicholas Popper points out in his study of the *History*, Ralegh's historiographical practice was at the cutting edge of modern, continental historiography associated with both Italian humanism and French legal history (17), and yet Ralegh, too, thinks in terms of providence and the strictly economic model of divine justice inscribed in the structure of history. For Ralegh, to undertake historical analysis is to determine "How Kings and

Kingdomes have florished and fallen; and for what vertue and piety GOD made prosperous; and for what vice and deformity he made wretched, both the one and the other ... In a word, wee may gather out of History a policy no lesse wise than eternall" (A2r–v).

18 See Holger Schott Syme, "'But, what euer you do, Buy': *Richard II* as Popular Commodity." Syme points out that stage histories popular in the 1580s and 1590s continued to be printed and sold well into the seventeenth century. Such an observation complicates considerably the familiar argument about history plays: that they had a brief vogue in the 1580s and 1590s before falling out of fashion in London.

19 The language of parasitism comes from D.R. Woolf, who identifies a number of "parasite genres" such as drama that "feed on" the chronicle in early modern England and ultimately "kill it" by providing more accessible and more affordable means to access historical material. See *Reading History in Early Modern England*, 26–36. It bears mention that earlier generations of historians took seriously early modern history plays, even if they treated them as largely parasitical on the more significant stream of early modern historical thought.

20 Blair Worden offers this anecdote in "Ben Jonson among the Historians," where he includes a similar account of the relationship between poetry and historiography in the period.

21 Note, for instance, that more than 50 per cent of the prose on pages 299–309 – all dealing with the moral/didactic value of history – is quoted directly from Keckerman and Vossius.

1 *Richard II*, Problem Tragedy

1 On the political implications of Richard's frequently moved body, see Paul Strohm, "The Trouble with Richard: The Reburial of Richard II and Lancastrian Symbolic Strategy."

2 On the possible topicality of *Richard II*, see Paul Hammer, "Shakespeare's *Richard II*, the Play of 7 February 1601, and the Essex Rising." On the plausibility of the conversation reported by Lambarde, see Jason Scott Warren, "Was Elizabeth I Richard II? The Authenticity of Lambarde's 'Conversation.'"

3 When the queen turned to Bacon for his testimony on the character of Hayward's history, Bacon ultimately argued, contra-Coke, that the volume wasn't treasonous but that it was, instead, stolen largely from Tacitus. Undeterred in the prosecution, the court subsequently imprisoned Hayward, suggesting that Coke's argument about historical parallels was more convincing. See Bacon, *The apology of Sr. Francis Bacon, Kt. in certain imputations concerning the late Earl of Essex.*

4 See Hadfield, *Shakespeare and Republicanism* for a discussion of the long history of republican thought in England. See too James Philips, "The Practicalities of the Absolute: Justice and Kingship in Shakespeare's *Richard II*," where he identifies a tradition of thought in England that limits the authority of sovereignty and emphasizes claims of the "ancient constitution."

5 For a similar reading of Hall's relative sophistication, see Paulina Kewes, "Narrative Historiography and the Rules of Succession" in *This Great Matter of Succession: Drama, History, and Elizabethan Politics* (forthcoming), where she shows that "Hall's step-by-step narrative of Lancaster's rise shows how election can work in practice. Parliament, it appears, is legally empowered to regulate succession; and heredity is an important but not a decisive factor" (11). Peter Herman – in a bracingly revisionist mode – goes so far as to suggest that Hall doubts the "authority and the pieties of providential historiography" (*ODNB*). That the *ODNB* includes such an argument about Hall might seem surprising: critics working on Shakespeare, following Tillyard even when they disagree with him, tend to treat Hall as a writer who espouses the "Tudor Myth."

6 On Tillyard's debt to Holinshed, see Desmet, "Shakespeare the Historian," 8.

7 On this ambiguity in Hall, see Dominique Goy-Blanquet, *Shakespeare's Early History Plays: From Chronicle to Stage*, where she argues that "Hall tends to read divine judgements in the misfortunes of the wicked. He never jests with the decrees of Providence ... Each transgression – murder, perjury, betrayal – evinces a reminder that the culprits soon paid for the price of their heinous crimes, sometimes by a just and natural turn of affairs, more often through" providence (154).

8 On the use of legal history by early modern historians, see Grafton, *What Was History?*

9 Donald Jellerson's "Spectral Historiopoetics of the *Mirror for Magistrates*" is distinct from this tradition where he argues for the collection's "dialogic sensibility" (¶ 4).

10 Suggesting this antiquarian sympathy, Bolton wrote commendatory verses for Camden's *Britannia* – "*Camdeno Suo Britannia*" (9): a second Apollo, Camden "shines [a light] on England" ("fulgere per Anglos") and "defeat[s] chaos" with history ("vincendo Chaos").

11 Contra Doty, see Paulina Kewes, "Narrative Historiography and the Rules of Succession" in *This Great Matter of Succession* (forthcoming). For Kewes, historiographers such as Hall and Holinshed in the mid- to late-sixteenth century were already thinking in terms of "popularity," though the popularity is founded on a philosophical tradition that recognizes the legitimacy of parliamentary electoral authority.

12 See Dowden, *Shakespeare: A Critical Study of His Mind and Art*; Frye, *A Natural Perspective*; and Tillyard, *Shakespeare's Last Plays*.

2 *A Chaste Maid in Cheapside* and the Histories of London

1 William Cecil, for instance, employed William Camden to establish the Welsh origins of his family, and the Stanleys – patrons of The Queen's Men – found their ancestors celebrated in that company's *True Tragedie of Richard the Thirde*. See Lawrence Manley, "Motives for Patronage: The Queen's Men at New Park, October 1588."

2 On the relationship between civic institutions and antiquarian practice in 1570s London – a "reformation of the archive" – see Andrew Gordon, *Writing Early Modern London*, where he recounts the story of "a concerted effort to re-organise and manage an expanding urban archive," which enabled innovative antiquarian research (124); see esp. 123–32. See also table 2 in Stuckey, "This Society Tendeth: Elite Prosopography in Elizabethan Legal History," which tabulates the close relationships between the Elizabethan Society of Antiquaries, the practice of law, and civic appointments. As Stuckey notes, most members of the historiographically innovative society were "by profession, record keepers, heralds and above all lawyers" (3) – the sort of men, that is, who would administer the city's records. As the table shows, the society also included an alderman, Benedict Barnham, and the recorder of the city of London, William Fleetwood.

3 The *Remembrancia* records payments to Edward Hewes for work as City Chronologer, though Woolf makes the compelling conjecture that the position went to Howes (*Reading* 33 n.76).

4 On Middleton's relationship with Cokayne, see Roebuck, "Middleton's Historical Imagination," 126–7.

5 See, for instance, Gary Taylor's introduction to the *Collected Works*, where he claims that Middleton had been the City Chronologer "for two decades before the post was created" (45). See also Alison Chapman, who suggests that, "Judging simply from the tenor" of his early pamphlets, "it is easy to see why Middleton later in life fared well as London's City Chronologer" (243); and Mark Hutchings' "Thomas Middleton, Chronologer of His Time," where he argues, referring to Middleton's plays, that Middleton was "the principal chronicler" of London and England during the first two decades of James' reign (17).

6 On the lost plays, see the Lost Plays Database: http://www.lostplays.org/index.php/Caesar%27s_Fall and http://www.lostplays.org/index.php/Randall,_Earl_of_Chester_(Chester's_Tragedy).

7 On civic pageantry and its relation to the civic men who "fill up Fame's voluminous book," see Gordon, *Writing Early Modern London*, 192–3.

8 As Michael Berlin notes in his introduction to "The Sun in Aries" in the *Collected Works*, the pageant situates Barkham "within a symbolic temporal

cycle in which the new Lord Mayor is the prime actor, serving by his presence to renew the office which he now holds" (1586).

9 This sense of matter's temporal promiscuity and palimpsestic character is the quickening premise of Harris' *Untimely Matter in the Time of Shakespeare*. In terms of urban infrastructure, see specifically chapter 3, "The Writing on the Wall: London's Old Jewry and John Stow's Urban Palimpsest."

10 See, for instance, Mardock, Harris, and Andreas Huyssen who remind us that "neutral civic space" is always an ideological fantasy, precisely because, once it becomes "civic" or lived in, space is necessarily made meaningful by the variety of practices that invest it with human signification as well as by earlier attempts to make it signify (Harris 101, 108). The recalcitrant residua of earlier lifeworlds inscribed materially in ruins and urban structures trouble our sense that a playwright might "discursively manage" a space, as does the sheer multiplicity of voices attempting to make the city meaningful. In Mardock's words, the city exists amid "contests to produce place and to practice space, to write, read, and rewrite the city" (12).

11 On this point, see Paster, who argues that the "ultimate function of these pageants is less to celebrate an individual than to remind the rulers and population of a town or city about their collective higher purpose" (*Idea* 128).

12 Gordon describes a similar strategy at work in Middleton's *Honourable Entertainments* (*Writing*, 165–9)

13 This observation is ultimately the foundation to Grantley's monograph on early modern London, *London in Early Modern English Drama*.

14 For more arguments that *Chaste Maid* is exclusively satirical, see Manley, Brian Morris and Roma Gill, Alizon Brunning, and George Rowe. According to this critical tradition, the play's plots, filled as they are with hypocritical Puritans, dishonest promoters, untrustworthy tutors, and fecund philanderers, ultimately engender a typically satirical (i.e., unromantic) city comedy. As Rowe argues, for instance, *A Chaste Maid* is a comedy whose form is "belied by its content ... a tissue of patterns and roles – social, linguistic, literary – which no longer have significance" (132).

15 On this point, see also Manley, who argues that the "incongruity of romantic illusion with urban reality" is a "major source of humour" in the play (*Literature* 433).

16 Note that Margot Heinemann, recognizing this tonal anomaly in *The Puritan Widow*, argued that Middleton was not the author. See *Puritanism and Theatre: Thomas Middleton and Opposition Drama under the Early Stuarts*.

17 On the semantic richness of gold in city comedy and its capacity to recall morality plays, see Elizabeth Hanson, "'There's Meat and Money Too': Rich Widows and Allegories of Wealth in Jacobean City Comedy."

18 On Middleton's heterogeneous tone and questions of repentance, see Gossett, "Middleton and Dramatic Genre": "Middleton's religious attitudes emerge even in comedy, where they tend to darken the form. Occasionally he does not seem to be playing with the genre so much as losing control of it. For example, in *Mad World* (1605), Penitent Brothel has a familiar role: the clever seducer of a jealous man's wife. But unlike Jonson's Volpone the following year, Brothel is appalled by his sin even while plotting to achieve his goal ... Equally serious are the conversion and repentance of Sir Walter Whorehound in *A Chaste Maid in Cheapside* and the Colonel in *A Fair Quarrel*" (237).

19 On the theological ambivalence of *The Winter's Tale* and its final scene, see Gareth Roberts, "'An art lawful as eating'? Magic in *The Tempest* and *The Winter's Tale*" and Ruth Vanita, "Mariological Memory in *The Winter's Tale* and *Henry VIII*."

3 Epic Tragedies in Marlowe's *Dido, Queen of Carthage*

1 For a more modest account of Camden, the Elizabethan Society of Antiquaries, and their methodological innovations, see Stuckey, "'This Society Tendeth': Elite Prosopography in Elizabethan Legal History," where he notes that, prior to professionalization, "the milieu was one of awakening, of 'discovery', so while the enthusiasm of these scholars cannot entirely counterbalance technical weaknesses in analyses which are obvious today, it is submitted that the group were genuinely great explorers in their field" (57).

2 On the feud between Leland and Polydore, see Phillip Schwyzer, "British History and 'The British History': The Same Old Story."

3 On Selden's critique of Geoffrey, see Woolf, *Reading History in Early Modern England*, 99–101.

4 See also Elizabeth Bellamy, *Translations of Power: Narcissism and the Unconscious in Epic History*, where she argues that, in sixteenth-century England, "[t]he Trojan disaster becomes a kind of fortunate fall ... The *translatio imperii* is constituted within a vast temporality in which history advanced teleologically from Troy as its posited origin to the inexorable fulfillment of empire in the current Royal House" (23–4).

5 See, for instance, Syrithe Pugh, "Marlowe and Classical Literature," where she argues that Marlowe "transforms Virgil's episode fully into tragedy, the genre with which it self-consciously aligned itself, removing like Ovid the epic framework justifying Aeneas' desertion" (84).

6 Mathew Martin's rich engagement with *Dido* makes a makes a similar point about trauma and repetition but to different ends. For him, the observation is best understood vis-a-vis Freud and modernity, where he traces "the modern subject's historiographical and hermeneutic procedures" which "are bifurcated between working through trauma in the form of stabilizing linear

narrative and acting trauma out as destabilizing performative fiction" (323). Here, I argue that Marlowe ironizes the *translatio imperii* by exploring the repetition of catastrophe bound up with fantasies of triumphal repetition.

7 See Paulina Kewes, "Marlowe, History, and Politics," where she notes that Marlowe is at bottom a historical playwright, exploring the history "of late medieval Turkey and Persia in *Tamburlaine, Parts One and Two* (1587), Continental Reformation in *Doctor Faustus* (c. 1588), the founding myth of Rome in *Dido, Queen of Carthage* (c. 1589), or a noted Mediterranean siege in *The Jew of Malta* (c. 1589)." More obviously, he focuses on history "in his last two works for the stage, *Edward II* (1592), and *The Massacre at Paris* (1593), a blood-soaked chronicle of near-contemporary France" (138).

8 The dating of Marlowe's play and its intended audience have long been a topic of debate. Martin Wiggins' account of the possibilities and probabilities is the most compelling. See Wiggins, "Marlowe's Chronology and Canon," 7–14.

9 The critical tradition tends to read this moment in characterological terms, as when Anthony Dawson argues that the staging of Aeneas in Marlowe's play "has psychologized" this moment in Virgil's poem, "and in a way trivialized it." For Dawson, this moment is about grief, and it tells the story "not so much of a defeated Troy but of a deracinated individual ... All this derives first from the fact that Aeneas is grief-stricken and focused on his own feelings" ("Priamus" 64). See also Donald Stump, who argues that this scene demonstrates a truth of character: Aeneas has been transformed by Marlowe into a "deluded exile who distresses children and embarrasses his fellow soldiers" (82). Bartels offers a similarly psychologizing reading of the scene when she argues that Aeneas is "in a way right" when he sees Priam "alive," wagging his hand just outside Carthage's walls because "Priam and Troy do live on in Carthage in a figurative sense, as a part of the culture's knowledge, legend, and art" (39). The psychological readings ignore, however, that Aeneas's "hallucination" speaks more truly to the sense of historical unfolding that the remainder of Marlowe's play stages.

10 Dawson recognizes a sense of repetition in the play that he locates in an anxiety over the imagined relationship between destiny and loss that is played out in early modern England. According to Dawson, Virgil's story is attractive to Marlowe and Shakespeare because it speaks to "the growing sense in the Elizabethan period of England's global, Protestant destiny, combined with the nagging feelings of loss associated with the demise of Catholicism, the erasure of images, the disappearance of embodied comforts before the mastery of a more rigorously austere religious aesthetic" ("Priamus" 75). While Dawson deftly teases out the sense of loss that coincides with any sense of progress, I pay more specific attention to the uncanny sense of repetition that characterizes Marlowe's vision of history in the play itself.

11 Tracing clusters of images in Books II and IV of the *Aeneid*, Victor A. Estevez points out the parallels that Virgil draws between the fall of Troy and the fall of Carthage. While, as Estevez points out, Virgil emphasizes that both Troy and Carthage are fallen cities by regularly invoking images of wounds and fire in Books II and IV, Marlowe expands on this sense of repetition, as I discuss here, by almost parodically elaborating the Virgilian repetition of image clusters to include the repetition of characters or of precise scenarios.

12 The nature of this wall, if it was actually onstage, remains unclear. After surveying the critical literature surrounding this conjectured wall and pointing out some of the (many) dramaturgical problems that such a wall might pose, Smith ultimately agrees with Chambers, Craik, and Hunter that the wall should be on stage and that it was "a fairly open ornamental structure" (178). On the dramatic difficulties that such iconic, stylized, ornamental walls might pose, see the Rude Mechanicals' production of *Pyramis and Thisbe*.

13 Marjorie Garber also makes this point that Aeneas might be read as a second Trojan horse in "Infinite Riches in a Little Room: Closure and Enclosure in Marlowe" (20).

14 Since Bernard Weinberg's comprehensive account of Renaissance literary theory, critics have widely recognized the overwhelming influence of the rhetorical tradition on theories of aesthetics, specifically around the Horatian notion that poetry should "teach and delight." Theories of art were uniformly "rhetoricized" (Weinberg 40), and the study of poetics was a study of "rhetorical poetics" (Plett 94, *passim*); this rhetoricized poetics insisted that art should be moralized.

15 Don Cameron Allen identifies the two distinct traditions of writing on Dido in the period, the first and far more prevalent indebted to Virgil's and Dido's accounts, and a second history of the virtuous Carthaginian queen based on a pre-Virgilian, Justinian tradition in which she lived three hundred years before the action of the *Aeneid* and immolates herself to protect the sanctity of her bond to Sichaeus from Iarbas. The Virgilian tradition is obviously the salient tradition here. See Allen, "Marlowe's *Dido* and the Tradition."

16 Susanna Braund makes a similar point about Virgil's tragic inheritance in *Latin Literature*, pointing out echoes of Euripides in Virgil's poem and drawing attention to the tragic structure of books I–IV.

17 On the largely negative critical account of Marlowe's play in relation to Virgil's poem, see, for instance, Swinburne, who detects in Marlowe's play "a servile fidelity to the text of Virgil's narrative" that "has naturally resulted in the failure which might have been expected from an attempt at once to transcribe what is essentially inimitable and to reproduce it under the hopelessly alien conditions of dramatic adaptation" (1:276). Marlowe's

more recent critics, including his Revels editor, similarly mistake his play as a failure at points where it seems unable to emulate epic, offering instead a poor product that "must have been begun," as some sort of challenge, "from a decision to turn parts of Virgil's epic poem into a form suitable for the stage" (xxxvi). Focusing less on the aesthetic problems that such translation poses and emphasizing instead its ideological import, Clare Kinney points out that there is "something inherently transgressive in the very notion that a tragic drama can offer a *mimesis* of epic mythology" (272); Troni Grande makes a similar claim when claiming that Marlowe takes "a traditional, authoritative genre" in epic and rewrites it within a dramatic tradition that is necessarily "popular" and "carnivalesque" (84).

18 On the association between Dido and other figures of female eroticism, and on "irrationality and disorder" in the *Aeneid*, see also Mihoko Suzuki, *Metamorphoses of Helen*, esp. 92–149.

19 I borrow this phrase from Melinda Gough, whose PhD dissertation – "Daughters of Circe" – traces the heirs of Circe in early modern English epic and theatre.

20 Alison Findlay also doubts that the play fails aesthetically, offering instead a sense of sublime possibility in Dido, despite the catastrophe and despite her being played by boys: "The demands of the Dido part make me doubt that the actors playing the protagonists would have been indistinguishable in age and maturity, as Kinney suggests. Instead, I propose that Marlowe's text deliberately offers the lead boy actor an opportunity to star centre-stage as a woman and, from this unusual theatrical starting point, generates alternative histories based on different configurations of gender, sexuality and power" (246).

21 On Marlowe's ironic engagement with tragic moralism, see Laurie Maguire and Aleksandra Thostrup, "Marlowe and Character." They note that Marlowe's moralizing "prologues and epilogues" "unmoor us hermeneutically": "We are instructed to applaud Tamburlaine and his achievements 'as you please'; Machiavelli invites us to grace Barabas 'as he deserves'; Faustus, like his fortunes, is antithetically 'good or bad'. But how do we know how to interpret – actions, morality, character – on Marlowe's stage?" (39).

4 Military Catastrophe and Elegiac History in *The Atheist's Tragedy*

1 This date follows Morris and Gill's New Mermaids edition of the play, and it assumes that the play was first performed not long before its registration and publication in 1611. Appealing to internal evidence offers only a certainty that the play was written sometime between 1603 – when the battle at Ostend that it describes took place – and 1611. All other considerations, including its putative relation to *Lear*, are too impressionistic to offer a good date. Historically, questions of the play's date have been muddied by discussions

of *The Revenger's Tragedy*, a play, now attributed to Middleton, that Tourneur was once thought to have authored. *The Atheist's Tragedy*, an apparently "less mature" play than *The Revenger's Tragedy*, was previously thought to be written prior to 1606. The date remains possible, but seems unlikely.

2 There is considerable historical disagreement over the date at which the military revolution "began" in earnest. David Eltis has argued that the revolution began in the early sixteenth century rather than in its latter half, an argument that contradicts previous claims by historians such as Michael Roberts and, most famously, Geoffrey Parker. The debate over the date and the meaning of "the military revolution" is framed well in Clifford J. Rogers's collection of seminal writing on the revolution, *The Military Revolution Debate: Readings on the Military Transformation of Early Modern Europe*, which offers a variety of dates from the fourteenth to the eighteenth century. Regardless of the date, we know that the field of battle was transforming rapidly because of technological and strategic innovation in the late sixteenth and early seventeenth centuries. On the acceleration of battlefield innovation over the course of the sixteenth century, see Michael Murrin, *History and Warfare in Renaissance Epic*, 2–5.

3 For at least the past twenty years, performance theorists have made this argument in various ways. See, for instance, Peggy Phelan in *Unmarked: The Politics of Performance*, where she insists that, in the theatre, the body is always recalcitrant, signifying in excess of its purported meaning and "fail[ing] to convey meaning exactly" (13). In this sense, the body on stage is curiously unmarked in that it "exceeds" semiosis, or "both the gaze and the language" (27).

4 I owe this observation to Peter Cockett and to Jennifer A. Low's *Manhood and the Duel*, which suggests that actors were often well versed in fencing, able to stage the moves of well-trained fencers "realistically" (61).

5 *Extremities Vrging the Lord General Sir Fra. Vere* ... contains a similar anecdote: "we haue alreadye endured aboue 161500 Canonodoes" by December 1601, "and yet all our bastions and defences [are] stil firme and tenable, hauing only their outward faces somewhat discountenanced by the fury of the many shot most of them haue endured, especially the sandbill, which is so farced with bullets, that (our men labouring to driue in spiked pallisadoes) doe often stumble upon 6 or 8 in one hole together" (B4).

6 Ronald Broude and Mike Pincombe each find "a small body of politically oriented morality plays" at the root of early modern revenge tragedy (Pincombe 13); both draw this inheritance through *Respublica* and *Horestes* (Broude 49).

7 On the influence of the morality tradition – broadly construed – on *The Atheist's Tragedy*, see Peter Murray, *A Study of Cyril Tourneur*, where he argues that the "dramatization of D'Amville's 'career' is in the allegorical

and symbolic medieval tradition of metrical tragedies and of morality, miracle, and saints' plays" (59). He subsequently describes the play as a *de casibus* tragedy (63). Thomas Rist and Robert Ornstein also identify the play as an heir of *de casibus* tragedy (Rist 107; Ornstein 117).

8 Brian Walsh is an exception to this generalization, as are Teresa Grant and Barbara Ravelhofer in their recent collection of essays. In *Shakespeare, The Queen's Men, and the Elizabethan Performance of History* for instance, Walsh reads Shakespeare's *Richard III* as "an exemplary case ... of *theatrum historiae*: history understood through the dynamics of theatre" (140). Grant and Ravelhofer similarly recognize that that the "style and characterization of Senecan tragedy was transposed wholeheartedly into English humanist plays which sought to grasp history, native and non-native, with classical means" (17).

9 As Motley notes, "Bentivoglio, Grotius, and many others give Vere, as a matter of course, the credit for this feat" but Motley follows Fleming's account because Fleming is "a man whom I should judge incapable of falsehood" (4.85 n.63). Whether or not one trusts Fleming's character, his is the only extant, first-hand account of the attack, and is based on immediate (if potentially biased) experience of the "feat"; as such, it deserves to be given some sort of priority. Grimeston also attributes the strategem to Vere: "The enemie being hotte at the assault, and the water risen; Generall *Vere* caused the sluces to be taken up" (B1v, italics in original).

10 Besides the bodies dumped into the sea, Tourneur may have gleaned most of these details from Grimeston, or he might have found them in pamphlets on the siege. If we follow Thomas Seccombe in the *Dictionary of National Biography* (First Series, Vol. 57) and imagine that Tourneur was brother or cousin or son of Richard Turnor – the one-time governor of Brill who was present at Ostend – then the details might also have come by word of mouth between relations. Wherever these specifics came from, however, the precision of Borachio's description suggests a familiarity and a real concern with the battle and the siege more broadly.

11 On the sea as an icon of the sublime in early modern England, see Steve Mentz, *At the Bottom of Shakespeare's Ocean*, 56–7.

12 On relations between Spain and England before 1615, see Eric Griffin, *English Renaissance Drama and the Specter of Spain: Ethnopoetics and Empire*, 1–27.

13 As Linda Woodbridge points out, revenge tragedy was often sceptical of the value or propriety of revenge, though it indulged in the pleasures of revenge before (generally) condemning it (*Revenge* 30–1).

14 On the italicization of lines in playtexts to mark them as truisms, see DeGrazia, *Hamlet without Hamlet*, 27.

15 I borrow the phrase from Scott McMillin and Sally-Beth MacLean, who use it in *The Queen's Men and Their Plays* to describe plays written by the Queen's Men. "Narrative overdetermination" in this sense refers to a play's internal self-commentary, as characters explain stage-action for the audience (133–8).

16 Tourneur's remembrance of Cecil is available – misattributed to Wotton – in *The Life and Letters of Sir Henry Wotton* (2.487–9).

17 Tourneur's version of Vere's life was ultimately adopted as historical fact in the monument at Westminster, which treats Vere and his brother, Horace, as valiant heroes. Captain Sir John Ogle offered a less enthusiastic response to Vere, under whom he served, but ultimately sees Vere's false parley as a matter of necessity: "Yet there was no hope but in recourse to some strategem, such as has always been held to be within the rules of honourable warfare, if not accompanied by any breach of word or faith" (Belleroche 452). Vere was playing tough but not dirty, according to Ogle, because he never broke any vows: "And yet did he [Vere] there [at Ostend] do many things worth the observation and reputation of so great a captain as he was: among the rest, that of his parley was of most eminent note, and was most noted so worst censured and that as well by sword and gown men" (in Belleroche 451).

18 The story of Spenser's penury comes from Jonson's "Conversations with Drummond," where Jonson claims that Spenser died for "lack of bread." Literary historians have often questioned the veracity of Jonson's claim, pointing out that Spenser was given an annual pension of £50 by Queen Elizabeth.

19 On the similarity, see A.C. Hamilton, "Spenser and Tourneur's *Transformed Metamorphosis*," 132–3.

Conclusion

1 "Tragedy, as Aristotle defined it, is both a certain kind of action and a work characterized by fear and pity, two passions intimately related to one another" (Fisher 9).

2 See also Allison Scott, who argues that Jonson's turn to masques marks his interest in the "external authority of the court" over solely aesthetic or personal ends (454).

3 On the "monumentality" of the folio *Workes*, see also Meskill, "Ben Jonson's 1616 Folio: A Revolution in Print?" and *Ben Jonson and Envy* (140); Martin Butler, "Introduction: From *Workes* to Text"; Mardock, *Our Scene is London* (10); Marjorie Swann, *Curiosities and Texts: The Culture of Collecting*

in Early Modern England (chap. 5); Jennifer Brady, "'Noe Fault, But Life': Jonson's Folio as Monument and Barrier."

4 See Corbett and Lightbown, *The Comely Frontispiece*: "The presence of the obelisks, which are monuments, and the laurels, the traditional crown of the poet, is surely to signify the author's desire that the folio may bring him a poet's immortality" (151).

5 On *Bartholomew Fair*'s biblical hermeneutics and Selden, see Rosenblatt, *Renaissance England's Chief Rabbi: John Selden*, esp. "Selden, Jonson, and the Rabbis on Cross-Dressing and Bisexual Gods."

Works Cited

Line references to Shakespeare's plays come from *The Norton Shakespeare*, 2nd edition, ed. Stephen Greenblatt et al. (New York: W.W. Norton, 1997), unless otherwise noted.

Line references to Middleton's plays come from *Thomas Middleton: The Collected Works*, ed. Gary Taylor and John Lavagnino (New York: Oxford UP, 2010). For the source of quotations from Middleton's pageants, see below.

Line references to Jonson's works come from *The Cambridge Edition of the Works of Ben* Jonson, 7 vols., ed. David Bevington et al. (New York: Cambridge UP, 2012).

Adorno, Theodor. *Metaphysics: Concept and Problems*. Stanford: Stanford UP, 2000.

Allen, Don Cameron. "Marlowe's *Dido* and the Tradition." *Essays on Shakespeare and Elizabethan Drama in Honour of Hardin Craig*. Ed. Richard Hosley. Columbia: U of Missouri P, 1963.

Anderson, Thomas P. *Performing Early Modern Trauma from Shakespeare to Milton*. Burlington, VT: Ashgate, 2006.

Anon. *Extremities vrging the Lord General Sir Fra. Veare to offer the late anti-parle with the Arch-duke Albertus*. London: William White and Thomas Purfoot, 1602.

– *Newes from Ostend*. London: Valentine Simmes, 1601.

– *Remembrancia*. London: E.J. Francis & Co., 1878.

– *The Return from Parnassus: Or, the Scourge of Simony*. London: G. Eld for John Wright, 1606.

Archer, Ian. "The Nostalgia of John Stow." *The Theatrical City: Culture, Theater and Politics in London, 1576–1649*. Ed. David L. Smith, Richard Streier, and David Bevington. New York: Cambridge UP, 1998. 1–34.

Arendt, Hannah. *The Human Condition*. 2nd edition. Chicago: U of Chicago P, 1998.

Aristotle. *Poetics*. Trans. James Hutton. New York: W.W. Norton, 1982.

Bacon, Francis. *The apology of Sr. Francis Bacon, Kt. in certain imputations concerning the late Earl of Essex*. London: Matthew Lownes, 1605.

– *The Historie of the Raigne of King Henry the Seuenth*. London: W. Stansby, 1622.

Baldwin, William, et al. *The Mirror for Magistrates*. Ed. Lily Bess Campbell. New York: Barnes and Noble, 1960.

Barbour, Reid. *John Selden: Measures of the Holy Commonwealth in Seventeenth-Century England*. Toronto: U of Toronto P, 2002.

Barry, Lording. *Ram-Alley: or merrie-tricks*. London: G. Eld, 1611.

Bartels, Emily. *Spectacles of Strangeness: Imperialism, Alienation, Marlowe*. Philadelphia: U of Pennsylvania P, 1993.

Barton, Anne. *Ben Jonson: Dramatist*. New York: Cambridge UP, 1984.

– *Shakespeare and the Idea of Play*. Santa Barbara: Praeger, 1976.

Bellamy, Elizabeth. *Translations of Power: Narcissism and the Unconscious in Epic History*. Ithaca: Cornell UP, 1992.

Belleroche, Edward. "The Siege of Ostend; Or the New Troy, 1601–1604." *Proceedings of the Huguenot Society of London* 3 (1888–91): 427–539.

Bergeron, David. *Pageants and Entertainments of Anthony Munday*. London: Garland, 1985.

Bevington, David. *Shakespeare: The Seven Ages of Human Experience*. 2nd ed. Malden, MA: Blackwell, 2005.

Blundeville, Thomas. *The true order and methode of wryting and reading hystories*. London: William Serres, 1574.

– *A Very Brief and Profitable Treatise declaring how many Counsels and what name of Counsellors a Prince that will govern well ought to have*. London: William Seres, 1570

Bolton, Edmund. *Hypercritica*. London: Anthony Hall, 1722.

Brady, Jennifer. "'Noe Fault, But Life': Jonson's Folio as Monument and Barrier." *Ben Jonson's 1616 Folio*. Ed. Jennifer Brady and W.H. Herendeen. Newark: U of Delaware P, 1991. 192–216.

Braund, Susannah M. *Latin Literature*. New York: Routledge, 2002.

Brissenden, Alan, ed. *A Chaste Maid in Cheapside*. By Thomas Middleton. London: Methuen, 2002.

Brooks, Douglas. *From Playhouse to Printing House: Drama and Authorship in Early Modern England*. New York: Cambridge UP, 2000.

Broude, Ronald. "Revenge and Revenge Tragedy in Renaissance England." *Renaissance Quarterly* 28.1 (1975): 38–58.

Brown, Judith. "Pretty Richard (in Three Parts)." *Shakesqueer: A Queer Companion to the Complete Works of Shakespeare*. Ed. Madhavi Menon. Durham, NC: Duke UP, 2011. 286–93.

Brunning, Alizon. "'O, how my offences wrestle with my repentance!': The Protestant Poetics of Redemption in Thomas Middleton's *A Chaste Maid in Cheapside*." *Early Modern Literary Studies* 8.3 (2003): n.p.

Budra, Paul. A Mirror for Magistrates *and the De Casibus Tradition*. Toronto: U of Toronto P, 2000.

Burke, Peter. *The Renaissance Sense of the Past*. London: Edward Arnold, 1969.

Butler, Martin. "Introduction: From *Workes* to Texts." *Re-Presenting Ben Jonson: Text, History, and Performance*. Ed. Martin Butler. New York: St Martin's Press, 1999. 1–20.

Cahill, Patricia. *Unto the Breach: Martial Formations, Historical Trauma, and the Early Modern Stage*. New York: Oxford UP, 2008.

Camden, William. *Britannia*. Trans. Philémon Holland. London: George Bishop and Joannis Norton, 1610.

Campbell, Lily B. "Theories of Revenge in Renaissance England." *Modern Philology* 28 (1931): 281–96.

Caruth, Cathy. *Unclaimed Experience: Trauma, Narrative, History*. Baltimore: Johns Hopkins UP, 1996.

– "Violence and Time: Traumatic Survivals." *Assemblage* 20 (1993): 24–5.

Cavarero, Adriana. *Relating Narratives: Storytelling and Selfhood*. New York: Routledge, 2000.

Certeau, Michel de. *Heterologies*. Trans. Brian Massumi. Minneapolis: U of Minnesota P, 1986.

Chapman, Alison A. "Writing Outside the Theatre." *Thomas Middleton in Context*. Ed. Suzanne Gossett. New York: Cambridge UP, 2011. 243–9.

Chaucer, Geoffrey. *The Legend of Good Women. The Works of Geoffrey Chaucer*. 2nd ed. Ed. F.N. Robinson. Boston: Houghton, 1957.

Cheney, Patrick. *Marlowe's Counterfeit Profession: Ovid, Spenser, Counter-Nationhood*. Toronto: U of Toronto P, 1997.

– *Shakespeare's Literary Authorship*. New York: Cambridge UP, 2008.

Clegg, Cyndia. "Introduction." *The Peaceable and Prosperous Regiment of Blessed Queene Elisabeth: A Facsimile from Holinshed's Chronicles*. Ed. Cyndia Clegg. San Marino: Huntington Library Press, 2005.

Cogswell, Thomas. "Middleton's Political Prose: 1620–7, A Brief Account." *Thomas Middleton: The Collected Works*. Vol. 1. New York: Oxford UP, 2007. 1907–11.

Connor, Francis. *Literary Folios and Ideas of the Book in Early Modern England*. New York: Palgrave Macmillan, 2014.

Corbett, Margery, and R.W. Lightbown. *The Comely Frontispiece: The Emblematic Title Page in England, 1550–1660*. New York: Routledge, 1979.

Coyle, Martin, ed. *William Shakespeare: Richard II*. New York: Columbia UP, 1995.

Craig, Hugh. "Jonsonian Chronology and the Styles of *A Tale of a Tub*." *Representing Ben Jonson: Text, History, Performance*. New York: Palgrave Macmillan, 1999. 210–32.

Croft, Pauline. "The Reputation of Robert Cecil: Libels, Political Opinion, and Popular Awareness in the Early Seventeenth Century." *Transactions of the Royal Historical Society* 1 (1991): 43–69.

Cummings, Brian. "Last Words: The Biographemes of Shakespeare." *Shakespeare Quarterly* 65.4 (2014): 482–90.

Davis, Alex. *Renaissance Historical Fiction*. Cambridge: D.S. Brewer, 2011.

Dawson, Anthony. "Priamus Is Dead: Memorial Repetition in Marlowe and Shakespeare." *Shakespeare, Memory, and Performance*. Ed. Peter Holland. New York: Cambridge UP, 2006. 63–86.

Dawson, Anthony, and Paul Yachnin. Introduction. *Richard II*. Ed. Anthony Dawson and Paul Yachnin. New York: Oxford UP, 2011. 1–128.

– *The Culture of Playgoing in Shakespeare's London: A Collaborative Debate*. New York: Cambridge UP, 2001.

DeGrazia, Margreta. *Hamlet without Hamlet*. New York: Cambridge UP, 2003.

– "Shakespeare's Timeline." *Shakespeare Quarterly* 65.4 (2014): 379–98.

Dekker, Thomas. *The Shoemaker's Holiday*. Ed. Jonathan Gil Harris. London: Methuen, 2008.

Dekker, Thomas, and Thomas Middleton. "The Patient Man and the Honest Whore." Ed. Paul Mulholland. *Thomas Middleton: Collected Works*. Ed. Gary Taylor and John Lavagnino. New York: Oxford UP, 2007. 280–327.

Dekker, Thomas, and John Webster. *Westward Ho!* London: John Hodges, 1607.

Derrida, Jacques. *The Work of Mourning*. Chicago: U of Chicago P, 2001.

Desmet, Christy. "Shakespeare the Historian." *Shakespeare Survey* 63 (2010): 1–11.

– "Shakespeare and Aristotle." *Literature Compass* 1 (2004): 1–9.

Diehl, Huston. "'Reduce Thy Understanding to Thine Eye': Seeing and Interpreting in *The Atheist's Tragedy*." *Studies in Philology* 78 (1981): 47–60.

Dinesen, Isak. *Out of Africa*. New York: Modern Library, 1992.

Dollimore, Jonathan. *Radical Tragedy: Religion, Ideology, and Power in the Drama of Shakespeare and His Contemporaries*. 3rd ed. New York: Palgrave Macmillan, 2010.

Donaldson, Ian. *Ben Jonson: A Life*. New York: Oxford UP, 2013.

Doty, Jeffrey S. "Shakespeare's *Richard II*, 'Popularity,' and the Early Modern Public Sphere." *Shakespeare Quarterly* 61.2 (2010): 185–205.

Douglas, Gavin. *The xiii bukes of Eneados*. London: William Copland, 1553.

Dowden, Edward. *Shakespeare: A Critical Study of His Mind and Art*. London: Henry S. King & Co. 1875.

– *Poly-Olbion*. London: Humphrey Lownes, 1612.

Duppa, Brian, et al. *Jonsonus Virbius*. London: Henry Seile, 1638.

Dutton, Richard. *Ben Jonson: Authority: Criticism*. New York: Palgrave, 1996.

– *Ben Jonson: To the First Folio*. New York: Cambridge UP, 1984.

Ellinghausen, Laurie. "'Shame and Eternal Shame': The Dynamics of Historical Trauma in Shakespeare's First Tetralogy." *Exemplaria* 20.3 (2008): 264–82.

Eltis, David. *The Military Revolution in Sixteenth Century Europe*. London: I.B. Tauris, 1998.

Erler, Mary C., ed. *Records of Early English Drama: Ecclesiastical London*. Toronto: U of Toronto P, 2008.

Estevez, Victor A. "Queen and City: Three Similes in *Aeneid* IV." *Vergilius* 20 (1974): 25–8.

Fancy, Peter. *The Age of Life and Man*. London: T. Mabb, 1650?

Ferguson, Arthur. *Clio Unbound: Perception of the Social and Cultural Past in Renaissance England*. Durham, NC: Duke UP, 1979.

Findlay, Alison. "Marlowe and Women." *Christopher Marlowe in Context*. Ed. Emily Bartels and Emma Smith. New York: Cambridge UP, 2013. 242–51.

Fineman, Joel. "The History Father Anecdote: Fiction and Fiction." *The Subjectivity Effect in Western Literary Tradition: Essays toward the Release of Shakespeare's Will*. Cambridge: MIT Press, 1991. 59–87.

Fisher, Jasper. *Fuimus Troes*. London: Robert Allot, 1633.

Fisher, Philip. *The Vehement Passions*. Princeton: Princeton UP, 2002.

Frassinelli, Pier Paolo. "Realism, Desire and Reification: Thomas Middleton's *A Chaste Maid in Cheapside*." *Early Modern Literary Studies* 8.3. Humanities Research Centre, Sheffield Hallam University, January 2003. Web. 16 October 2008. http://purl.oclc.org/emls/08-3/fraschas.htm.

Freud, Sigmund. *Beyond the Pleasure Principle*. Ed. James Strachey. New York: W.W. Norton, 1989.

Frye, Northrop. *A Natural Perspective: The Development of Shakespearean Comedy and Romance*. New York: Columbia UP, 1965.

Fussner, F.S. *The Historical Revolution: English Historical Writing and Thought, 1580–1640*. New York: Columbia UP, 1962.

Gager, William. *Dido*. Ed. and trans. Elizabeth Sandis. *Early Drama at Oxford*. University of Oxford, 25 March 2019. http://edox.org.uk/dido/.

Gamel, Mary-Kay. "The Triumph of Cupid: Marlowe's *Dido Queen of Carthage*." *American Journal of Philology* 126 (2005): 613–22.

Garber, Marjorie. "'Infinite Riches in a Little Room': Closure and Enclosure in Marlowe." *Two Renaissance Mythmakers, Selected Papers from the English Institute, 1975–1976*. Ed. Alvin Kernan. Baltimore: Johns Hopkins UP, 1977.

Gibbons, Brian. *Jacobean City Comedy*. London: Rupert Hart-Davis, 1968.

Gordon, Andrew. *Writing Early Modern London: Memory, Text, and Community*. New York: Palgrave Macmillan, 2013.

Gossett, Suzanne. "Middleton and Dramatic Genre." *Thomas Middleton in Context*. Ed. Suzanne Gossett. New York: Cambridge UP, 2011. 235–42.

Gosson, Stephen. *The schoole of abuse*. London: Thomas Dawson, 1587.

Gough, Melinda. "Daughters of Circe: Effeminacy and Poetic Efficacy in Renaissance Epic and Theatre." PhD diss. Yale U, 1990.

Goy-Blanquet, Dominique. *Shakespeare's Early History Plays: From Chronicle to Stage*. New York: Oxford UP, 2003.

Grady, Hugh. "Shakespeare's Links to Machiavelli and Montaigne: Constructing Intellectual Modernity in Early Modern Europe." *Comparative Literature* 52.2 (2000): 119–42.

Grafton, Anthony. *What Was History? The Art of History in Early Modern Europe*. New York: Cambridge UP, 2007.

Grafton, Anthony, and Lisa Jardine. *From Humanism to the Humanities: Education and the Liberal Arts in Fifteenth- and Sixteenth-Century Europe*. Cambridge, MA: Harvard UP, 1986.

Grande, Troni. *Marlovian Tragedy: The Play of Dilation*. Lewisburg: Bucknell UP, 1999.

Grant, Teresa, and Barbara Ravelhofer. Introduction. *English Historical Drama: 1500–1660*. Ed. Teresa Grant and Barbara Ravelhofer. New York: Palgrave, 2008. 1–30.

Grantley, Darryll. *London in Early Modern English Drama: Representing the Built Environment*. New York: Palgrave, 2008.

– "Middleton's Comedy and the Geography of London." *Thomas Middleton in Context*. Ed. Suzanne Gossett. New York: Cambridge UP, 2011. 28–36.

Griffin, Benjamin. *Playing the Past: Approaches to English Historical Drama, 1385–1600*. London: D.S. Brewer, 2001.

Griffin, Eric. *English Renaissance Drama and the Specter of Spain: Ethnopoetics and Empire*. Philadelphia: U of Pennsylvania P, 2009.

Grimeston, Edward. *A True Historie of the Memorable Siege of Ostend*. London: George Eld, 1604.

Grossman, Marshall. *The Story of All Things: Writing the Self in English Renaissance Narrative Poetry*. Durham: Duke UP, 1998.

Gurr, Andrew. *Playgoing in Shakespeare's London*. 3rd ed. New York: Cambridge UP, 2004.

Hadfield, Andrew. *Shakespeare and Republicanism*. New York: Cambridge UP, 2008.

– "Why Does Literary Biography Matter?" *Shakespeare Quarterly* 65.4 (2014): 371–8.

Hall, Edward. *The vnion of the two noble and illustre famelies of Lancastre [and] Yorke*. London: Richard Grafton, 1548.

Halpern, Richard. "The King's Two Buckets." *Representations* 109 (2009): 67–76.

Hamilton, A.C. "Spenser and Tourneur's *Transformed Metamorphosis*." *Review of English Studies* 8.30 (1957): 127–36.

Hammer, Paul E.J. "Shakespeare's *Richard II*, the Play of 7 February 1601, and the Essex Rising." *Shakespeare Quarterly* 59.1 (2008): 1–35.

Hammill, Graham. "Time for Marlowe." *English Literary History* 75.2 (2008): 291–314.

Hampton, Timothy. *Writing from History: The Rhetoric of Exemplarity in Renaissance Literature*. Ithaca: Cornell UP, 1990.

Hanson, Elizabeth. "'There's Meat and Money Too': Rich Widows and Allegories of Wealth in Jacobean City Comedy." *English Literary History* 72.1 (2005): 209–38.

Happé, Peter, ed. *A Tale of a Tub. Cambridge Edition of the Works of Ben Jonson*. Ed. David Bevington, Martin Butler, and Ian Donaldson. New York: Cambridge UP, 2012. 543–654.

Harding, Vanessa. "Cheapside: Commerce and Commemoration." *Huntington Library Quarterly* 71.1 (2008): 77–96.

Harris, Jonathan Gil. *Untimely Matter in the Time of Shakespeare*. Philadelphia: U of Pennsylvania P, 2008.

Hayward, John. *The first and second parts of John Hayward's the life and raigne of King Henrie IIII*. Ed. John J. Manning. London: Royal Historical Society, 1991.

Heinemann, Margot. *Puritanism and Theatre: Thomas Middleton and Opposition Drama under the Early Stuarts*. New York: Cambridge UP, 1982.

Helgerson, Richard. *Self-Crowned Laureates: Spenser, Jonson, Milton, and the Literary System*. Los Angeles: U of California P, 1993.

– "Weeping for Jane Shore." *South Atlantic Quarterly* 98.3 (1999): 451–76.

Hendricks, Margo. "Managing the Barbarian: *The Tragedy of Dido, Queen of Carthage*." *Renaissance Drama* 23 (1992): 165–88.

Herman, Peter. "Rastell's *Pastyme of People*: Monarchy and the Law in Early Modern Historiography." *Journal of Medieval and Early Modern Studies* 30:2 (2000): 275–308.

Heylyn, Peter. *Mikrokosmos a little description of the great world*. Oxford: William Turner, 1639.

Heywood, Thomas. *An Apology for Actors*. London: Nicholas Okes, 1612.

– *A chronographicall history of all the kings*. London: J. Okes, 1641.

– *Troia Britannica*. London: W. Jaggard, 1609.

Higden, Ranulph. *Polychronicon*. Ed. Churchill Babington. Trans. John Trevisa. London: Longmans, Green, 1869.

Higgins, Michael H. "The Influence of Calvinistic Thought in Tourneur's *Atheist's Tragedy*." *Review of English Studies* 19 (1943): 255–62.

Hodgdon, Barbara. *The End Crowns All: Closure and Contradiction in Shakespeare's History*. Princeton: Princeton UP, 1991.

Holinshed, Raphael. *The Chronicles of England*. London: Henry Denham, 1587.

Hopkins, Lisa. "Englishmen Abroad: Mobility and Nationhood in *Dido, Queen of Carthage* and *Edward II*." *English: Journal of the English Association* 59: 324–48.

Howard, Henry. *Certain bokes of Virgiles Aeneis turned into English meter*. London: Richard Tottel, 1557.

– *Surrey's Fourth Boke of Virgill*. Ed. Herbert Hartmann. New York: Oxford UP, 1932.

Howard, Jean. *Theatre of a City: The Places of London Comedy, 1598–1642.* Philadelphia: U of Pennsylvania P, 2007.

Howard, Jean, and Phyllis Rackin. *Engendering a Nation: A Feminist Account of Shakespeare's English Histories.* New York: Routledge, 1997.

Howard, Michael. *War in European History.* 2nd ed. New York: Oxford UP, 2009.

Howard-Hill, Trevor. *Middleton's "Vulgar Pasquin": Essays on* A Game at Chess. Newark, DE: U of Delaware P, 1995.

Hoy, David Couzens. *The Time of Our Lives: A Critical History of Temporality.* Cambridge: MIT Press, 2009.

Hutchings, Mark. "Thomas Middleton, Chronologer of His Time." *Thomas Middleton in Context.* Ed. Suzanne Gossett. New York: Cambridge UP, 2011. 17–27.

Huyssen, Andreas. *Present Pasts: Urban Palimpsests and the Politics of Memory.* Redwood City, CA: Stanford UP, 1980.

James, Heather. *Shakespeare's Troy: Drama, Politics, and the Translation of Empire.* New York: Cambridge UP, 1997.

Jardine, Lisa. *Francis Bacon: Discovery and the Art of Discourse.* New York: Cambridge UP, 1974.

Jellerson, Donald. "The Spectral Historiopoetics of *The Mirror for Magistrates.*" *Journal of the Northern Renaissance* 2. January 2010. Web. 16 October 2015. http://www.northernrenaissance.org/the-spectral-historiopoetics-of-the-mirror-for-magistrates/.

Kamps, Ivo. *Historiography and Ideology in Stuart Drama.* New York: Cambridge UP, 1996.

– "The Writing of History in Shakespeare's England." *A Companion to Shakespeare's Works: The Histories.* Ed. Richard Dutton and Jean Howard London: Oxford: Blackwell, 2003. 4–25.

Kelley, Donald R. *Foundations of Modern Historical Scholarship: Language, Law, and History in the French Renaissance.* New York: Columbia UP, 1970.

– Introduction. *History and the Disciplines: The Reclassification of Knowledge in Early Modern Europe.* Ed. Donald R. Kelley. Rochester: U of Rochester P, 1997. 1–10.

– "The Problem of Knowledge and the Concept of Discipline." *History and the Disciplines: The Reclassification of Knowledge in Early Modern Europe.* Ed. Donald R. Kelley. Rochester: U of Rochester P, 1997. 13–28.

– "The Theory of History." *The Cambridge History of Renaissance Philosophy.* Ed. Charles B. Schmitt and Quentin Skinner. New York: Cambridge UP, 1988. 746–61.

Kermode, Frank. *The Sense of an Ending.* New York: Oxford UP, 1967.

Kewes, Paulina. *This Great Matter of Succession: Drama, History, and Elizabethan Politics.* New York: Oxford UP, forthcoming.

– "History and Its Uses." *The Uses of History in Early Modern England*. Ed. Paulina Kewes. San Marino: Huntington Library Press, 2006, 1–30.

– "Marlowe, History, and Politics." *Christopher Marlowe in Context*. Ed. Emily Bartels and Emma Smith. New York: Cambridge UP, 2013. 138–54.

Kinney, Clare. "Epic Transgression and the Framing of Agency in *Dido, Queen of Carthage*." *Studies in English Literature* 40.2 (2000): 261–76.

Knights, L.C. *Drama and Society in the Age of Jonson*. London: Chatto & Windus, 1937.

Kottman, Paul. "Defying the Stars: Tragic Love as the Struggle for Freedom in *Romeo and Juliet*." *Shakespeare Quarterly* 63.1 (2012): 1–38.

– *A Politics of the Scene*. Stanford: Stanford UP, 2008.

– "Slipping on Banana Peels, Tumbling into Wells: Philosophy and Comedy." *diacritics* 38.4 (2008): 3–14.

Kyd, Thomas. *The Spanish Tragedy*. Ed. Michael Neill. New York: W.W. Norton, 2013.

LaCapra, Dominick. *Writing History, Writing Trauma*. Baltimore: Johns Hopkins UP, 2001.

Lambarde, William. *A Perambulation of Kent*. London: Edmund Bollifant, 1596.

Lancashire, Anne. *London Civic Theater: City Drama and Pageantry from Roman Times to 1558*. New York: Cambridge UP, 2002.

Leech, Clifford. *Shakespeare: The Chronicles*. London: Longmans, Green, 1962.

Leggatt, Alexander. *Citizen Comedy in the Age of Shakespeare*. Toronto: U of Toronto P, 1973.

– *Shakespeare's Political Drama: The History Plays and the Roman Plays*. New York: Routledge, 1989.

Le Goff, Jacques. *Time, Work, and Culture in the Middle Ages*. Trans. Arthur Goldhammer. Chicago: U of Chicago P, 1980.

Leinwand, Theodore B. *The City Staged: Jacobean Comedy, 1603–1613*. Madison: U of Wisconsin P, 1986.

Leland, John. *Joannis Lelandi Antiquarii de rebus britannicis collectanea*. 6 vols. Ed. Thomas Hearn. London: Joseph Richardson, 1770.

Levine, Joseph M. *Humanism and History: Origins of Modern English Historiography*. Ithaca: Cornell UP, 1987.

– "Thomas More and the English Renaissance: History and Fiction in *Utopia*." *The Historical Imagination in Early Modern Britain*. Ed. Donald R. Kelley and David Harris Sacks. New York: Cambridge UP, 1997. 69–92.

Levy, F.J. *Tudor Historical Thought*. San Marino: Huntington Library Press, 1967.

Lopez, Jeremy. "Imagining the Actor's Body on the Early Modern Stage." *Medieval and Renaissance Drama in England* 20 (2007): 187–203.

Low, Jennifer A. *Manhood and the Duel: Masculinity in Early Modern Drama and Culture*. New York: Palgrave, 2003.

Lowenstein, Joseph. *Ben Jonson and Possessive Authorship*. New York: Cambridge UP, 2002.

Luis-Martinez, Zenón. "Shakespeare's Historical Drama as *Trauerspiel*: *Richard II* – and After." *English Literary History* 75.3 (2008): 673–705.

Lupton, Julia Reinhard. "Judging Forgiveness: Hannah Arendt, W.H. Auden, and *The Winter's Tale*." *New Literary History* 45.4 (2014): 641–63.

– *Thinking with Shakespeare*. Chicago: U of Chicago P, 2013.

Maguire, Laurie, and Aleksandra Thostrup. "Marlowe and Character." *Christopher Marlowe in Context*. Ed. Emily Bartels and Emma Smith. New York: Cambridge UP, 2013. 39–48.

Manley, Lawrence. "John Stow's Survey of London: Of Sites and Rites." *The Theatrical City: Culture, Theatre, and Politics in London, 1576–1649*. Ed. David L. Smith, Richard Strier, and David Bevington. Cambridge: Cambridge UP, 1995. 35–54.

– *Literature and Culture in Early Modern London*. New York: Cambridge UP, 1995.

– "Motives for Patronage: The Queen's Men at New Park, October 1588." *Locating the Queen's Men: Material Practices and Conditions of Playing, 1583–1603*. Ed. Helen Ostovich, Holger Schott Syme, and Andrew Griffin. Burlington, VT: Ashgate, 2009. 51–64.

Mardock, James. *Our Scene Is London: Ben Jonson's City and the Space of the Author*. New York: Routledge, 2008.

Marlowe, Christopher. *Dido, Queen of Carthage and The Massacre at Paris*. Ed. H.J. Oliver. Revels Plays Series. London: Methuen, 1968.

Martin, Mathew. "Translation and Trauma: Oedipus, Hamlet, and Marlowe's *Dido, Queen of Carthage*." *LIT: Literature, Interpretation, Theory* 23.4 (2012): 305–25.

May, Todd. *Death*. New York: Routledge, 2014

McElroy, Bernard. *Shakespeare's Mature Tragedies*. Princeton: Princeton UP, 1973.

McMillin, Scott, and Sally-Beth MacLean. *The Queen's Men and Their Plays*. New York: Cambridge UP, 1998.

Mentz, Steve. *At the Bottom of Shakespeare's Ocean*. London: Bloomsbury, 2009.

Meskill, Lynn S. *Ben Jonson and Envy*. New York: Cambridge University Press, 2009.

– "Ben Jonson's 1616 Folio: A Revolution in Print?" *Études Épistémè* 14 (2008): 177–91.

Middleton, Thomas. *Sunne in Aries*. London: Edward Allde, 1621.

– *Triumphs of love and antiquity*. Nicholas Okes, 1619.

– *The tryumphs of honour and industry*. Nicholas Okes, 1617.

Middleton, Thomas, and Thomas Dekker. "The Patient Man and the Honest Whore." *Thomas Middleton: The Collected Works*. Ed. Gary Taylor and John Lavagnino. New York: Clarendon Press, 2007. 285–327.

Morris, Brian, and Roma Gill. Introduction. *The Atheist's Tragedy*. By Cyril Tourneur. Ed. Brian Morris and Roma Gill. New York: Norton, 1976.

Motley, John Lothrop. *History of the United Netherlands: From the Death of William the Silent to the Twelve Years' Truce, 1609*. 4 vols. New York: Harper and Brothers, 1880.

Mullaney, Steven. "Affective Technologies: Toward an Emotional Logic of the Elizabethan Stage." *Environment and Embodiment in Early Modern England*. Ed. Mary Floyd-Wilson and Garrett Sullivan. New York: Palgrave Macmillan, 2006. 71–89.

– *The Place of the Stage: License, Play, and Power in Renaissance England*. Ann Arbor: U of Michigan P, 1995.

Murray, Peter. *A Study of Cyril Tourneur*. Philadelphia: U of Pennsylvania P, 1964.

Murrin, Michael. *History and Warfare in Renaissance Epic*. Chicago: U of Chicago P, 1994.

Neill, Michael. *Issues of Death: Mortality and Identity in English Renaissance Tragedy*. Oxford: Clarendon Press, 1997.

Neufeld, Matthew. "Putting the Past to Work, Working through the Past." *Huntington Library Quarterly* 76.4 (2013): 483–97.

Neville, Alexander. "Tragedy and God's Judgements." *English Renaissance Literary Criticism*. Ed. Brian Vickers. New York, Cambridge UP, 1999. 125–7.

Newman, Karen. "*A Chaste Maid in Cheapside* and London." *Early Modern English Drama: A Critical Companion*. Ed. Garrett A. Sullivan, Patrick Cheney, and Andrew Hadfield. New York: Oxford UP, 2006. 237–47.

– "Goldsmith's Ware: Equivalence in *A Chaste Maid in Cheapside*." *Huntington Library Quarterly* 71.1 (2008): 97–113.

Oliver, H.J., ed. Introduction. *Dido, Queen of Carthage and The Massacre at Paris*. By Christopher Marlowe. Revels Plays Series. London: Methuen, 1968.

Ornstein, Robert. "*The Atheist's Tragedy* and Renaissance Naturalism." *Studies in Philology* 51.2 (1954): 194–207.

– *The Moral Vision of Jacobean Tragedy*. Madison: U of Wisconsin P, 1960.

Parker, Geoffrey. *The Military Revolution, 1500–1800: Military Innovation and the Rise of the West*. 2nd ed. New York: Cambridge UP, 1996.

Parry, Graham. *The Trophies of Time: English Antiquarians of the Seventeenth Century*. New York: Oxford UP, 1995.

Paster, Gail Kern. *The Body Embarrassed: Drama and the Disciplines of Shame in Early Modern England*. Ithaca: Cornell UP, 1993.

– *The Idea of the City in the Age of Shakespeare*. Athens: U of Georgia P, 1985.

Patterson, Annabel. *Reading* Holinshed's Chronicles. Chicago: U of Chicago P, 1994.

Phelan, Peggy. *Unmarked: The Politics of Performance*. New York: Routledge, 1993.

Phillips, James. "The Practicalities of the Absolute: Justice and Kingship in Shakespeare's *Richard II*." *English Literary History* 79.1 (2012): 161–77.

Pincombe, Michael. "English Renaissance Tragedy: Theories and Antecedents." *Cambridge Companion to Renaissance Tragedy*. Ed. Emma Smith and Garrett A. Sullivan Jr. New York: Cambridge UP, 2010. 3–15.

Plett, Heinrich F. *Rhetoric and Renaissance Culture*. New York: Walter de Gruyter, 2004.

Polydore Vergil. *Historia Anglica*. Ed. and trans. Dana F. Sutton. University of Birmingham Philological Museum. 4 Aug. 2005. Web. 31 Oct. 2015. http://www.philological.bham.ac.uk/polverg/.

Popper, Nicholas. *Walter Ralegh's* History of the World *and the Historical Culture of the Late Renaissance*. Chicago: U of Chicago P, 2012.

Porter, Stephen. *Shakespeare's London: Everyday Life in London, 1580–1616*. Gloucestershire: Amberley Publishing, 2009.

Price, Hereward T. *Construction in Shakespeare*. Ann Arbor: U of Michigan P, 1951.

Pugh, Syrithe. "Marlowe and Classical Literature." *Christopher Marlowe in Context*. Ed. Emily Bartels and Emma Smith. New York: Cambridge UP, 2013. 80–9.

Puttenham, George. *The Arte of English Poesie*. London: Richard Field, 1589.

Quint, David. *Epic and Empire: Politics and Generic Form from Virgil to Milton*. Princeton: Princeton UP, 1993.

Rackin, Phyllis. *Stages of History: Shakespeare's English Chronicles*. Ithaca: Cornell UP, 1990.

Ramazani, Jahan. *The Poetry of Mourning: The Modern Elegy from Hardy to Heaney*. Chicago: U of Chicago P, 1994.

Reed, Robert Rentoul, Jr. *Crime and God's Judgement in Shakespeare*. Lexington: UP of Kentucky, 1984.

Ribner, Irving. *The English History Play in the Age of Shakespeare*. London: Methuen, 1965.

Rist, Thomas. *Revenge Tragedy and the Drama of Commemoration in Reforming England*. Burlington, VT: Ashgate, 2008.

Roberts, Gareth. "'An art lawful as eating'? Magic in *The Tempest* and *The Winter's Tale*." *Shakespeare's Late Plays: New Readings*. Ed. Jennifer Richards and James Knowles. Edinburgh: U of Edinburgh P, 1999. 126–42.

Roberts, Michael. *The Military Revolution, 1560–1660*. Belfast: Marjory Boyd, 1956.

Roebuck, Thomas. "Middleton's Historical Imagination." *The Oxford Handbook of Thomas Middleton*. Ed Gary Taylor and Trish Thomas Henley. New York: Oxford UP, 2012. 116–29.

Rogers, Clifford J., ed. *The Military Revolution Debate: Readings on the Military Transformation of Early Modern Europe*. Boulder, CO: Westview, 1995.

Rosenblatt, Jason P. *Renaissance England's Chief Rabbi: John Selden*. New York: Oxford UP, 2006.

Rowe, George. *Thomas Middleton and the New Comedy Tradition*. Omaha: U of Nebraska P, 1979.

Sacks, Peter. *The English Elegy: Studies in the Genre from Spenser to Yeats*. Baltimore: Johns Hopkins UP, 1985.

Schrickx, Willem. "Cyril Tourneur, War Correspondent, Spy, and Author of *Extremities urging Sir Francis vere to the Anti-parle*." *Neophilologus* 78.2 (1994): 315–27.

Schwyzer, Philip. *Archaeologies of Renaissance Literature*. New York: Oxford UP, 2007.

– "British History and 'The British History': The Same Old Story?" *British Identities and English Renaissance Literature*. Ed. David J. Baker and Willy Maley. Cambridge: Cambridge UP, 2002. 11–23.

Scott, Allison V. "Jonson's Masque Markets and the Problems of Literary Ownership." *Studies in English Literature* 47.2 (2007): 451–71.

Scott-Warren, Jason. "Was Elizabeth I Richard II? The Authenticity of Lambarde's 'Conversation.'" *Review of English Studies* 66 (2012): 208–30.

Selden, John. *Analecton Anglobritannicon libri duo*. Frankfurt: Prodeunt ex Officina Paltheniana, 1615.

– *The historie of tithes*. London: N.p., 1618.

Sidney, Sir Philip. *A Defence of Poetry*. Ed. Jan van Dorsten. New York: Oxford UP, 1973.

Simoni, Anna. *The Ostend Story: Early Tales of the Great Siege and the Mediating Role of Henrick van Haestens*. Utrecht: Hes & de Graaf, 2003.

Skelton, John. *Respublica*. Ed. Leonard Magnus. London: EETS e.s. 94, 1905.

Smith, Logan Pearsall. *The Life and Letters of Sir Henry Wotton*. 2 vols. Oxford: Clarendon Press, 1907.

Smith, Mary E. "Staging Marlowe's *Dido, Queene of Carthage*." *Studies in English Literature* 17.2 (1977): 177–90.

Somogyi, Nick de. *Shakespeare's Theater of War*. Burlington, VT: Ashgate, 1998.

Stanyhurst, Richard, trans. *Thee first foure bookes of Virgil his Aeneid*. Leiden: John Pates, 1582.

Stow, John. *The Chronicles of England*. London: [Henry Bynneman for] Ralphe Newberie, 1580.

– *A Survey of London. Reprinted from the Text of 1603*. 2 vols. Ed. Charles Lethbridge Kingsford. Oxford: Oxford UP, 1908.

Strohm, Paul. "The Trouble with Richard: The Reburial of Richard II and Lancastrian Symbolic Strategy." *Speculum* 71.1 (1996): 87–111.

Strong, Roy. *Henry, Prince of Wales and England's Lost Renaissance*. New York: Thames and Hudson, 1986.

Stuckey, Michael. "'This Society Tendeth': Elite Prosopography in Elizabethan Legal History." *Prosopon: The Journal of Prosopography* 1 (2006): 1–58.

Stump, Donald. "Marlowe's Travesty of Virgil: Dido and Elizabethan Dreams of Empire." *Comparative Drama* 34.1 (2000): 79–107.

Suzuki, Mihoko. *Metamorphoses of Helen: Authority, Difference, and the Epic*. Ithaca: Cornell University Press, 1992.

Swann, Marjorie. *Curiosities and Texts: The Culture of Collecting in Early Modern England*. Philadelphia: U of Pennsylvania P, 2001.

Swinburne, Algernon Charles. *The Complete Works of Algernon Charles Swinburne*. Ed. Edmund Gosse and Thomas James Wise. 18 vols. London: William Heineman, 1927.

Syme, Holger Schott. "'But, what ever you do, Buy': *Richard II* as Popular Commodity." *Richard II: New Critical Essays*. Ed. Jeremy Lopez. New York: Routledge, 2012. 223–44.

Taylor, Gary. "Thomas Middleton: Lives and Afterlives." *Thomas Middleton: Collected Works*. Ed. Gary Taylor and John Lavagnino. New York: Oxford UP, 2010. 25–58.

Taylor, Gary, and Rory Loughnane. "The Canon and Chronology of Shakespeare's Works." *The New Oxford Shakespeare: Authorship Companion*. Ed. Gary Taylor and Gabriel Egan. New York: Oxford UP, 2017. 417–602.

Taylor, Gary, and Trish Thomas Henley. "Unintroduction: Middletonian Dissensus." *The Oxford Handbook of Thomas Middleton*. Ed. Gary Taylor and Trish Thomas Henley. New York: Oxford UP, 2012. 1–15.

Thomas, Allen. *The History and Antiquities of London, Westminster, Southwark, and Parts Adjacent*. 4 vols. London: Cowie and Strange, 1827–9.

Tillyard, E.M.W. *Shakespeare's History Plays*. London: Chatto & Windus, 1944.

– *Shakespeare's Last Plays*. London: Chatto & Windus, 1938.

Tourneur, Cyril. *The Atheist's Tragedy*. Ed. Brian Morris and Roma Gill. New York: Norton, 1976.

– *A funerall poeme. Vpon the death of the most vvorthie and true souldier; Sir Francis Vere, Knight*. London: John Windet, 1609.

– *"A Griefe on the Death of Prince Henrie." Three elegies on the most lamented death of Prince Henrie.* London: Nicholas Okes and Felix Kingston, 1613. A2–A4r.

– *The transformed metamorphosis*. London: Valentine Simmes, 1600.

Ure, Peter. Introduction. *Richard II*. Ed. Peter Ure. London: Methuen, 1969.

Vanita, Ruth. "Mariological Memory in *The Winter's Tale* and *Henry VIII*." *Studies in English Literature* 40 (2000): 311–37.

Vickers, Brian, ed. *English Renaissance Literary Criticism*. New York, Cambridge UP, 1999.

– "Incomplete Shakespeare: Or, Denying Coauthorship in *1 Henry VI*." *Shakespeare Quarterly* 58.3 (2007): 311–52.

– "Rhetoric and Poetics." *The Cambridge History of Renaissance Philosophy*. Ed. C.B. Schmitt and Quentin Skinner. New York: Cambridge UP, 1988. 715–45.

Vine, Angus. *In Defiance of Time: Antiquarian Writing in Early Modern England*. New York: Oxford UP, 2010.

Virgil. *The Aeneid*. Trans. Robert Fitgerald. New York: Vintage, 1990.

– *The XIII bukes of Eneados*. Trans. Gavin Douglas. London: William Copland, 1553.

– *Thee first four bookes of Virgil his Aeneis*. Leiden: John Pates, 1582.

Walsh, Brian. "Performing Historicity in Dekker's *Shoemaker's Holiday*." *Studies in English Literature, 1500–1900* 46.2 (2006): 323–48.

– *Shakespeare, The Queen's Men, and the Elizabethan Performance of History*. New York: Cambridge UP, 2010.

Waswo, Richard. *The Founding Myth of Western Civilization: From Virgil to Vietnam*. Hanover, NH: Wesleyan UP, 1997.

Weimann, Robert. *Author's Pen and Actor's Voice: Playing and Writing in Shakespeare's Theatre*. Ed. Helen Higbee and William West. New York: Cambridge UP, 2000.

Weinberg, Bernard. *A History of Literary Criticism in the Italian Renaissance*. 2 vols. Chicago: U of Chicago P, 1961.

Wells, Robin Headlam. *Shakespeare's Humanism*. New York: Cambridge UP, 2005.

Wells, Susan. "Jacobean City Comedy and the Ideology of the City." *ELH* 48 (1981): 37–60.

Wheare, Degory. *The Method and Order of Reading both Civil and Ecclesiastical Histories*. London: M. Flesher (for Charles Brome), 1685.

Wheeler, Richard. *Shakespeare's Development and the Problem Comedies: Turn and Counter-Turn*. Los Angeles: U of California P, 1981.

White, Hayden. "The Value of Narrativity in the Representation of Reality." *Critical Inquiry* 7.1 (1980): 5–7.

Wiggins, Martin. "Marlowe's Chronology and Canon." *Christopher Marlowe in Context*. Ed. Emma Smith and Emily Bartels. New York: Cambridge UP. 7–14.

Wilson, Emily. *Mocked with Death: Tragic Overliving from Sophocles to Milton*. Baltimore: Johns Hopkins UP, 2004.

Womersley, David. "Against the Teleology of Technique." *The Uses of History in Early Modern England*. Ed. Paulina Kewes. San Marino: Huntington Library Press, 2006. 91–104.

Woodbridge, Linda. *English Revenge Drama: Money, Resistance, Equality*. New York: Cambridge UP, 2010.

– "Introduction to *A Chaste Maid in Cheapside*." *Thomas Middleton, Volume 1: The Collected Works*. 2 vols. Ed. Gary Taylor and John Lavagnino. New York: Oxford UP, 2007. 907–11.

Woolf, D.R. "From Hystories to the Historical: Five Transitions in Thinking about the Past." *The Uses of History in Early Modern England*. Ed. Paulina Kewes. San Marino: Huntington Library Press, 2006. 31–67.

– *The Idea of History in Early Stuart England: Erudition, Ideology, and 'The Light of Truth' from the Accession of James I to the Civil War*. Toronto: U of Toronto P, 2000.

– "Little Crosby and the Horizons of Early Modern Culture." *The Historical Imagination in Early Modern England: History, Rhetoric, and Fiction, 1500–1800*. Ed. D.R. Kelley and D.H. Sacks. New York: Cambridge UP, 1997.

– *Reading History in Early Modern England*. New York: Cambridge UP, 2000.

– *The Social Circulation of the Past: English Historical Culture, 1500–1730*. New York: Oxford UP, 2003.

Worden, Blair. "Ben Jonson among the Historians." *Culture and Politics in Early Stuart England.* Ed. Kevin Sharpe and Peter Lake. Stanford: Stanford UP, 1994. 67–75.

– "Historians and Poets." *The Uses of History in Early Modern England.* Ed. Paulina Kewes. San Marino: Huntington Library Press, 2006. 69–90.

– *The Sound of Virtue: Philip Sidney's* Arcadia *and Elizabethan Politics.* New Haven: Yale UP, 1996.

Yates, Frances. *Shakespeare's Last Plays: A New Approach.* New York: Routledge, 1975.

Žižek, Slavoj. *Looking Awry: An Introduction to Jacques Lacan through Popular Culture.* Cambridge: MIT Press, 1992.

Index

www.ingramcontent.com/pod-product-compliance
Lightning Source LLC
LaVergne TN
LVHW041113090826
844660LV00061B/874/J

* 9 7 8 1 4 8 7 5 0 3 4 8 2 *